PEN AND BLOOD

PEN AND BLOOD

CONVERSATIONS WITH KILLERS

ALAN R. WARREN

COPYRIGHT

House of Mystery Publishing

Seattle, Washington, USA

Vancouver, British Columbia, Canada

ISBN (eBook): 978-1-998680-02-3
ISBN (Paperback): 978-1-998680-03-0

Cover design, formatting, layout, and editing by Evening Sky Publishing Services

CONTENTS

Introduction vii

BOOK 1

Ian Brady - The Moors Murders

1. The Crimes 3
2. Nothing Like Good Planning 5
3. Lost Soul 9
4. Who Was Ian Brady 13
5. Pauline Reade 19
6. John Kilbride 29
7. Keith Bennett 37
8. Lesley-Ann Downey 41
9. Edward Evans 55
10. Trial & Prison 71

The Letters 89

BOOK 2

Stephen Port - Grindr Serial Killer

1. The Crimes 121
2. Anthony Walgate 123

3. Gabriel Kovari 135
4. Daniel Whitworth 143
5. Jack Taylor 153
6. Arrest, Interrogation, and Prison 161

The Letters 195

BOOK 3

David Shearing - The Wells
Gray Park Murders

1. The Crime 301
2. Missing Family 303
3. Investigation 311
4. Who was David Shearing? 323

The Conversations 327

Bibliography 419
About the Author 427
Also by Alan R. Warren 429

INTRODUCTION

Where do serial killers come from? That's the question that everyone is trying to answer. At this point in the world, we don't know. Television psychologists often seem to have the answer within the half-hour allotted for the program. They frequently make it sound clear-cut, straightforward, and even like an easy solution. Only it's not. Nor is it ever that simple.

One of the most common answers they give is that the child was physically abused by their father or psychologically abused by their mother. Firstly, how one can ascribe physical abuse only coming from the father and not the mother is nonsensical, and vice versa; it's just as absurd for the psychological abuse only coming from the child's mother.

You can't always believe in theories from

crime shows that take such easy paths to find an answer to something so complex and not understandable to the average person who has never thought about committing several murders during their lifetime.

This simplified explanation provided by these crime shows isn't to say that these problems don't exist and can't contribute to what leads a person to commit murder. Depending on the person, they can significantly contribute to developing a mind and creating its construct, which would permit this behavior. Often, when a child is overpowered and physically abused by one or both parents, it's more about how they respond to such violence. One child might find it a source of power, a way to take control of their situation. In contrast, others will shut off their abilities to feel emotions when beaten.

In the case of a sociopath—one who doesn't feel emotions—there is no pain when they're attacked, just as there is no remorse when others are attacked in any way. The prefrontal cortex is believed to no longer control the urges to lash out and hurt another. Afterward, there is no remorse or empathy for the pain caused. Instead, a cool, calculated logic is used to cover up or conceal the crime.

During the teenage years, a child will start

to lash out. They will not jump straight to murdering another human. Instead, they look towards small animals that they have the power to control. With no possibility of a survivor remaining to tell others of the attack, it puts them in a position where it's much easier to get away with their violent crime. As they continue to age, sexual awareness can become part of their crimes. Sometimes, if they attach a specific sexual behavior to an act of violence, it will lead to serial killers who act out their crime to achieve sexual gratification.

Also, in their early years, a sociopath begins to develop the ability to fake their emotions around others. Someone in their family dies, an aunt or grandfather, and they see their mother or father crying at the funeral or getting upset about the death. They learn to copy these behaviors so that nobody questions why they are not crying as well.

This book brings you word-for-word discussions with three killers: Ian Brady (The Moors Murders), Stephen Port (Grindr Serial Killer), and David Shearing (The Wells Gray Park Murders). It includes letters they wrote from prison after they were convicted of their murders, and actual dialogue via interviews and exchanges. The letters and conversations will demonstrate several of the behaviors mentioned. Even though these killers had different kinds of victims and their methods varied, they all needed to control their victims through manipulation.

Stephen Port is a serial killer of the modern era in the UK who used modern technology, such as social media dating apps, to meet his victims. Port was also well aware of the isolated feeling certain men felt when they were still very young and trying to deal with feelings of being gay. Once Port was able to gain their trust online, he would invite them over to his apartment and drug their drink without them being aware of it. Once they were visibly intoxicated from the booze and drugs or even unconscious, he would have sex with them. This act of drugging them gave Port the feeling of power, which was the only way he could have sex. His victims died soon afterward from the drugs he gave them. He would then take their bodies to a local park, where he would make the victims look like they had overdosed and died in the park. Because many people were using and overdosing on drugs in that same park, the police didn't detect that there was an active serial killer at work. And since the victims were gay, the police didn't look too closely into their deaths, leaving Port free to continue his killings for years.

On the other hand, Ian Brady was different because he used an accomplice, Myra Hindley. From 1963 to 1965, they pursued their victims directly, in person. Even though the couple targeted a younger set of victims, usually teenagers, they were still driven by a sexual drive towards them. Brady wanted his victims to know he was in control and had the power to do whatever he wanted. He wasn't hiding his abuse from them. Unlike Port, who lured his victims and drugged them into an unconscious state before abusing them, Brady wanted them to see it and experience it fully. He wanted them to be conscious and aware of what he was doing to them and took most of his pleasure from the control he exerted during his sexual assault. Brady could also get quite violent. The more they struggled or seemed to be hurting from the attack, the more abusive he would get.

The third killer covered in this book is David Shearing, who was convicted of murdering a family of six people while they were camping at Wells Gray Park, British Columbia, Canada, in 1982. When Shearing murdered the four adults to reach his primary targets, the two young girls, for sexual assault purposes, all of these criminal acts are usually viewed as a continuous event, meaning the deaths that occurred have a strong connection to the sexual assault and may even have been a necessary part of his planned sexual assault. In legal terms, what's considered is the overall context of the crimes, not just the immediate cause of death. If it was Shearing's primary intention to assault the two young girls sexually, and he had to commit homicide to do it, then it would be considered first-degree murder. That said, detectives had no concrete evidence of how or when the murders took place. So, he was only charged with second-degree murder in all six counts.

All three of these murderers had the same primary focus, which was to assault children and young adults sexually before murdering them. All three of these murderers wanted to isolate their victims before committing their crimes against them. In all cases, control over their victims was the strongest aspect that drove them. The only difference was in the way they achieved that control.

One unique point often unmentioned when it comes to Ian Brady's murders was that even though he worked with an accomplice to carry out his actions, Brady, like Port, was attracted to the same sex. Yet, many of the reports about his killings didn't talk about this. Possibly because, during the 1960s, homosexuality was still illegal, and any discussion about it was avoided as much as possible.

The primary differences between all three killers were the method of killing, the age of the victims, and the nature of the crime. Port needed his victims to be subdued or incapacitated before he would act on them, whereas Brady and Shearing wanted their victims to know what they were going to do to them.

Their victim choices were different in age. Brady and Shearing preferred younger victims, anywhere from six to sixteen, prepuberty, whereas Port usually wanted a man around his age. Port also didn't want any violent scenes during his crime. He didn't want to become physical with his victims, whereas Brady enjoyed being aggressive and sadistic toward them. After Shearing sexually assaulted his young victims, he shot them in the head.

Shearing was also different from Brady and Port in that Shearing was willing to murder others to get to his primary victims, the children. The adult victims, who were in the way of Shearing to get to the children, were just collateral damage to him. It didn't matter who they were or what they did. Shearing needed to get them out of the way to reach his chosen victims. On the other hand, Brady and Port chose to find a victim who was alone or to get their victims alone first. Regardless of their MO, all three of these killers needed to be alone with the children to act out their fantasies.

One other, even more critical difference in the Shearing murder case is that, unlike Port and Brady, Shearing goes up for a chance to get parole every two years. Do we think that those who sexually assault children get cured while in prison?

BOOK 1

IAN BRADY - THE MOORS MURDERS

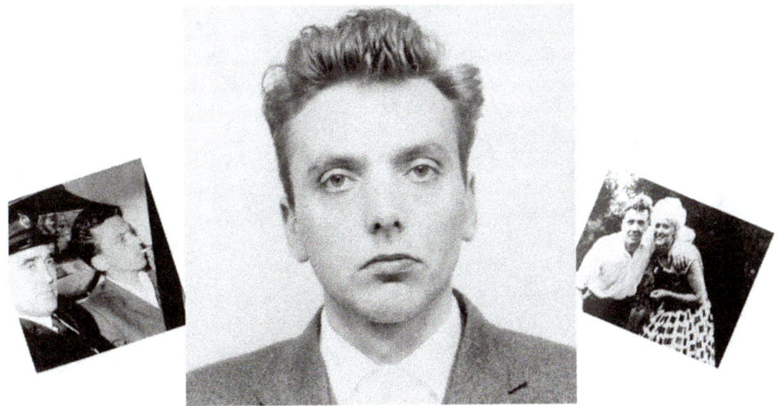

1

THE CRIMES

In 1965, in Manchester, England, the Police were called to a possible crime scene at the residence of Ian Brady and Myra Hindley, his girlfriend. In the upstairs spare bedroom, they found the remains of 17-year-old Edward Evans, who had been cut into pieces with an axe.

After an investigation and search, the Police found two suitcases that were full of graphic pictures of a young 10-year-old girl, Lesley Ann Downey, who had been missing for months. The photos showed her tied up and tortured. Also found were recordings of the assault on tape, which, when heard at the police station, made people cry and throw up.

The horrors that were about to unfold

shocked the UK and the entire world. Soon, they would become known as the "Moors Murders" and became one of the most infamous serial murder cases to come out of Britain.

2

NOTHING LIKE GOOD PLANNING

It was a plain, chilly Fall afternoon when the charming Ian Brady was settling in with a bottle of fine German wine with his beautiful blonde girlfriend, Myra Hindley, at their home. Myra lit some candles, creating the perfect mood for their nightly plans.

With this couple, their evening plans were not what a typical couple in 1960s Manchester would make. They wouldn't light a fire, cozy up to a romantic movie, or cuddle in their beds while reading a good book. Their plans were far more sinister and probably not what you would think.

That night, they were planning to have an "event," maybe two or three if things went well, maybe even more. But before they had any events, they needed to create a list of things necessary to pull off not just an event but the perfect event.

What kind of "event" are you asking? Well, it was the event of murder. And not just any murder, but a perfectly planned murder made just for Brady and Hindley.

"Alright, first things first. We need a plan!" Brady said with a firm voice.

"Yeah, Like what? I mean, can't we go and do it?" Hindley answered with a light, whimsical feel as she sat on the sofa sipping her cocktail.

Brady turned his head rapidly and looked her directly into her eyes. "I said we need a plan, and we need it to be written. We can't make any mistakes, do you understand that?" He answered sternly.

Brady then grabbed a paper and pen from the desk and threw it at her, landing it on her lap. "Here! Start writing."

"Fine, fine. Where do I start?"

"The first thing we need to ensure is that there can be no thread that will connect our starting point with where we end up."

"Right, okay, that makes sense."

"Second, we have to ensure we leave no evidence behind. So, no tire tracks, footprints, or fingerprints at the scene. We must be cautious not to leave any hair or fingerprints either."

"Right, so we wear gloves and perhaps a hat?"

"If we need to, you might need to cover your hair. Perhaps a scarf?"

"Right, cover my beautiful hairdo. I'm not having that!"

Brady bent down, grabbed Hindley's arm, and glared at her directly into her eyes. This time, he had an angry look she had seen before. Only a few times before. It was like he was completely different, as if his whole face had changed. "Are you not taking this seriously? Are you not taking proper note?"

"Yes, I am!" Hindly answered him softly.

"Fine. See that you do!" Brady almost shouted at her as he let go of her arm with a hard push, which made her lose grip on the pen she used to write down the rules.

"Next," Brady continued as he began to pace back and forth in front of her. We must have duplicates of all of the clothing we use. I mean everything: shoes, socks, and even our underwear." Brady stopped as he said that and glared at Hindley.

"I got it." She snidely answered.

"We will be burning all of our clothing and dumping the ashes into the river after the crime." Brady finished.

"Oh, perhaps we should buy cheaper clothes for the murders then?"

Ignoring what she just asked, Brady continued with a new thought: "Your car. "

"Yes,"

"It must be thoroughly washed and polished inside before and after the event."

"Right, got it."

"Now for the weapons. We must ensure that we clean the inner and outside of our guns. We have to score the bulletheads to make sure that there are no ballistic markings on impact."

"Okay, you know how to do that?"

Brady continued talking without answering her. "We also need plastic sheets for the car, in case we need to cover the seats. Oh, yeah, and we need to steal some license plates from other vehicles to use during an event."

3

LOST SOUL

On the morning of Friday, March 5, 2010, Winnie Johnson was awakened by what sounded like a voice calling out to her. She had sat down on her sofa the night before and drifted off to sleep while thinking about the memorial service that was finally going to happen forty-six years after her son, Keith Bennett, had disappeared.

She soon realized she heard short gusts of wind blasting across her roof, loud, low roars, and no one calling her. As she sat up slowly, she could see it was still very dark. She walked towards her living room window, opened her curtains, and saw it was cloudy. It had been a bitterly cold winter with plenty of snow. The news reported the worst winter Manchester had seen since 1987. She wrapped her robe around herself and tied the rope tightly, as it had been disheveled sometime during her night on her sofa.

Winnie walked over to the fireplace mantle, picked up the picture of her son, and walked back to her sofa, focused on Keith's eyes in the image. She was trying to connect with and get his answers, as she had done for so many years.

As Winnie sat back on her sofa, she quietly said, "Look at my eyes. They are tired and have no answers. They don't know much, but I love you, and I guess that's all they'll know."

She sighed and placed the picture on her coffee table. Winnie was not going to cry. She had cried now too many times, and no matter how hard she cried, no matter if she screamed and yelled, nothing would change. Nothing was going to change. Winnie would play over the last time she saw her son: she was walking to the market, and her son was running off to meet his friends to see a movie. She remembered waving at him and smiling. Every time she rewound and relived this in her mind, she wanted to change it. She desperately tried to change it and would try and change letting him go to the movies. She wanted to tell him, "No, you cannot go. You are to stay with me and help me shop." But even when she re-imagined Keith coming to the market with her, he would disappear from the store, and she would end up in the same place. Keith was gone.

Just before 11:00 a.m. that same day, Councilor Jim McArdle helped Winnie into the memorial for Keith at the Manchester Cathedral. Her hair was combed flat across her head and held back with a band, keeping it out of her face. She was wearing a black and white speckled dress with a long magenta sweater over it.

Winnie stood before a large crowd, including her family, friends, and neighbors, and the room fell silent. She was trembling and felt a little dizzy. It was all so overwhelming. Not only was this the memorial she had always prayed for, but it was also the last step in closing the case. Winnie reached out her right arm and held onto the stand dedicated to her son. She held on tightly to help keep her balance as she spoke.

Winnie spoke to the crowd. She expressed her love for her son, and she believed he was with her to this day, watching over them, and he was in the church now. She went on to thank everyone for being there, not only at the service but with her through her journey to find her lost son, or as she called him, her "Lost Soul."

After the memorial, Winnie was off to the

Saddleworth Moors, where Brady identified the spot as Keith's resting place. When she arrived, a small group of people assembled. It was a large, beautiful grassy field with a wood post barbed wire fence running beside the road they traveled to get there. The people had all brought tokens of love and sorrow, such as flowers, teddy bears, and some pictures of Keith, and tied them to the posts of the fence.

Winnie now stood in the same spot she had stood in years before when she came dressed in work clothes with a shovel to dig in search of her son's remains. Ian Brady had decided to help detectives find the remains of the other two victims he had murdered, one of them being Keith Bennett. They had no success in finding Keith's body that day and still have not seen him today.

Keith Bennett is now known as the "Lost Soul."

4

WHO WAS IAN BRADY

Ian Duncan Stewart was born on Sunday, January 2, 1938 in Glasgow, Scotland. Ian's mother, Maggie Stewart, was an unmarried waitress who struggled to pay her bills, and eventually, she gave Ian away to her neighbors, the Sloan family, when he was just 2 months old. Later in life, Ian told a journalist he "loathed the first day of each week," as by Scottish law, Sundays were closed to prevent any prospect of merriment on the Sabbath. "Sunday was not the day to be born on, especially not this Sunday, and I found myself illegitimate before taking my first breath. In my case, of course, most people would prefer the term bastard."

The Sloan family was an average middle-class family with four children who lived close enough to Maggie she could keep in contact with her son. Ian started to develop a dark side to his behavior when he was about four years old by torturing small animals. He broke one dog's leg, set another dog on fire, and even decapitated a cat.

When Ian was nine years old, the Sloans moved to the suburbs of Glasgow, so he no longer had easy access to his mother. After the Sloans settled into their new home, Ian started to attend the Shadowlands Academy for gifted children, and initially, things seemed to go well for him. But Ian's violent behavior continued in their new home. Instead of it being directed towards animals, however, he now tortured younger neighbor kids.

Ian started breaking into people's homes and stealing things. He was caught at age 15 and had to go to juvenile court. He decided to quit school and work any job he could get, including as a tea boy at a shipyard and as a messenger for a butcher.

Everything came to a sudden halt when Ian was arrested for using a switchblade knife on his then-girlfriend for going to a dance with another boy. The court put Ian on probation and sent him back to his mother's house to live in Manchester.

Ian's mother, Maggie, had married an Irish man named Patrick Brady. Patrick was a fruit seller at the Smithfield Market and hired Ian as a fruit porter. Within a few months, however, Ian was caught stealing a bag of lead seals from the store, fired, and arrested. At the time, Ian was 17 years old, so he was sentenced to two years in a British youth prison in Hatfield, which was designed to help reform young offenders rather than to punish them.

In keeping with what was becoming normal behavior for Ian, he also got into trouble at the youth prison. He was found to be brewing alcohol in the prison and was sent to a different and more strict young offender prison in Hull.

On November 14, 1957, Ian was released from that prison and returned to his home in Manchester, where he started a new job and studied to be an accountant. It wasn't long before he began working as a clerk at Millward's Merchandising, a wholesale chemical plant in Gorton, just south of Manchester.

Around this time, Ian began to read about the Nazis. He even taught himself German so he could read Adolf Hitler's *Mein Kampf*. Brady was also a big fan of the works of the Marquis de Sade, who was known for his very vivid accounts of sexual violence.

About three years later, in January 1961, Millward's hired a typist named Myra Hindley. Myra was around 20 years old, tall, and had peroxide blonde hair. Brady admitted to never liking her hairstyle and noticed she had heat marks on her legs from sitting too close to her fireplace at home. She worked in a small room beside Brady, taking dictation and typing his letters. Brady never paid much attention to Hindley; he thought of her as just another of the female workers.

On the other hand, Myra had written in her diary that she was very attracted to Brady. She would write things like "Ian looked at me today" or "I wonder if Ian is courting. Still feel the same." She would also write, "I love Ian all over again. He has a cold, and I would love to mother him."

On December 23rd, Millward's had their annual Christmas party. The staff would usually spend a few hours at a pub nearby and then return to the mill for some drinks. This year, after they returned, a few typists danced and drank in the office. Brady joined them, and he kissed them all.

When Myra walked into the room, Brady kissed her, too. They made a plan to meet later that night at a different pub. After a few drinks, he took her to the movie *King of Kings*, a biblical film. In the coming weeks, Brady took Myra out to see several films. They would stay up all night having discussions about religion and the Nazis.

5

PAULINE READE

Ian and Myra's house had to be cleared of anything incriminating that could be found by the Police. They would place these items into suitcases and take them to the railway stations. Brady wanted alibis to be established and remain valid for 14 days, then they could put it to a vague status, as most people can't remember what they did last week unless something special was happening.

The master plan was placed into a large envelope along with a contact list, maps of the planned places they were going to rob, photographs, an address book, and tapes. They then hid the envelope amongst other papers in a locked room at Millward's, where they both worked. These were the documents that Myra destroyed in the first five days after Brady was in prison and while she was still free.

Myra joined the Rifle Club to get a license to amass weapons to rob a bank. Brady wanted her to get one rifle, a .45, and a .38 snub nose gun, as he didn't trust automatics. But Brady and Hindley's planned robberies would never happen. Instead, they moved on to something much more personal: rape and murder. How this change occurred is still not known. The van they rented for robberies had become a place that would carry a body instead of their guns or the money they would have taken from their planned bank heists.

Next door to the couple lived Joan and Amos Reade. Their oldest daughter, Pauline, was 16, and their son, Paul, was 13. Pauline attended the same school as Maureen Hindley and had been in a short relationship with David Smith, who worked as an apprentice in her father's bakery.

On Friday, July 12, 1963, Pauline was going to a local dance at the Railway's Workers' Social Club on Chapman Street, about a 10-minute walk from her home. Pauline called two of her friends to ask them to go with her to the dance, but both were not allowed to go because there was going to be alcohol served at the dance, and their mothers disapproved.

Pauline finished getting herself ready at about 7:45 p.m. and left for the dance. She wore a black blouse, a pink and gold shirt, a knitted cardigan, a blue coat, and a pair of white stiletto heels. As Pauline walked down Gorton Lane, she was enjoying the warm sun on her face, which also partially blinded her from seeing anything in front of her.

As she walked beside a parked black van, she could hear the driver's side window squeak as it rolled down. Myra called out to Pauline and asked her where she was going. Pauline recognized Myra, stopped, and told her about the dance. Pauline relaxed into a conversation about school and their mutual friends.

Myra then pointed to some 78 rpm records (the popular medium for music at this time) that were sitting on the passenger seat of her van and offered to give them to Pauline if she would come to Saddleworth Moor to help her find an expensive glove that she had lost when she was out there earlier that morning. Pauline was early for the dance, so she thought she could fill her spare time helping Myra find the glove. She collected the records, placed them on her lap, entered the van, and they headed for the moor.

Meanwhile, Ian Brady was at his parents' home, creating an alibi. He deliberately asked them what time it was before he left so they would remember when he was there if they were ever asked. According to Brady, when he got to the place on Gorton Lane where Myra should have been, he saw that the van was gone and knew she must have found a victim already. He headed for the moor.

Brady arrived at the moor and parked his bike beside Myra's van. He still wasn't sure who the victim was going to be. Would it be a boy or a girl? He lifted the goggles off his face, removed his gloves, and walked towards Myra and Pauline. They were both sitting in the van smoking. He walked over, squeezed in beside Myra, and lit himself a cigarette.

After Myra introduced Brady to Pauline, she told them they had better start searching for her lost glove before it got too dark. They put out their cigarettes and headed into the moor, with Brady walking about 15 feet in front of the girls. Everything was going very casually, as they still saw cars traveling by on the road. They slowly made it over a small hill and out of sight of the road, and Myra gave Brady the signal "Groucho." Brady walked up behind Pauline, grabbed her head, and put her in a stranglehold.

Pauline fell to the ground and stared into

Brady's eyes in shock. Brady told her to stay quiet, and she would be alright. She turned her eyes to Myra, but instead of getting help from her, Myra just smiled and told Pauline to keep quiet.

Pauline shouted that she was "unwell," which meant it was her time of the month. Myra just got down on her knees beside Pauline and started to unbutton her coat. Brady stood up and watched over the moor while Myra finished undressing Pauline.

Myra started to fondle Pauline's breasts. Pauline laid down and was submissive, letting Myra now kiss her breasts. After Myra completely stripped Pauline down, Brady got undressed and joined her in having sex with Pauline.

The sun had fallen behind the mountains, and it was getting dark. Brady stood up and told Pauline to get dressed. She started to put her clothes back on, and when she reached for her necklace, Myra grabbed it from her and told her, "You won't need this where you're going!" The outburst made Brady mad enough to slap Myra across the face, and she went silent.

Brady returned to the van to get what he needed to finish the job and left the girls alone.

Myra picked up a knife she had in the truck and attempted to stab Pauline in the chest, but the knife didn't penetrate as the blade was bent. Myra then punched Pauline in the face a few times, which caused Pauline's nose to start bleeding.

When Brady returned and saw that Myra had not killed Pauline yet, he took his knife and cut her throat. Blood started to gush out of Pauline's neck, but she was still alive. So Brady slashed her neck again. This time, it severed her carotid artery, and she was dead in seconds.

Myra told Brady that the girl they had just killed was Pauline Reade. At first, Brady didn't remember who she was. Then he realized they had just eliminated the competition for David Smith for Myra's sister, Maureen.

It was too dark to take pictures of Pauline, so he told Myra to return the knife and camera to the van and get the spade. When she returned, Brady dug into the soft peat until he reached about five feet. He grabbed Pauline by her shoulders while Myra held her legs, and they put her into the hole. Brady started shoveling peat onto Pauline's body until she was fully buried, and Myra pulled up handfuls of grass by the roots and stomped them over top of the grave to make sure that there was no sign of a disturbance.

The couple counted how many steps it took to get back to the van so that they could find the grave again if they had to. Then they changed all the clothes they were wearing during the rape and murder. Myra headed back home with her van, but Brady stayed at the moor and buried the spade he had used to bury Pauline's body.

When Myra pulled up and parked her van in front of their home, she noticed Pauline Reade's mother searching the street for her daughter. By the time Brady got back home, nobody was on the street looking for Pauline. At 2:30 in the morning, Ian and Myra were cutting up the clothes they wore and burning them. Meanwhile, Pauline's father got out of bed and went to the social club to look for his daughter.

Myra has a slightly different memory of what happened that night at the moor with Pauline Reade. She claimed that she was waiting on Gorton Lane, and when Pauline got close to the van, it was Brady, who was parked and sitting on his motorbike across the street. Myra said he flashed headlights to signal her he chose who he wanted. She was to get that person.

Myra also claimed she drove Pauline to the moor, and Brady followed them there. When they parked, Brady and Pauline looked for the glove alone and were gone for about one hour. Brady returned alone and took her out to where Pauline was already dead and told her to stay with the body while he went and got the spade to bury her with.

It was then that Myra figured that Brady had raped Pauline as well since her clothes were all disheveled. Myra claimed she became scared for her life and her family, as she could no longer trust what Brady would do.

Several weeks passed, and the Police still had no leads on the missing Pauline Reade. Brady and Myra were able to get over the panic and excitement of committing the murder and soon moved on to their next victim.

Around this time, Myra was in a minor traffic accident and became friends with the policeman who wrote her a citation. Myra claimed she eventually fell in love with this police officer, who would come to her house and leave out the back when they heard Brady's motorbike approaching.

In Myra's later version, she claimed that she met the policeman when he came to look at her van, which she had decided to sell. Brady claimed that he encouraged the affair between Myra and the policeman so that they would be privy to inside information. It should be said that the police officer came forward after Myra was arrested and was cleared of any involvement in the murders.

A couple of months later, Brady and Myra decided it would be safe to head back to the moor and return to their routine of drinking and hanging out there. They were in shock when they arrived to see that North Sea Gas had been digging a trench for a new pipeline and narrowly missed their hidden spade buried in a shallow grave there. Even more terrifying to the couple was just how close it was to where they buried Pauline Reade, who lay buried just a few yards away.

The couple spent the day at Saddleworth taking pictures of Myra and her dog, Puppet, on and around the grave. On their ride home, something resonated with Brady for years to come. As they turned a sharp corner from the moor, a young girl strolled across the road just when Brady floored the bike. She was walking so lightly that it was like she was floating. Immediately, Brady slammed on the brakes and came to a sliding halt. The girl turned and looked at him in the eyes and said, "Sorry, God bless." Then she continued across the road as if nothing had happened.

6

JOHN KILBRIDE

Years before, one of Brady's girlfriends had given him a sealed pack of Tarot cards. "I used them from a psychological point of view, not occult. The combination of intricate designs and colors, plus the multi-interpretational relationship of meanings, made the cards a meditative and psychological conduit, providing a conduit to the subconscious, reflecting inner doubts or confidence in some immediate project at hand. Based on a study of such self-serving amateurs, I do not hesitate to state that one could achieve a higher percentage of success with a pack of Tarot cards," Brady claimed in his book, *Gates of Janus*.

Autumn arrived softly in Gorton. It was still mild and dry. The only way you could tell summer was over was the leaves falling from the trees, covering the roads. One night, while drinking wine, the couple pulled out their master plans, placed a map on the living room table, and started to plot for their next victim.

They decided to go to a different area this time. They didn't want it too close to where Pauline went missing and to avoid being recognized by someone they knew; the further they went, the better. They soon decided on a town five miles from Gorton, Ashton-Under-Lyne. The couple grabbed their jackets and decided to go and check out the city.

When they arrived in their newly selected town, they came across the Ashton Market. They agreed that the market was the perfect place to pick someone up because a long, dark street ran behind it with no houses. They carefully made their plans and decided to make the following Saturday, November 23, 1963, the day of their next killing.

Brady rented a car for the trip to Ashton Market to find a victim, as they thought it would be best to change their vehicle every time they wanted to commit a murder. The couple went to Manchester on the Friday night before, just in case the Police checked to see who had rented cars on the day the person went missing. When they were at the station renting the car, they first heard about President Kennedy of the United States being shot. When they arrived home and turned on the television, all programming had been preempted, and it was all about the Kennedy assassination and the possibility of World War III starting.

Sheila and Pat Kilbride were married and in their 30s. They lived in Ashton-Under-Lyne with their six children, two miles from the Ashton Market. Their oldest child, John Kilbride, was 12 years old and had just started attending a Roman Catholic secondary school.

Saturday, November 23rd, started like every other Saturday morning for the Kilbride family: with a family breakfast, and then everyone did their chores for the day. John asked his mother if he could go to the movies with his friend, John Ryan. They went to see *The Mongols* with Jack Palance. The movie ended at about 4:30 p.m. that afternoon, and the boys decided to go to the market to try to make some money. They knew many vendors would pay kids to help pack away their wares after the market closed.

A dark fog had descended over the market sometime around 6:00 p.m., and John Ryan decided he wanted to go home. When he left, John Kilbride was standing beside a large garbage bin.

Only two witnesses to what happened next existed: Ian Brady and Myra Hindley. Both versions of the events are included.

BRADY

According to Brady, everything went as planned. Myra told the boy at the market that she had lost her glove while Brady watched the crowd to ensure nobody was watching the two talking. Myra took Kilbride to her car, and they got in together. Myra then picked up Brady at a prearranged place and headed to the moor.

Brady claimed that when they arrived, they parked, and the three of them walked into the moor. John Kilbride kept asking the couple what they were doing there and where they were going. John was getting scared because it was getting dark, plus he couldn't see well enough to find a glove.

Brady then gave the "Groucho" signal, and Myra grabbed the boy. He started to struggle and kick at her. Brady then joined in and helped bring him to the ground. Brady pulled the boy's pants and underwear down, and with Myra holding his legs, Brady sexually assaulted John. After the assault, Brady strangled the boy to death with his bare hands.

Brady then went to find the spade and returned to dig a grave for John's body. When the hole was deep enough, the couple placed his body into it face down. Before Brady covered the body with dirt, he slapped the boy's backside and shouted out, "Take that, you bastard!"

HINDLEY

Myra claimed she wore a black wig that day and waited on a side street while Brady picked up John Kilbride. She claimed that Brady got him into the car by offering him some sherry to help him find a lost glove. Then they drove to Saddleworth Moor and parked.

Myra claimed she stayed in the car while Brady and John walked into the moor. While waiting with the car, she opened the trunk and took out a rifle they had placed there earlier that day. After half an hour, she flashed her car lights into the moor. She said she saw three flashes from a flashlight, and Brady returned to the car within minutes. He was carrying the spade and one of the boys' shoes.

Brady told her that he had tried to cut the boy's throat with his knife, but it had a serrated blade and was too blunt, so he had to strangle the boy with his shoestring. One flaw about Myra's version of events is that records show the rifle she had was bought in 1964, after this murder. Ian Brady also denied Myra's claim that Brady used a knife; why would he use a short, blunt knife? After all, he nearly decapitated Pauline Reade with a knife, and he would have had no problem killing a young boy with a knife as well.

The couple returned home and followed the same routine as they had after Pauline Reade's murder, burning all their clothes and the victim's shoes as well. They cleaned the car thoroughly and returned it to the auto rental.

The Kilbrides called the Police the following day, on Sunday. The Kennedy assassination overshadowed the reports in the news of the now-missing boy, but the locals were still able to find about 100 volunteers to help look for him. The Police even used a psychic, Annie Lansley, in this case. She saw John Kilbride's resting place on a downward slope, with a skyline completely barren and no trees in sight, a main road nearby, and a stream. Brady later commented that he thought Lansley was accurate but didn't believe in the psychic stuff. He added that she would have been next on their list if she had been correct about their next victim.

In the months following the murder of John Kilbride, Brady himself broke one of his own rules and wrote Kilbride's name in his master plan book. Once found, the name in the book would later cause the couple problems with the Police.

7

KEITH BENNETT

Keith Bennett was a 12-year-old boy, the oldest of four children, who vanished on June 16, 1964. He lived in Longsight with his stepfather, Jimmy Johnson, and mother, Winnie, who was seven months pregnant when Keith disappeared.

Winnie planned to go to play bingo on the night her son disappeared. She left the house at 7:45 p.m. and took Keith with her. Keith was heading to stay with his grandmother for the night, as he did once a week. Keith had broken his glasses the night before at a swimming competition. He wore a T-shirt, blue jeans, a white leather jacket, and black shoes. Winnie and Keith parted ways at the crossroads.

Myra was parked on the street, waiting for the right victim to come along. She would lure them into her vehicle and take them to their death. When she saw Keith Bennett, she offered him some money if he could help her lift some boxes. He quickly got into the car with her, and they drove off.

BRADY

After they parked, Brady said all three of them walked into the moor. While they were walking, Keith told the couple that he had to be at his grandmother's within the hour as he was supposed to spend the night with her. Myra assured him they would get him back in time and that he would not have to worry.

Brady knew precisely where they were walking to, as the couple had planned this murder the same as they had the two previous ones. The three of them walked for about three miles before Brady stopped and started to whistle a tune.

The tune was the signal for Myra to overtake the boy. Keith started to scream in panic, and Brady grabbed the boy's neck from behind. Keith fell onto the ground and began to kick and scream, just like John Kilbride had. While Myra was wrestling with the boy on the ground, Brady jumped on his back and put his hands around his neck. Myra then pulled the boy's pants down and held onto his legs while Brady proceeded to sexually assault the boy, keeping his hands around Keith's neck. After Brady finished, he strangled the boy with his bare hands.

Brady stood up and dressed while Myra turned the boy's body around so he could lie on his back. Brady grabbed his camera and started to take pictures of Keith. The couple buried Keith Bennett just as they had the two previous murders. This time, Brady marked the grave with a large stone. The two walked back to the car in the dark, went home, and followed the same steps as the other murderers by burning their clothes and cleaning the car thoroughly.

HINDLEY

Myra claimed that Brady was already in the car's back seat when she picked up Keith Bennett. She said it was Brady who saw Keith and told Myra he was the one. She then drove to the Saddleworth Moor and parked the car.

Myra then claimed that Brady and Keith walked ahead of her into the moor. She kept a distance behind them to watch for anybody around. At one point, Brady signaled to Myra to stop following them and stay where she was.

She stayed in that spot until Brady returned about half an hour later. He was carrying the spade, but Keith wasn't with him. Myra said she asked Brady if he had sex with the boy, and he wouldn't answer her. She went on to say that she never did see Keith's body, and the two of them walked back to the car and drove home.

Brady developed the pictures he had taken of Keith, and Myra said the boy was covered in blood. The photos were too blurry and didn't please Brady, so he destroyed them.

The morning after Keith went missing, his grandmother went to see Winnie to find out why Keith never came to her house for the night. The two women were upset and started looking for Keith, checking his school and the local medical clinic. Nobody had seen him.

Keith's stepfather became the prime suspect for the Police. They checked under the floor of their house and even dug up their garden. The rumors around the town ran rampant. Neighbors thought the boy had been killed by his stepfather and dumped in the river.

8

LESLEY-ANN DOWNEY

Brady and Hindley had murdered three people so far – raped them, killed them, and buried them in the spot where they died. All three murders had been committed outside, but the next killing would be different. It would be committed indoors.

In August 1964, Myra's sister, Maureen, now 18, married David Smith, who was 16. Maureen was seven months pregnant. None of Maureen's family attended the wedding. Brady devised a plan to take Maureen and David out for the day as a honeymoon present. The four of them ended up out at the moor with several bottles of wine.

The women stayed where they parked and talked while the men walked away into the distance and spent several hours together. According to Brady, this was the first time he brought up the opportunity for Smith to make money by helping him out.

When the four arrived home, the men stayed downstairs for hours, discussing plans while the sisters went to bed. It was the first of many drinking nights the two couples would have. About the same time, Myra, who had been living with her grandmother, moved to a new house, and Brady moved in with them.

One night, when the couple was out shopping, they saw an advertisement for a fair happening in the area on Boxing Day, December 26th. They were both excited that many children would be coming to the fair. It was time to go home and make plans for another murder.

On December 26th, around 2:00 p.m., Myra took her grandmother to her son's house across town and returned to pick her up later that night, around 9:30 p.m.

Ten-year-old Lesley-Ann Downey lived with her mother, Ann, and brother Tommy. Ann had been dating Alan West, whom she eventually married. On December 26th, the day of the fair, Lesley, Tommy, and a few other friends went to the fair as they had done in previous years. Lesley wore her red dress with lace, a pink sweater, red shoes, and a blue coat. She had six pennies for spending money.

After the kids ran out of money, they headed home. Lesley noticed a show going on and wanted to stay and watch it. She told the others to head back, and she would catch up to them.

We don't know the exact chain of events after Brady and Hindley found Lesley. However, the police found a tape recording of the three of them in one of the bedrooms. Also, there were pictures of Lesley found that showed her tied up and wearing a leather outfit, which was thought to have been taken after the tape recording was made. In the nine pictures found, Lesley was naked and posed in various ways, such as praying, kneeling, and one with her arm stretched out.

Myra's Story

Myra claimed that Brady found Lesley and was with the girl first. Brady dropped some boxes beside Lesley and asked if she would help pick them up for some money. The three of them placed the boxes into the car and drove off.

When they arrived at their house, Myra

claimed that Brady had taken Lesley upstairs into a bedroom and had left Myra alone downstairs. She claimed that Brady told her to keep an eye out for anybody who might come by the house and to fill the bathtub with warm water. She did what she was told and waited in the bathroom, and when the water in the tub became cold, she drained it and filled it up again. Myra became worried and went into the bedroom. She saw Lesley lying on the bed face down and figured she was dead. Myra saw a lot of blood running down her legs, which made her think that Lesley had been raped.

When they went to dispose of the body at Saddleworth Moor, Brady went over the hill and disappeared in the distance. He had gone to get the spade. At that moment, a policeman pulled up beside Myra, who was waiting by the car, and asked if everything was okay. She was in a panic, as Lesley's body was still in the trunk, but the quick-thinking Myra replied that she was just letting her spark plugs dry out. The officer believed her and drove off.

Myra then drove to pick up her grandmother. It was after 11:00 p.m. when she finally arrived there. When her uncle answered the door, Myra told him how bad the roads were, and that's why she couldn't get there sooner. She told her uncle that it would be way too dangerous to drive her grandma home now, which caused the two of them to argue, as Myra was still going to drive home. He couldn't understand why she couldn't take her grandma with her now.

Myra left alone anyway so she could return home to Brady and do their regular ritual of burning all the clothes and evidence left at their home. Her grandmother had to sleep on the floor at her son's house. The next morning, at around 10:30, Myra went to pick up her grandmother.

Like other stories Hindley told about the previous murders, this story doesn't fit with any of the evidence. The tape recording found later proved she was involved throughout the crime and not downstairs watching out the window, making sure nobody came to the house.

Brady's Story

Brady said that Myra picked up Lesley at the fair by herself and was with Myra in the car when they picked up Brady a few blocks away. The three of them went back to Myra and Brady's new home. Brady claimed that Myra took part in raping Lesley. He said that it was Myra who strangled Lesley with a silk cord while Brady held the girl down. He also added that Myra went to the pub afterward and played with that same silk cord in public.

According to Brady, after they were done with her, the tub was needed to wash Lesley's body before disposal to remove any hairs or fibers she might have picked up while in their house. The couple carried the body out to the car, drove out to the moor, and buried Lesley not far from where Pauline Reade's body was.

Transcript Of The Tape Recording

BRADY: "Get out of the fucking road! Get in the fucking basket!"

The sound of a door banging, then some heavy footsteps crossing a floor, then somebody blowing into a microphone. A few more footsteps followed with a very quiet woman's voice, so soft that it was not understandable.

In the distance, you can hear some more footsteps lightly walking across the room. Some light whispered conversation was happening at the same time.

> LESLEY-ANN DOWNEY: "Don't! Mum - ah!" followed by a high-pitched little girl's scream.

HINDLEY: "Shut up!"
LESLEY: "Oh, please. Oh, help."
HINDLEY: "Shh. Shh. Shut up!"

You could now hear the little girl scream loudly again.

HINDLEY: "Shut up. Shut up."

You could hear a gurgling sound, and then the child began to cry.

HINDLEY: "Keep quiet, and you'll be alright. Go on."

The sound of heavy footsteps running up some stairs and then entering the room while the child continued to cry.

BRADY: "Here."
HINDLEY: "Hush hush, go on."

The child continued to cry lightly, almost like a moaning sound.

> HINDLEY: “You are alright, hush, hush. Put it in your mouth, hush, and shift that hand.”

The child continued crying.

> HINDLEY: “Put it in your mouth and keep it in, and you’ll be alright. Put it in! Stop it. If you don’t shh.”

The child was now making a muffled sound.

> BRADY: “Put it in at the same time.” The woman screamed, “Put it in.”
>
> BRADY: “Put it in, keep it in. Stop it now! Stop it now!”
>
> HINDLEY: “I’m only doing this, and you’ll be alright. Put it in your mouth. Put it in, in!”

You could hear Brady and the woman talking with each other quietly, but too low to hear what they were saying.

HINDLEY: "Will you stop it, stop it! Shut!"

BRADY: "Quick. Put it in now!"

You could now hear a whimpering from the child and then a retching sound, almost like someone trying to throw up.

LESLEY: "What's this in for?"

BRADY: "Put it in."

LESLEY: "Can I just tell you something? I must tell you something. Please take your hands off me a minute, please, please, mummy, please. I can't tell you."

The child let out a loud grunt.

LESLEY: "I can't tell you, I can't

breathe. I can't, Dad. Will you take your hands off me?"

BRADY: "No, tell me."

LESLEY: "Please, God."

BRADY: "Tell me."

LESLEY: "I can't while you got your hands on me."

BRADY: "Why don't you keep it in?"

LESLEY: "Why? What are you going to do with me?"

BRADY: "I want some photographs, that's all. Put it in."

LESLEY: "Don't undress me, will you?"

HINDLEY: "That's right, don't—"

LESLEY: "It hurts me. I want to see mummy, honest to God."

BRADY: "Put it in!"

LESLEY: "I swear on the Bible."

BRADY: "Put it in and hurry up now! The quicker you do this, the quicker you'll get home."

LESLEY: "I've got to go because I'm going out with my mamma. Leave me, please. Help me, will you?"

BRADY: "Put it in your mouth, and you'll be alright."

LESLEY: "Will you let me go when this is out?"

BRADY: "Yes. The longer it takes you to do this, the longer it takes you to get home."

LESLEY: "What are you going to do with me first?"

BRADY: "I'm going to take some photographs. Put it in your mouth."

LESLEY: "What for?"

BRADY: "Put it in your mouth, right in."

LESLEY: "I'm not going to do it."

BRADY: "Put it in. If you don't get that hand down, I'll slit your neck!"

LESLEY: "Won't you let me go? Please."

BRADY: "No, no. Put it in. Stop talking. What's your name?"

LESLEY: "Lesley."

BRADY: "Lesley, what?"

LESLEY: "Ann."

BRADY: "What's your second name?"

LESLEY: "Westford. Westford."

BRADY: "Westford?"

LESLEY: "I have to get home before 8 o'clock. I got to get, or I'll get killed if I don't. Honest to God."

BRADY: "Yes."

The sound of the woman's footsteps walking out of the room and going down some stairs, some clicks, and then the woman came back up the stairs and into the room again.

BRADY: "What is it?"

HINDLEY: "I've left the light on."

BRADY - "You have?"

HINDLEY: "So that -" (the rest of the sentence is not clear enough to tell what she said)

The child then started to cry and said, "It hurts my neck."

BRADY: "Hush, put it in your mouth, and you'll be all right."

HINDLEY: "Now listen, stop crying."

LESLEY: "It hurts me."

HINDLEY: "Hush! Shut up, now put it in. Pull that hand away and don't dally, and just keep your mouth shut, please. Wait a bit. I'll put this on again. Do you get me?"

LESLEY: "No! I-"

HINDLEY: "Shh, hush. Put that in your mouth, and again, packed more solid."

LESLEY: "I want to go home. Honest to God. I'll (muffled speech) before 8 o'clock."

HINDLEY: "No, it's alright."

BRADY: "Eh!"

It was then that music started playing. At first, it was some country-style music, followed by "Jolly St. Nicholas" and then the song "Little Drummer Boy." Throughout the music, you could hear muffled noises and people speaking, but their voices were too quiet to hear what they were saying.

Suddenly, there were three loud cracks, even-timed and systematic, and the music grew fainter. The last thing you could hear before the tape stopped was some footsteps across the floor.

Meanwhile, back at the Downey House, Ann Downey and Alan West were in a panic. Tommy had come home without Lesley. The two of them went to all the neighbors' houses, knocked on doors, and searched through the streets looking for her. They returned home at about 10:00 p.m. with no results, so they called the police.

The next day, the police took Alan West, Lesley's soon-to-be stepfather, in for questioning, and he was interrogated for several hours.

9

EDWARD EVANS

On April 24, 1965, David Smith and Maureen Hindley lost their six-month-old baby daughter to bronchitis in the hospital. Feeling as though they had no other support from their families and no other friends, the loss led Maureen and David to get even more involved with Maureen's sister, Myra, and Ian Brady.

The two couples started to go to the Saddleworth Moor regularly. The girls stayed near the car, and the men headed into the moor. Unawares, Brady began to take Smith to the places where he had buried the bodies of his previous victims. Sometimes, Smith would stand on top of someone's grave without knowing it. Brady started giving Smith books like *The Life and Ideas of Marquis de Sade*, emphasizing specific passages such as "Should murder punish murder?"

Often, after leaving the moor, the four returned to Myra and Brady's house, where the girls would retire to bed, and the men stayed in the living room drinking until daylight. During times like these, Brady started to discuss his plans to commit armed robberies and asked Smith if he would like to join in. On one night in particular, October 2nd, Brady told Smith that he had killed before and had the pictures to prove it. He also claimed that he would do another murder to prove it.

On Tuesday, October 5th, Smith returned a box of books to Brady. Months before, Brady had lent him the books, instructing him to read them and write down quotes he liked in a separate exercise book. After a few minutes, Brady took the books upstairs and returned with two suitcases. In the suitcases, there was the tape recording of Lesley Ann Downing, books of sexual perversions, gun cartridges, and a few letters.

Brady and Myra put the suitcases in the trunk of their car and headed to the Manchester Train Station, where they deposited them into a locker. Brady was still unsure about Smith's ability to murder someone, and he thought about taking Smith out for a drive, parking the car, handing him the gun, and telling him to kill a random stranger. If he couldn't do it, he would shoot Smith. But this idea was not a good one since it might lead the Police to Myra, as Smith was married to her sister.

On the morning of October 5th, Smith told Brady and Myra that they had received an eviction notice as they owed their landlord 14 pounds and 8 shillings. He wanted to borrow the money from them, but Myra told him they were broke. Brady told Smith that they could get the money from "rolling a queer"—they could go out and find a homosexual, offer him sex if he would come home with them, and steal his money. Because it was still illegal to be homosexual, the person they mugged would not go to the Police.

Their next murder was the first time the couple had not followed their master plan list, and Brady had not used his tarot cards to predict what would happen.

Edward Evans was a 17-year-old apprentice engineer who lived in the Ardwick area of Manchester with his mother, Edith, father John, and one sister and brother. On October

6, 1965, around 6:30 p.m., Edward went out with his friend, Michael Mahone, to see a soccer game at the Old Trafford soccer stadium. Edward wore a white T-shirt, blue jeans, brown Italian dress shoes, and a suede jacket.

Edward was to meet his friend at Auntie's Bar. According to the bar owner, George Smith, Edward showed up around 7:00 p.m., but his friend Michael did not. Edward ended up leaving the bar to go to the game alone.

At about 10:30 p.m. that evening, Myra and Brady went to the store to get some wine, then drove to the Manchester Train Station and parked. Ian exited the car and entered the station while Myra waited there. She had parked on a double yellow line, and a policeman came by and told her to move and that if she were still there when he returned, he would ticket her.

When Brady got into the station, within two minutes, he recognized a young man standing alone, leaning against a wall beside a cigarette machine. Brady had seen him at a Manchester gay pub several times, but the two had never spoken.

Brady walked over to the man, and they chatted briefly. The man was Edward Evans. According to Brady, he asked Evans to come back to his place for a drink, which was a covert way of inviting him back to have sex.

Edward agreed, and they got into the car with Myra. Brady told Edwards that Myra was his sister. When they arrived home, Brady told Myra to get David Smith and ask him to come. When they got out, Brady whispered to Myra to wait a while before they came over.

Up to now, the stories from Myra, Brady, and Smith were the same, but as usual, it changed when we got to the rape and murder.

HINDLEY'S STORY

Myra insisted that Smith was waiting at home, fully dressed, and that she had no idea about Brady and Smith's plan to murder Edward Evans. When she arrived at Smith's place, Maureen was surprised to see her sister and wanted to know why she was coming over so late. Myra said she had a message from their mother, who tried to come around Friday to borrow Maureen's shoes.

Myra said she asked Smith to walk back to her place with her, as it was dark out and the outside of the apartment building was not on. The corporation that runs the building confirmed that the lights were out that night at the trial. Smith agreed and told Maureen that he would return soon. He also took the stick he used when he walked his dog, which was about two inches thick and three feet long, with a string wrapped around the end.

When the two arrived at Brady and Myra's, Myra told Smith to wait across the street until she flashed the kitchen lights twice. Then he was to come in the front door. Myra disappeared around the back of the house, and Smith waited anxiously.

Brady gave her the signal that the murder was about to happen. Myra went into the kitchen, flashed the lights twice, and claimed that she never came out again until the murder was over and all the noise had stopped. According to Myra, she helped by getting the blankets that the men wrapped the body in and ran upstairs to make sure her grandmother was asleep. She yelled down to the men when it was safe to bring the body upstairs and place it in the spare room. She said the three of them spent three hours cleaning the living room and made plans on how and where they would dispose of the body the next night. David Smith then left for his home around 3:00 a.m.

BRADY'S STORY

According to Brady, he and Edward Evans entered the house, opened a bottle of wine, sat on the sofa, and started talking. Myra went upstairs and changed, then went over to get David Smith. He said that it only took the two men a few minutes before they began to have sex. They started kissing, and that led to them having oral sex. Later when the trial was held, forensic evidence of dog hairs from the house was found on Smith's anus and legs after his jeans were removed from his corpse.

Shortly after the men finished, they put their clothes back on and continued to drink. They could hear Myra and Smith coming up the front stairs, approaching the front door. Brady bounced up quickly, ran to the front door, and opened it.

Brady looked at Smith and shouted, "Do you still want those miniatures? They are in the kitchen." The couple entered the front door, headed down the hallway, and into the kitchen. Brady returned to the living room and walked behind the sofa, where Edward was still seated.

Brady then claimed that he had an axe lying under the back side of the sofa, and he reached down, picked it up, and brought it down with great force onto Edward's head. He was aiming for the back of his head to kill him instantly, but Edward turned around at the last second, causing the axe blade to bounce off his crown.

Edward started screaming out, so Brady kept swinging his axe. Myra and Smith came out of the kitchen and just stood and watched. The dogs in the kitchen were barking uncontrollably. Myra's grandmother, sleeping upstairs, was awakened by all the commotion and shouted down the stairs, asking what had happened. Brady said that Myra shouted something back at her grandmother, but he couldn't remember what Myra said as his mind was focused on killing Evans.

Edward was still alive after a dozen blows to his head, so Brady went into the kitchen and grabbed some electrical cord. Brady came back out into the living room and strangled Edward to death by wrapping the wire around his neck. Edward finally went quiet. Brady stood up and handed his axe to Smith. Brady said he later did this to ensure Smith's prints were on the handle.

The walls, floors, and carpets were splattered with blood. Brady then said, "This is the messiest murder I have committed." He reached down, took Edward's wallet from his jeans, and opened it to look through it. He took the wallet, shoes, and the axe and put everything into a large travel bag.

Brady had sprained his left ankle sometime during the night, so he decided that they would put Edward's body upstairs in the spare bedroom. He took the string that was on the end of Smith's dog stick and tied Edward's body up into a fetal position. Myra had spread a white cotton blanket on the floor, and Brady and Smith placed the body in the middle and wrapped it up. Then, they wrapped the body in a plastic sheet and another blanket.

The two men carried the body up to the empty spare bedroom while Myra held on to the door handle of her grandmother's door, just in case she decided to get up and come out to see what was happening. Brady claimed that he had to take his holster and gun off and put them down in the bedroom, as they got in his way when they were moving the body. Had he remembered to retrieve the weapon, he could have used it on the Police when they came to search the house.

They spent almost three hours cleaning up all the blood in the living room. Brady would comment later that he thought it was incompetence that the Police couldn't find traces of blood on their carpet.

Smith then left to go home, and Brady was

pleased with how Smith handled himself during the murder and how calm he remained. Brady and Myra drank wine until about 3:30 a.m. that night before falling asleep. It was then that Brady thought that there would be no rush to bury the body, as there was nothing to connect them to the victim. He thought he might like to burn Edward on their next bonfire night.

DAVE SMITH'S STORY

> "Brady opened the door, and he said in a very loud voice, "Do you want those miniatures?" I nodded my head to say yes, and he led me into the kitchen, gave me three miniature bottles of spirits, and said, "Do you want the rest?"
>
> When I first walked into the house, the door to the living room was closed. Ian went into the living room, and I waited in the kitchen. I waited about a minute or two, and then suddenly, I heard a hell of a scream. It sounded like a woman, high-pitched. Then the screams carried on, one after

> another, loud. Then I heard Myra shout, "Dave, help him!" very loud.
>
> When I ran in, I just stood inside the living room, and I saw a young lad. He was lying with his head and shoulders on the couch, and his legs were on the floor. He was facing upwards. Ian was standing over him, facing him, with his legs on either side of the young lad's legs.
>
> The lad was still screaming. Ian had a hatchet in his hands. He was holding it above his head, and he hit the lad on the left side of his head with the hatchet. I heard the blow; it was a terribly hard blow; it sounded horrible."

According to Smith, Brady persuaded him to help dispose of the body since he sprained his ankle in the fight with Evans and couldn't do it himself. Smith wasn't strong enough to carry Evans to Brady's car, so they decided to put the body upstairs in the spare bedroom, with Smith assuring Brady that he would indeed help him dispose of the corpse later.

Smith claimed he was scared that Brady would kill him once they were finished, but

Brady told him he could go. On the way home, Smith was so nervous about Brady attacking him that he would jump and yelp at any noise he heard.

Maureen was sleeping in their bedroom when Smith walked in. He went straight to the bathroom, started wildly throwing up, and moaned loudly, almost like a painful cry. His behavior woke up Maureen, who joined him in the bathroom. As she began to rub his back, she noticed that he was covered in blood.

"What happened?" she screamed in panic. Smith slowly stammered out that he had witnessed a murder and that it was her sister, Myra, and Brady who did the killing. Maureen fell into a deep shock but told him that they had to go to thc Police.

Smith agreed but was still terrified of the rage he saw in Brady's eyes when he killed Evans. He was worried that Brady would be watching them from their house, and if he saw them leaving, he would come after them. The couple decided to wait until daylight when many people would be out on the road, and they would have a better chance of getting away.

At 6:00 a.m., they slipped out the front door. Smith was armed with a kitchen knife, and Maureen a screwdriver. When they got to the nearest telephone booth, Smith called the Police and explained what he had witnessed the previous night.

A squad car drove to the booth, picked the couple up, and took them to the police station for questioning. After Smith explained what he had witnessed to the officer, they called Superintendent Bob Talbot, a well-known criminal detective in Britain.

Talbot met with Sergeant Carr and headed to the house where the murder was alleged to have happened. Smith told them that Brady had at least two guns and would leave the house to go to work at 8:30 a.m. Talbot arranged for twenty-four uniformed officers to attend the house while they searched.

Talbot and the other officers made it to the location and waited to catch Brady as he was leaving for work. After 8:30 came and went, and no Brady, he decided to approach the house. He saw a deliveryman dropping off loaves of bread down the street, so he borrowed his white delivery jacket before knocking on Brady's door.

Talbot went around to the back of the house and knocked on the back door. Myra answered the door and seemed surprised to see a bread-man at the door.

> DETECTIVE: "Is your husband in?"
>
> MYRA: "I haven't got a husband."
>
> DETECTIVE: "I am a police superintendent, and I have reason to believe there is a man in the house."
>
> MYRA: "There's no man here."
>
> DETECTIVE: "I have received a report that an act of violence took place here last night, and we are investigating it."
>
> MYRA: "There's nothing wrong here."
>
> Talbot pushed past Myra while taking off his white coat, and she then realized that he was indeed a detective.
>
> MYRA: "He's in the other room. He's in the other room in the bed."

The detective entered the living room and found Brady seated on a sofa pushed up against the wall, with no back on it. He was wearing a string vest and had a surprised look on his face. Myra claimed later that when the detective walked into the living room and saw Brady staring in shock, she finally felt free.

Talbot looked around the room and had a Sergeant look through the kitchen. Brady had an exercise book in front of him and a ballpoint pen. After Talbot introduced himself and told him why they were there, Ian started writing.

Talbot turned to Myra and said he wanted to search upstairs, so Myra led him to the staircase. The two walked up to the top landing, and Talbot tried the first door. It opened, and inside, sitting and drinking some tea, was Myra's grandmother. He excused himself, closed her door, and walked to the next room. When he tried the door, it was locked. He asked Myra if she had the key.

Myra explained that the room was always locked as she kept her firearms in there and that she had left her key at work. The two walked down the stairs and into the hallway. Talbot told her that he wouldn't leave until he could check the locked room. He offered to send an officer to her workplace to get the key. Myra said nothing.

Brady said, "You better give him the key. A fight got out of hand last night. It's upstairs." His wording was his hint to Myra so that she would know what story to go with when they found the body. The two walked back up the stairs, and this time, Myra unlocked the door and swung it open.

The room was set up like a regular spare bedroom with a bed, a dresser, and an armchair. The detective noticed under the window that there was a large parcel covered up with a blanket. He walked closer to it and saw a travel bag beside the end of the blanket. It was open and had a bloody axe in it.

Talbot went back down the stairs and told Brady to get dressed. He asked two officers to watch over him.

Brady and Myra did have a plan in case they got caught. They would shoot the Police in the head first, then Brady would kill Myra, then put the gun in his mouth and kill himself. The two detectives could have been killed if they had been able to carry out their plan. Fortunately, because Brady had left his gun upstairs while he and Smith moved the body, Brady wasn't armed.

The neighbors were all out on their front lawns looking on as more Police started showing up at the Brady house. Brady was escorted out to the police car wearing handcuffs. Myra's grandmother was confused about what was happening, and Myra walked her over to their neighbors.

10

TRIAL & PRISON

TRIAL

The trial began on April 19, 1966, and lasted two weeks. Judge Fenton Atkinson presided. The courtroom had to be fitted with safety glass to protect Hindley and Brady after the public had issued many threats. It was also to protect the prosecutors and witnesses against Brady. He often attempted to spit on them as they walked by on their way to the stand to testify.

Once, when Brady and Hindley were brought to the courthouse, two figures covered with blankets jumped on the police car that carried them. The two were arrested and identified as Patrick and Terry Downey, the father and uncle of victim Lesley Ann Downey. The two men were eventually released, but told they would be charged if they returned to the courthouse.

Both Hindley and Brady had been charged with three murders - Lesley Ann Downey, John Kilbride, and Edward Evans. *The murders of Pauline Reade and Keith Bennett were not yet known.* Each of the defendants had a defense lawyer. Brady's lawyer was David Lloyd Adamson, and Myra's lawyer was Phillip Curtis. Brady appeared in court wearing a grey suit, white shirt, and a vest. Myra appeared in a black and white spotted suit with a yellow blouse and wore her bleached blonde hair.

The couple had pleaded not guilty to all charges, which was no surprisc. For 15 days, the trial was heard in an open court so anybody could watch. Over 150 pieces of evidence and 86 witnesses were called to testify.

The prosecutor, William Mars-Jones, used David Smith as the chief witness, and he testified for about seven hours. Smith was now 18 years old and showed up in tight jeans and a velvet shirt. The prosecution made him go and put on a tie during a break in the proceedings. It was revealed after the trial that Smith was to be paid an enormous sum for his exclusive story, but only if the couple were convicted. Judge Atkinson called this finding a gross interference with the course of justice.

Maureen Hindley appeared in a new suit, had a bouffant hairstyle, and testified that Myra had changed after meeting and going out with Brady. It was as though she was trying to tell the court that Myra was a sweet and innocent woman who Brady had warped. Under cross-examination, she was asked about receiving 100 pounds for giving a story to the newspapers. She admitted to it but said it never changed her story.

David and Maureen Smith's admission of being paid by a newspaper for their stories was not damaging to the prosecution and did not affect the jury.

When it was Brady's turn to testify, it lasted eight hours, and Hindley testified for six hours. Hindley claimed throughout the trial that she was not responsible for any of the murders. She also claimed that she was not present in the room or on the tape of Downey being tortured. She claimed that she had been looking out the window and running a bath the whole time Brady was with Downey.

Much was made by the prosecutor about the tapes and books about Nazi figures that Brady owned. Brady responded that his fascination with Hitler and the Nazis was aesthetically-based, not political. He had admired the boldness and courage with which Hitler put his beliefs into effect in Germany.

Brady admitted to striking Edward Evans with an axe but insisted that since it was proven Evans died from strangulation, not the axe blows, he wasn't the one who killed him. The jury then heard the 16-minute tape of Lesley Ann Downey being assaulted and having her pictures taken by Brady and Myra. The prosecutor then explained that in the tape, when Myra and Brady were shouting at Lesley to "put it in," they were talking about Brady's penis, not a gag.

The jury retired to deliberate at 2:40 p.m. on May 6th and asked for three pieces of evidence: Brady's notebook, the disposal plan for Edward Evans' body, and Myra's shoes that had spots of Edward's blood on them. Two hours later, the jury asked for the dates that Myra bought her guns. The jury returned with their verdict by 5:00 p.m. that evening.

On May 6th, the jury found Ian Brady guilty of all three murders and Myra Hindley guilty of two of the murders (Lesley Ann Downey and Edward Evans).

The judge asked the couple to stand and asked if they had anything to say before sentencing. Brady said, "No, except that the guns were bought in July 1964." He then buttoned up his suit jacket and turned to look at Myra, who said nothing.

The judge then handed down sentencing:

> "Ian Brady, these were three calculated, cruel, cold-blooded murders. In your case, I pass the only sentence that the law now allows, which is three concurrent sentences of life imprisonment. Put him down."
>
> "In your case, Hindley, you have been found guilty of two equally horrible murders, and in the third as an accessory after the fact. On the two murders, the sentence is two concurrent sentences of life imprisonment, and on the charge of being an accessory after the fact to the death of Kilbride, a concurrent sentence of seven years imprisonment. Put her down."

Two days after they were sentenced, the judge released a letter to the Home Secretary:

> "Though I believe Brady is wicked beyond belief without hope of redemption, I cannot feel that the same is necessarily true of Hindley once she is removed from his influence. At present, she is as deeply corrupted as Brady, but it is not so long ago that she was taking instruction in the Roman Catholic Church and was a communicant and a normal sort of girl."

After the sentencing, Brady and Hindley spent one more night at Risley before being imprisoned. They could speak to each other one last time, only briefly in the hallway, before being taken away. Myra claimed that she only asked Brady not to kill himself in prison.

Myra Hindley was sent to Holloway Prison in London, and Ian Brady went to Durham Prison. They would never see each other again.

PRISON

Brady wrote his first letter to Myra on his sixth day in Durham Prison:

"Dear Myra, it's a beautiful morning, clear blue sky, a sharp early tang in the air and the sun's radiance hot on the skin. There's an old clock tower near here, the chimes ring out every quarter of an hour, that sound combined with the warbling of the birds helps to produce a pleasant backdrop and reduce the stark realities of the present cheerful country sounds."

I work in my cell during the day sewing mailbags, which may not be an ideal mode of work, but it's surprising how quickly time goes while doing it. Well, Myra, I hope you've gotten over the initial shock of your sentence. I at least got what I expected but you should never have been on any charge except for harboring. Keep your chin up. The day you are released will be the happiest day of my life. I expect none happier."

"So, clear your mind of well-justified hate and bitterness and approach each day in hope and each person as an individual. Never express despair; you have a future and I will see you begin life anew, and so, I'll dwell once

> more in freedom as seen through your eyes. But for now, keep your eyes looking towards the sky, ignore the grimy ground till you again tread grass underfoot. I'm counting on you, by gaining your freedom, to bring me back to life. So, don't let me down, Kiddo."
>
> Brady signed off "Ich werde sie nicht vergessen" (German for "I will not forget you").

Myra responded about one week later, but she was not so optimistic about her experiences in jail:

> "I don't for a minute think they'll grant my appeal, but I have nothing to lose by trying, and what's a year with sentences like ours? Anyway, I've been convicted and branded a murderess, so I'm not just sitting back and accepting it. We know each other, and one day, in the fullness of time, the truth will out. It must be so. I dreamed last night that Smith had died or left Maureen, and she came forward and said that

she lied about Ashton Market, etc. She had her baby last week, a boy. I think her conscience will start bothering her pretty soon."

"Here I am, Sunday, 7:30 p.m., there's a strong wind blowing, rattling the leaves on the many trees in the gardens outside my cell. It sounds just like home. There's a weeping willow in the center of the lane. I feel rather like one myself tonight. I feel desolate, not because I'm on my own, of course, but because you aren't here. I miss you all the time, but sometimes more than others. I hate Sundays anyway."

"You've read, of course, about all the publicity concerning the girl at school whose mother kept her off because she wasn't allowed to wipe her cutlery on a napkin? I read yesterday that the people have bought her story for 800 pounds and the BBC have paid her 130 pounds. What a waste of money."

I'll sign off again until tomorrow. I wear wax earplugs some nights. The girl in the next room sometimes spends her nights crying for her sister, so I put plugs in and cut that noise off.

> This cell is perfect for peace and quiet. I wish I could remain here indefinitely. However, if I move to the star wing, I hope to remain under rule 43 (*isolation from fellow prisoners, as they were both child sex offenders*) and cherish any solitude. It suits me fine."

Myra Hindley appealed her convictions in 1966 but was denied. She wrote letters to Brady once a week, and he wrote Myra every Friday until March 1972, when she wrote to Brady telling him that their love affair was over. She had started to believe in God, and she knew he would never accept such a change in her.

Myra then applied to be placed into the general population, which was granted. She could now walk around in prison without any escorts. The first thing she did with her newfound freedom was enroll in the Open University to take a Humanities degree class.

In January 1973, Myra found a new love, a lesbian prison officer, Patricia Cairns. The two of them quickly became close, and by November, they devised a plan to help Myra escape prison. They had the dream of going to Brazil to work as missionaries.

Maxine Croft, a 22-year-old woman in the same prison as Myra and a prison trustee, was brought into the plan by Cairns. She was serving three years for writing bad checks. As a trustee, Maxine had access to parts of the prison that were out of bounds for most prisoners, and she was allowed day paroles to London. Maxine returned from her outing, realizing that she was almost free. She was so stressed that she ended up telling prison officials about Cairn's plan to get Myra out of prison.

Patricia Cairns was fired from her job at the prison, arrested, and charged with conspiring to affect the escape of Myra Hindley. All three of them went to trial in April 1974 and pleaded guilty. Cairns was given a six-year sentence, Maxine Croft got an extra 18 months, and Myra got an additional 12 months added to her sentence. Maxine appealed her sentence, won, and was released immediately.

In 1983, David Astor, a friend of Myra's defense attorney, Frank Longford, started visiting Myra. Astor was also giving her money, which the church hid.

Ian Brady was sent to prison, where he spent nearly two decades until he was moved to the Ashworth Psychiatric Hospital, a high-security facility. He was diagnosed as a psychopath. He repeatedly stated that he did not ever want to be released and that he wanted to be allowed to die. Brady went on a hunger strike in 1999 and had to be force-fed, and this continued right through until 2012.

Brady claimed that the murders were not part of a never-ending series of serial killings but merely an existential exercise. He also claimed that he and Hindley had moved past the murders by the end of 1964 and had wanted to commit armed robberies in the future.

On November 29, 1984, a *Sunday People* journalist, Fred Harrison, was the first person in nine years to be allowed to visit Brady. Harrison reported that he thought Brady looked at least 90 years old. It was on his second visit to Brady that he was told about the murders of Pauline Reade and Keith Bennett and that Brady and Myra had committed them.

It took several more visits to get more of the details behind the murders and other murders that Brady was involved in, which nobody else knew anything about. In June 1985, Harrison started publishing his findings in a series of articles called "My Secret Murders." When Brady heard about the articles, he no longer accepted visits from Harrison. Harrison published a book about one year later called *Brady and Hindley: Genesis of the Moor Murders*.

What Brady had confessed to about the murders of Reade and Bennett was not about clearing his conscience or trying to give some relief to the victims' families. Instead, it was more selfish. In 1985, Myra had applied for parole. Rumor had it that it might get approved. So Brady decided he would act. By his confessing that the two of them had killed at least two others, the parole board denied Myra's application.

The relatives of Pauline Reade and Keith Bennett had read the articles written by Harrison and were impatient for the police to reopen the cases and find the bodies. They insisted that the police bring Brady and Myra back to the moor to show them where they buried the bodies.

In the Winter of 1986, Myra Hindley received a letter from Bennett's mother, Winnie, asking Hindley for help locating her son's remains. Myra was so moved by this letter that she decided to help. However, it is rumored that she heard about Brady's confession and wanted to get credit for discovering the bodies. It might even lead to her getting out on probation.

Hindley then made a 17-hour taped confession to the police, in which she described all five murders in great detail. She was taken to the moor twice so that she could show the police where the bodies were buried, but for three months, nothing was found.

Myra was taken to the moor on December 16, 1986, first by car in the early morning to an airport and then taken to the moor by the police helicopter. There was a leak to the press when this was to happen, so there were reporters all over the moor and even a helicopter rented by the media.

Myra was taken a second time to the moor on March 24, 1987, where she spent most of the time walking around the areas she had pointed out on the first visit. Myra's taped confession would be released in the next month, so police felt pressure to have the bodies of the victims before the public knew.

On July 1, 1987, Pauline Reade's body was found in an area that Hindley had shown the police. It was only about 300 feet from where Lesley Ann Downey's body was found.

After police found Pauline's body, Brady decided he would help the police, too. He was taken to the moor two times as well. He could not find Keith Bennett's grave; whether he didn't remember or was taking the police on a wild goose chase was unknown. The search for Bennett was called off on August 24, 1987.

In November 1987, the police acquired permission to take Brady out to the moor again to see if he would show them where Bennett was buried. On December 8, 1987, at 5:00 a.m., police took Brady to the moor again. They spent nine hours searching and found nothing.

In 2001, Brady published The Gates of Janus through Feral Publishing in the United States. It contains his studies and analyses of several serial killers. Madame Tussauds in London sent a letter to Brady asking for his details, such as eye color, etc., and a set of his clothes, as they were making a wax model of him for their House of Horrors.

Myra Hindley died in prison of bronchial pneumonia brought on by heart disease when she was 60 years old in November 2002. Ian

Brady died on May 15, 2017, in Ashworth Hospital.

Dave Smith was never charged in the murders but was rumored by the people in Manchester to have played a part in them. Smith was called names and ridiculed by all his neighbors and even strangers who just passed him on the street. One of his neighbors, William Lees, bothered him so much that Smith ended up stabbing him several times and was arrested and sentenced to three years in prison in July 1969. He died in Ireland in 2012.

Maureen Smith decided she would leave Smith when he was put in prison. By then, they had three children, and she was unable to handle raising them, so she gave them away to government child care. When Smith got out of prison in 1972, he gained custody of the three children and divorced Maureen in 1973. He later remarried. But just after getting custody of his children, Smith got arrested again. He had been living with his father, who had cancer. Smith gave him a milk drink containing over twenty crushed sodium amytal pills, killing his father. Smith ended up spending only two days in prison for the mercy killing.

Maureen also remarried a man named William Scott in 1974, who was 22 years older than she was, and they had a daughter, Sharon.

In 1980, Maureen suffered a brain hemorrhage. Myra was granted permission to visit her in the hospital, but Maureen had already passed by the time she arrived.

The house the couple shared on Wardle Brook Avenue was demolished by the local city council in 1987.

Keith Bennett's grave has still not been located.

THE LETTERS

Swiss psychiatrist, psychotherapist, and psychologist Carl Jung once said, "Everything that irritates us about others can lead us to an understanding of ourselves." German-Swiss poet and novelist Hermann Hesse said, "If you hate a person, you hate something in him that is part of yourself. What isn't part of ourselves doesn't disturb us." I have to wonder if anything like this was running through Ian Brady's mind when he wrote his letters from prison. After reading Brady's letters and his book, *The Gates of Janus*, I found applying both quotes to him easy. Throughout all his writings, when Brady disliked someone, another prisoner, the publisher of his book, or just anybody with whom he disagreed, he always called them a pedophile.

Throughout the "Moors Murders," several of Brady's victims were minors, both boys and girls. He sexually assaulted them and was convicted of the crimes. Therefore, Brady was an actual pedophile. So, was he lashing out at others, blaming them for what he did himself, and perhaps hated most about himself?

A great example is in Brady's Letter #2, in which he calls out Peter Sotos, who wrote the Afterword of his book for his publisher, claiming Sotos was a convicted pedophile. In truth, Sotos was not a pedophile. He was an American author with over 30 books published, a songwriter, and a musician in the British band "Whitchouse."

Sotos became controversial in 1984 when he began publishing a newsletter, *Pure*, which was the first to be dedicated primarily to serial killers. He then continued on this path by writing books about sexually motivated serial killers. One of those books was called *Little*, which discussed the murder of Leslie Ann Downey by Ian Brady. His writing the book is more likely why Brady didn't like Sotos.

When Brady's publisher had Sotos write the Afterword for his book, it upset him even more. The totality of Sotos' criminal history consists of his being arrested, charged, and convicted of possession of child pornography. He was found with a photocopy of a child pornography magazine that he used in the second edition of his *Pure* newsletter. Whether Sotos was using the material for reference for his magazine or was viewing the material for self-pleasure is unknown. Sotos was never charged with any other offense.

Throughout the Moors Murder trial, Brady refused to admit to ever sexually assaulting the young boys, and he refused to discuss it. The media wouldn't reference sex between Brady and his same-sex victims as they believed it would upset their readers or viewers. It was still the 1960s, and any act of homosexuality was illegal.

Another point that Brady seemed to want to make in his letters was that he was an animal lover. He opposed the common belief that all serial killers abused pets or small animals when they were children. He claimed that this was not true. Because he liked animals, it could not be said that all serial killers abused animals. However, according to the FBI's National Incident-Based Reporting System, which began collecting detailed information from all levels of policing agencies, about eighteen thousand in total, cruelty offenses to animals would often lead to more significant crimes.

It was a long-held belief of the National Sheriff's Association that if a person was harming an animal, there was a good possibility that it would lead to the person hurting a human. Police had seen this pattern for years and were primarily responsible for adding it to the FBI's database. The Michigan State University, which did a study on animal cruelty, reported these findings:

- 100% of sexual homicide offenders examined had a history of cruelty towards animals.
- 70% of all animal abusers have committed at least one other criminal offense, and almost 40% have committed violent crimes against people.
- 63.3% of men who had committed crimes of aggression admitted to cruelty to animals.
- 48% of rapists and 30% of child molesters reported committing animal abuse during childhood or adolescence.

- 36% of assaultive women reported cruelty to animals, while 0% of non-assaultive women did.
- 25% of violent, incarcerated men reported higher rates of "substantial cruelty to animals" in childhood than a comparison group of non-incarcerated men (0%).
- Men who abused animals were five times more likely to be arrested for violence towards humans, four times more likely to commit property crimes, and three times more likely to have records for drug and disorderly conduct offenses.

Researchers also found that, at the very least, when a young person shows a fascination for cruelty to animals, it is a definite red flag to indicate that this person had a far more significant chance of being a rapist or serial killer.

It is interesting to note that the same study also found similarities among school shooters that are more common in recent years. Most of the shooters had committed violent acts towards animals before escalating their violence towards their schoolmates, teachers, and even their parents. An example of this was in the case of the Columbine shooters Eric Harris and Dylan Klebold, who shot and killed twelve students. Both had told their classmates about them not only torturing animals but also mutilating their remains after killing them.

So, was Brady's insistence that he was an animal lover just another defensive behavior in his letters? Was he trying to convince me that he was not a rapist?

In Brady's third letter, he mentions that most prisoners feel more at home in prison than free in society. According to Ron Zifer, the program manager for the Prison Fellowship's Academy, most prisoners sentenced to a ten-year or longer term go through five steps to cope:

1. Denial - This stage usually lasts up to three years before they finally accept that they will be in prison for several years.
2. Anger - During this stage, they often lash out by bullying or attacking other prisoners who appear weaker than they do. They frequently threaten lawsuits or legal actions and can file

grievances with the prison or guards.

3. Bargaining Phase - After a few years, the prisoner looks towards God. They try to create a bargain with God if they can get out of prison. The blame for why they got into trouble and prison also begins, such as, "*If only I had a father.*"
4. Depression & Withdrawal - After a few more years pass, and they realize the bargains they made with God don't work, it often causes the prisoner to get depressed. They start to withdraw from others and feel sorry for themselves and everything they lost.
5. Acceptance - Zifer says the fifth and final stage is when the prisoner starts to accept what has happened to them and that they will be in prison for many years or even the rest of their lives. This acceptance is where things become more comfortable for them, and they start to settle into routines, such as taking classes or beginning to work. Some of them will turn to religion and start to go to church.

Stage 5 was the stage where Brady was at the time of his letters, so it was easy for him to say he preferred being in prison rather than free. He often mentioned throughout his letters how the people who believed they were free because they weren't in prison were fooling themselves. Being in prison took away many responsibilities, like working and paying bills. He argued he had more freedom in jail.

In his fourth letter, Brady claimed that his dislike of free society continued. He mentioned the prison in Liverpool as the *only* industry left.

> "Yes, prison seems to be the only industry left in Liverpool, and as I'm the only high-profile prisoner that Ashworth holds to use my name to demonize the mainly chemically embalmed or professional freeloaders stored here and to glorify and justify the overmanned mercy care trust and POA [Mental Prison and its workers] parasite."

It's almost as if Brady was saying he was the only star left at the prison; therefore, *he* was the reason the prison was a flourishing industry for Liverpool. Brady liked to brag about being well-read in all his letters but seemed most proud of his readings of Hitler, Goebbels, and Nietzsche. All those people were extremists and believed themselves superior to or better than others. Brady's personality was a perfect match to what he liked to read.

Philosopher Friedrich Nietzsche's theory of the Übermensch opposed typical religious ideals. He argued that humans needed to be grounded in the human ideal instead of the mindless acceptance of what religion teaches. He believed God to be dead, which to him meant that the time for humans to rely on a God to set values was no longer needed. Christian values were reactionary to life, making them destructive. The new goal should be advancing the human race with each generation, which would be achieved through artificial selection.

Adolf Hitler and the Nazi party would use this philosophy to describe how to achieve a superior Aryan German master race. Unfortunately, the idea created the concept of inferior humans or the "Untermenschen." Taken to the extreme, eventually, this would lead to the belief that the superior humans should enslave, dominate, and use the inferior humans to aid them in creating this exceptional race.

Brady, believing himself to be one of those who were superior to others, gave himself permission to murder and sexually assault any of those he deemed inferior. Therefore, in his mind, he should not be punished for his actions. His ego also played into his control over anyone around him, including Myra Hindley.

LETTER 1

NOT ALL SERIAL KILLERS MISTREAT ANIMALS!

"July 2, 2015

Dear Cody,

Thanks for your letter. Yes, more psychiatrists, criminologists, and merely political parents reinforcing the state line integrally in order to obtain official posts as peer commissioners as reliable rubber stampers. I receive letters from many university students and lecturers asserting that my book, *Gates of Janus*, would have been worth ten times more if it was written by FBI profilers, psychiatrists, psychologists, etc., all trying to create a media career for themselves by claiming to have a unique insight into the criminal mind. In reality, thinking that they themselves think and act as criminals not surprising, of course, as criminal instincts are indications or partially active in the minds of every same person. As for always publicly stated, you can't treat honest, respectable people when it comes to serial global slaughter and theft, as all history illustrates, if you want the real news on Al-Jazeera, a freebie channel on 133 with dozens of political, tribal, social wars, etc. raging daily throughout the world. You're about to conclude that most of the same people are in prison. The real underworld of major crime is obviously above politicians, bankers, military, corporate, etc., who are all psychopathic or psychotic.

The whole African Continent consists of 50-odd countries run by insane dictators, and you need only look as much as Tony Blair and George Bush as recent representations of war criminals in the West. Study the leaders of the world, not the petty criminals in its prisons. The police and the intelligence and military forces that protect the elite status of the establishment all this is self-evident to many, of course, but not the sleep-walkers.

Yes, I know the areas well *[Mosley and Greenfield areas in Manchester]* leading the hottest field and other major cities in north Bolton? Some excellent architecture up in York, up your way. River Abbey is worth a visit. Yes, its academic stereotypical smears that all serial killers mistreat animals. We usually mistreat anyone who does. As documented. Yes, I had a criminal record in Glasgow and was on an apprenticeship at the shipyard in Golvin. I also worked at Smithfield Market in Manchester, but it was someone else who implicated me in a petty crime falsely leading to Borstal, where I ran gambling and booze. Eventually, I worked in the offices as I always insisted that one should have a legal source of income as well.

I was educated at Shaolin's Academy in Glasgow, but again, I chose my own path studying psychology and other subjects suitable to my plans.

(Do you make any money from your book?)

No, I'm donating all money for *Gates of Janus* to charities.

(Can I visit you in prison?)

No, I halted all social visits and phone calls in 1998 when Ashworth (Mental Hospital) became a regressive prison.

(Asked about Manchester)

Yes, Tip Street was always a criminal haunt, running down to Smithfield. The Kings Pub on Oldham Street *[Cody used to work the door there]*.

(Asked if he ever visited Germany)

Yes, I visited Berlin, Munich, Hamburg, and Nuremberg.

(Do you have any firearms?)

When police surrounded the house and blocked all roads, I was caught in bed downstairs while two pistols, a .45 and a .38, and a rifle were all upstairs. Elsewhere, we also had a 303 rifle and a Browning 9-millimeter automatic with unlimited ammunition.

(Do you know other areas of Manchester?)

Yes, I know Oldham and Shaw, etc., and I enclosed a signed label for sticking in Janus *(his book)*.

Thanks for the envelope, Smithfield *[Smithfield Market was where Brady worked at one time, and the envelope was a souvenir that Cody sent to him in prison]*.

(Are you religious?)

No, I'm not religious. As I've said, when men make plans, the Gods laugh.

Best Wishes

Ian Stewart Brady"

1

To: Lady Lachey — From: Stuart-Brady

2nd July 13

Dear Lady,

Thanks for your letter and the photos.

Yes, most psychiatrists and criminologists are merely political parrots, reinforcing the state line unquestioningly in order to obtain official posts, fees, commissions, or celebrity status etc. I received letters from many university students and lecturers, remarking that my book, "The Gates of Janus" was "worth ten written by former FBI profilers, penal psychiatrists/psychologists, etc." all hoping to create a lucrative media career for themselves by claiming to have unique insight into "the criminal mind" — in reality meaning that they themselves think and act as criminals. Not surprising, of course, as criminal instincts are ubiquitous, latent or partially active in the minds of many "sane" civilians. As I've always publicly stated, you can't beat "decent, honest, respectable" people when it comes to serial global slaughter and theft, as all history illustrates. If you watch the real news on Aljazeera (Freeview channel [illegible]), with dozens of political, tribal, racial wars, etc, raging daily throughout the world, you'd perhaps conclude that most of the "crazy" people are in power. The real "underworld" of major crime is obviously above in politicians, bankers, military, corporate, etc, all probably psychopaths or psychotic. The whole African continent consists of fifty-odd countries run by vicious dictators. And you need only look at such as Tony Blair and George Bush as recent representatives of mad criminals in the west! Study the leaders of the world, not the comparatively petty criminals in prisons. And the police and intelligence and military forces which protect and perpetuate the whole status quo of the establishment.

LETTER 2

EVERYONE IS A PEDOPHILE!

“August 2, 2015

Dear Cody,

Thank you for your July letters.

No, I didn’t authorize any extended edition of the book. I donated the entire proceeds of the first edition to charity and all future proceeds. So, the publisher, by sending me no funds, all royalties for the second edition, and foreign translated editions, is in effect stealing from and defrauding charities of proceeds due to them *[the royalties from the first edition of Brady’s book all went to char-*

ities, the second edition was released by the publisher, Feral House, without Brady signing off on the book, and no royalties were sent to the charities - the publisher claims that it was an extended version].

As for the Afterword written by Sotos *[Peter Sotos is a controversial author also published by Feral House]*, it was widely attacked by all in the first edition. The publisher paid Sotos to write a deliberate attack in order to placate any right-wing criticisms. Sotos is a convicted pedophile, child pornographer, and police informer, and was publicly described as a toilet door scribbler who would produce any picture or obscenity for money, which reflects even more clearly the money-grabbing greed and treachery of the publisher, of course. *[It's ironic that Brady is calling out Sotos for being a pedophile, which is what Brady was.]*

Obviously, the death of Colleen Watson *[Brady's longtime friend who wrote a Foreword in Brady's book]* in 2014 obviously encouraged Parfrey *[referring to Adam Parfrey, the founder and owner of Feral House]* to increase his fraudulent exploitation to feel free to take any measures of public exposure you think fit in. My solicitors have also been instructed likewise and for legal action. As you know, my mighty is right, and prisoners are always exploited both for money and to distract attention from the major criminals in government, corporations, and the military force of law and order.

My solicitors made it plain through the media that Powell [a woman from South Wales who at one time got friendly with Brady and was telling stories on him] was then entirely dismissed from my legal affairs, etc.

(Can I visit you?)

No, as I stated, I stopped all visits and phone calls in 1998 when this place became a regressive prison, and despite many of my previous solicitors asking me to reconsider, I remain unchanged and without regret in this respect.

Thanks for the envelopes. If you

see any Schaefer pen refills in blue medium, I'm running out, and just two will do. Please excuse the bedridden handwriting.

Best Wishes

Ian Stewart Brady"

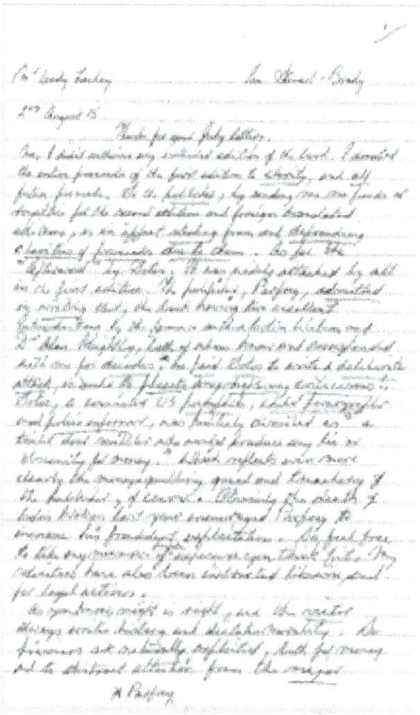

LETTER 3

PEOPLE PREFER BEING IN PRISON!

"October 12, 2015

Dear Cody,

Thanks for your letter.

[Cody had sent Brady a Christmas card and a bracelet with the flag of Scotland on it.]

The Christmas card you sent was held by Mercy Care POA. And the bracelet was also not permitted. I instructed the thief executive *(it should be the "Chief" executive, but Brady was upset)* office to return both prohibited items to you, so let me know when you receive them. You shouldn't bother sending in any other items, as all the attention-seeking officials without real jobs here will simply prohibit items to justify their own parasitic existences.

Second, it is common knowledge that the more corrupt, the more overtly corrupt and criminal the person is in our system, the more publicly moral and righteous they appear to the ignorant. Yes, I'm still bedridden, and now I have a chest infection. As I've said my solicitors and London legal executives will handle my funeral arrangements, and I've been kept informed.

(Cody had offered to do security at Brady's funeral with members of the criminal underworld - it wasn't a genuine offer. It was to find out Brady's plans for his funeral and to see if Brady trusted Cody enough to get access to his body and his estate.)

I'm glad you took my advice and avoided approaches by the media *(in the previous letter, you will read about Cody's offer to be on the Jeremy Kyle Show - Cody told Brady that he turned down the offer due to Brady's advice not to go on the show).* In my day, people actually went out of their way rather than speak to the media. Quite the opposite these days. As you said, the Andy Warhol prediction that everybody would be famous for 15 minutes has been surpassed, more like 15 seconds.

(Do you believe prisoners can become institutionalized?)

People that become institutionalized due so because, consciously and subconsciously, they prefer to be. More at home at prison than in the free, the outside world talking of freedom but regretting it.

(Do you have any tattoos?)

No, and I don't want one, who does?

(Do you celebrate your birthday?)

Birthdays? No, I've never bothered with them.

(Are they ever going to make a movie about you?)

No, I've stopped three Hollywood films to be made over the decades (he had refused to sign the rights away). Unfortunately, in the UK, television programs can be made, and films without release contracts being signed.

I also took legal action to have the three Hollywood films stopped.

I enclosed a classic "Easy Rider" DVD, the scenes in the cemetery in New Orleans reminded me of my second visit to America and time in New Orleans.

Best wishes

Ian Stewart Brady"

LETTER 4

PRISON BEST LIVERPOOL INDUSTRY!

"September 16, 2016

Dear Cody

Thanks for yours at first and eighth of September and the Laura Biden Assassin DVD Denmark Rolled.

Funeral arrangements are all detailed in my will in the hands of my solicitors and London legal executives. There are no sole heirs to my estate.

Enemy of the Gate? Yes, I've seen it, it's actually quite a good account of a battle within battle at Stalingrad, but what are my favorite films in general question? As I'm a film buff covering films from the 1920s to the present. There are too many to mention, including the UK, US, European, and world cinema. Apart from *Al Jazeera*, for real news, I watch documentaries, films, plays, and quality series, old and new. No reality programs or TV or celebrity trash or spectacles.

So that brings me onto the offer you receive from social media. *(Cody was contacted by on of the producers of the* Jeremy Kyle Show *because he was involved in gangs and the criminal fraternity. They wanted him to go on the program to speak to someone going down the same path as Cody. Cody was to try to help them. He had let Brady know about this offer, which he turned down.)* These people search the media for targets to appear on such programs as the *Jeremy Kyle Show* to publicly demonize and ridicule for the entertainment of the ignorant rabble. I have trusted contacts in the quality media but never the tabloids or got to television.

(Did you receive my Gobbles and Outlands book?)

Yes, I received the Gobbles and

Outlands books, and the pen refills, etc. and acknowledged in previous letters to you.

I'm kept well informed by outside sources of all instances of individual exploitation and betrayals of confidence and act according to circumstance or importance by legal and other means. I've had 50 years of experience, and some friends can't wait to be asked to assist by every method.

Try reading Trotsky's *Crime and Punishment*. I've read most of the world's classics. I no longer read much at this late stage. Yes, prison seems to be the only industry left in Liverpool, and as I'm the only high-profile prisoner that Ashworth holds to use my name to demonize the mainly chemically embalmed or professional freeloaders stored here and to glorify and justify the overmanned mercy care trust and POA *(Mental Prison and its workers)* parasite.

I had more freedom and trust in the Durham *(The former Prison Brady was in before being transferred to the Hospital Prison)* in the 1960s, which held the great train robbers, Mad

Frankie Fraser, the Richardsons, the Portland spies, etc. where Ronnie Kray and I did the cooking keeping busy and translating books into braille for schools for the blind.

Ashton on the line station *(the police station that first arrested Brady and Hindley for the murders)*, we were interrogated by chiefs for 12 hours there in 1965 unsuccessfully. Hyde police headquarters is now empty and disused *(this is where the infamous pictures of Brady and Hindley were taken in the hallways of this station).*

I enclosed the signed label you requested for Janus *(Brady's book).*

Best wishes

Ian Stewart Brady

P.S. Early Christmas card enclosed."

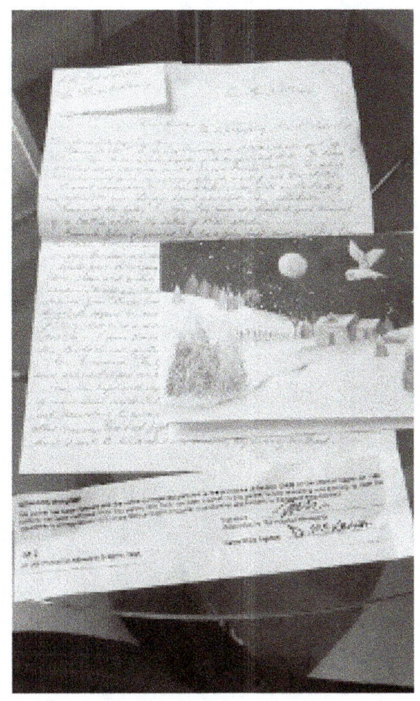

BOOK 2

STEPHEN PORT - GRINDR SERIAL KILLER

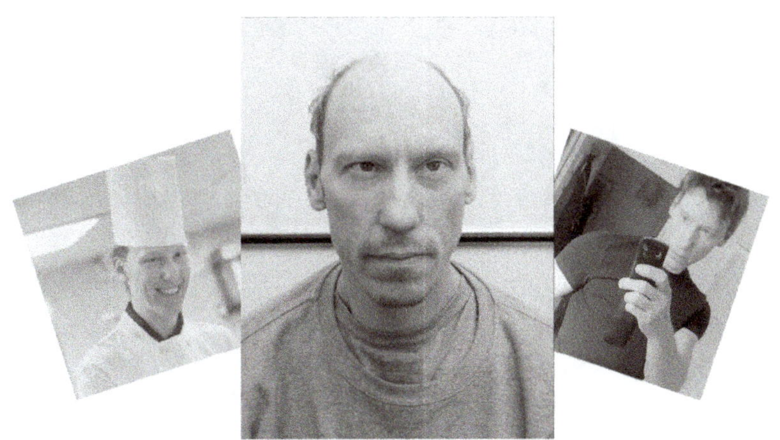

1

THE CRIMES

After any serial killer gets caught and the news spreads worldwide, people come forward to talk about their experiences or how they knew the killer. Stephen Port's case was no different.

Slowly, several men talked to different media outlets to tell their stories of how they knew Port and what had happened to them when they were with him. Strangely, some were just seeking attention and creating complete falsehoods about knowing the killer for an unknown reason.

After sifting through these cases, I found only two men with proof of their contact with Port. One was Fabio Porchat, now 28, who had a relationship with Port in 2012 when he was 19. He had moved from Brazil to London, where he got a job as a waiter. While he was working one night, he met Port. The two of them hit it off and began dating. Porchat eventually moved in with Port to his Barking apartment, and they stayed together for about one month. After they broke up, Porchat returned to Brazil to continue his life.

Sometime in 2019, he read about a man in London named Stephen Port, who was arrested as a serial killer. At first, he was excited because he thought his one-time boyfriend had made a movie or documentary about a serial killer. Needless to say, he was shocked to find out that instead, it was a documentary about his ex, Stephen Port, being a serial killer.

2

ANTHONY WALGATE

Early on the morning of June 19, 2014, the police received a phone call about a dead body found in front of an apartment building on Cooke Street.

> **999 Dispatcher:** "Emergency ambulance, what's the address of the emergency?"
> **Phone caller:** I think it's Cooke Street. There's a young boy. I think he's collapsed outside, and I don't know."
> **Dispatcher:** "Outside of which number?"
> **Caller:** "Um, 47 or 58."
> **Dispatcher:** "Sorry?"
> **Caller:** "47 or 58."
> **Dispatcher:** "47 Cooke Street."

Caller: "Yeah."
Dispatcher: "Right, What area?"
Caller: "Barking. Looks like he's collapsed or had a seizure or something, or he's just drunk."
Dispatcher: "Okay, what's the telephone number you are calling from?"
Caller: "I'll go get my car."
Dispatcher: "Alright, don't worry about that. What's the telephone number you are calling from?"

The caller puts the phone down and goes quiet.

Dispatcher: "Hello!?"

The 999 dispatcher calls the caller back.

Dispatcher: "Hello, it's the ambulance service. We were cut off there. Could you confirm your location?"
Caller: "Ahh, I've just driven away now."
Dispatcher: "Where was the fella outside of?"
Caller: "Uh, Cooke Street."
Dispatcher: "What number?"

Caller: "Um, I don't know, I didn't look."
Dispatcher: "You said 47 before?"
Caller: "Yeah, I did 47, yeah."
Dispatcher: "So you think they had a seizure? Is that correct?"
Caller: "Umm, uh yeah, yep."
Dispatcher: "So you were passing by in your car?"
Caller: "Yes."
Dispatcher: "Okay, and you've drove past now, so you're no longer there?"
Caller: "That's right."
Dispatcher: "How old did he look to you, sir?"
Caller: "Twenties."
Dispatcher: "Do you know if he was awake?"
Caller: "No."
Dispatcher: "Do you know if he was breathing?"
Caller: "No, I don't know."
Dispatcher: "Did you see anything happen at all?"
Caller: "No."
Dispatcher: "No, you just think he may have possibly had a seizure, and he was lying there on the floor?"
Caller: "Yes."

Dispatcher: "Okay, thanks for letting us know. We'll get someone there as soon as we can."
Caller: "Okay."
Dispatcher: "Thank you."

The caller hangs up on the dispatcher again, so the 999 dispatcher calls him back.

Dispatcher: "Hello, Sir. It's the ambulance service. Sorry to bother you again. It was definitely Cooke Street that the patient was on?"
Caller: "Yes. I passed him, and it was Cooke Street."
Dispatcher: "Okay, and were you just driving past and saw the patient lying there?"
Caller: "I was just driving out of my car park."
Dispatcher: "Is your car park there?"
Caller: "And I saw him lying on the floor."
Dispatcher: "Okay."
Caller: "I got out and had a look at him."
Dispatcher: "Yes."

Caller: "Called you and got back into my car."
Dispatcher: "Alright, no worries, no worries, just wanted to be sure. Thank you for your help, sir, and sorry to bother you again."
Caller: "Okay, no worries."
Dispatcher: "Bye-bye."

Two officers arrived on Cooke Street at the location they were given by dispatch and saw a man lying asleep on the sidewalk. One officer immediately jumped out of their car to see if the man was still alive, while the other officer looked around the area to see if he could find anything suspicious. The man was dead, and they saw no signs of any struggle.

The body was that of a young man who looked to be in his early twenties. He was sitting on the sidewalk with his back propped up against the outside wall of an apartment building. His shirt was pulled up and wrapped around his chest, which exposed his stomach. His pants zipper was left wide open. His head was facing downwards, looking as though he had been asleep. He might have been dragged by his feet while lying face down. Beside him was a black duffle bag and a bottle containing some liquid, but police could not find a cell phone at the location.

The ambulance arrived and took the body to the hospital, where he was officially declared deceased. The medical examiner performed an autopsy, ruling the death by overdose of the drug GBH. They had also found a bottle of GBH in his pants pocket.

In London, Barking had become known as a place where you would see the streets and parks frequented by male prostitutes and drug addicts. It was also an area you would stay away from after dark. There had been several overdoses in the area, so finding a young man dead from an overdose on the streets wasn't all that unusual. But one thing that stuck out for the police for this particular death was that the victim's underwear had been removed and put back on inside out. He also had 14 bruises on his body, so they decided to do a small investigation to see if there was anything unusual about this case. The first thing they would have to do was identify the victim.

For the first few days, police were unsuccessful in finding out anything about the dead man until Anthony Walgate's downstairs neighbor/friend came into the police station and reported him missing. She had tried calling his phone for two days and never got an answer. She went upstairs to his apartment several times to see him, but he hadn't been home for at least two days, not since he went to meet the man from Barking, whom he had met online.

When the police asked her why he was meeting this man he had met online, she explained that it was for paid sex. After that, the police seemed to lose interest in her missing friend. Likely because he was just a male escort who hadn't returned home.

Anthony Walgate, 23, was in his second year of design, fashion, and art at the University of Middlesex. Police discovered that he had been running ads on the *Sleepy Boys* app as a male escort to earn extra cash during his time in college. He often attended fashion shows with his two best girlfriends and his mother. Walgate's body was found the day before his mother, newly remarried, left for her honeymoon to Greece with her new husband.

Police decided to investigate the phone number from which they received the tip about the body on the sidewalk on Cooke Street. They found it belonged to the same Stephen Port who had booked the appointment with Walgate the prior evening. Two detectives went to Port's apartment at 62 Cooke Street to get a statement on the details of Port finding Walgate's body.

Port told them he had gotten off working the late shift around 4 a.m. When he arrived home, he saw the body lying on the sidewalk of his apartment building entrance. Port said he tried to wake the man by slapping him a few times, but got no response. Port also claimed the man was still alive as he heard him gurgling and making groaning noises. So he sat the man up against the apartment building wall, called the ambulance, and went into his apartment and bed.

Walgate's mother and friends decided to do their own investigating. They signed into Anthony's profiles on several gay hookup apps and tried to find the man he was planning to meet. They knew this unknown man went by the name "Joe Dean" and learned quickly that that profile had been deleted. They went to the police with this information, hoping to find out who this Joe Dean was.

Later that week, detectives learned that Port had booked an appointment under the profile name of Joe Dean with Anthony Walgate for an evening of sex. After Port booked that appointment, he searched online for drug rape pornography. Port went to the Barking Rail Station at 10 p.m. to meet Walgate and bring him back to his flat.

About ten days later, on June 26, the police

returned to Port's apartment, took him into custody, and brought him back to the police station for interrogation. While being questioned about the details of his discovery of Walgate's body, Port continued to answer with the same story. He never changed his story until they asked him if he had ever used the profile name "Joe Dean." Detectives told Port that they also knew he had made an appointment for sex with Anthony Walgate that same evening of June 17 and that he had reported finding his dead body in front of his apartment building. Port continued to deny that the man he had rented for sex was the same man he had found dead in front of his building. Later that evening, during the questioning, he asked the detectives if Walgate had had a fit in his apartment, and if it was an accident, would it still be his fault?

Eventually, Port started to change his story and admitted to having hired Walgate off an escort web app, and after Walgate got to his apartment, he began using drugs he had brought with him. Port said that the two engaged in sex twice during the night. Walgate got dressed to leave but fell asleep while wearing all his clothing, including his shoes. The next day, when Port awoke, Walgate was still sleeping, so Port didn't wake him and left for his job. When he returned from work, he found Walgate was still asleep. Port could not wake him. Later that night, he heard Walgate gurgling and making strange noises, so he panicked, dragged his body outside to the front of his apartment building, where he left him lying on the sidewalk, and then called the ambulance.

Detectives decided to arrest Port and charge him with perverting justice during a crime investigation, or lying to police on a suspicious death case, in simpler terms. The charge was a way of keeping Port in custody until they could figure out the details behind Walgate's death. After Port's arrest, the police returned to his apartment to complete a search and removed his computer for later examination. Unfortunately, the police neglected to search Port's computer during this investigation. It is uncertain why. We would never find out whether it was incompetence or a lack of caring about the victim. But if they had properly searched his computer, they would have found incriminating evidence. They would have found several web searches for "Unconscious boy," "drug and raped," "Gay teen knocked out raped," and "guy raped and tortured young nude boy."

Time passed, and the police didn't discover any new evidence or lay any charges, which upset Walgate's family and friends. A few said they called detectives frequently and were brushed off. One of Walgate's friends, China Dunning, said when she asked police if they had searched Port's computer, they responded by telling her that it was a costly procedure and probably not worth it.

During Port's trial for lying to the police, he admitted that he had Walgate in his apartment for sex and that Walgate took the GHB willingly. "When I met Mr. Walgate for sex, the young man had wanted to have some stuff to make him horny and high." Port claimed, "I saw that he had a little brown bottle." He said it wasn't until after Port returned from a night shift at the bus stop diner that he found Walgate stiff and rigid in his bed, making a gurgling noise. Port then panicked, dragged the body out of his apartment building, and placed him against the outside wall. Port did not check to see if Anthony was still alive; he just got into his car and started to drive, and that's when he decided to call the 999 ambulance service.

In a police interview that day, the jury heard that Port asked a detective: "Can I say for the scenario - if it was an accident, and if he did have a fit in my place, is that still my fault?" "Initially," Mr. Rees said, "the defendant denied having met Mr. Walgate but later admitted spending time in his flat with him, where Mr. Port claimed Mr. Walgate willingly took GHB/GBL."

Port was found guilty and given eight months in jail as a sentence, but he only served three months before being released with an electronic tag on his leg until June 2015. The police then closed the case.

Kate Whelan, Anthony Walgate's aunt, made an emotional appeal for people to take care when using dating websites and apps:

> "It was four years ago, and a predatory serial sex fiend murdered Anthony at the age of 23 while he was attending university and had an exciting future. Our lives will never be the same. We live daily with trauma, shock, anger, and pain. Please be careful if you are using dating apps. The internet is fabulous, but be aware that there are predators. Although your kids are young adults and you feel sensible, please reinforce the stranger danger warnings."

3

GABRIEL KOVARI

Gabriel Kovari, 22, originally from Slovakia, left his home because he felt the people there were too conservative and intolerant. He first went to Spain, where he lived with Thierry Amodio as his boyfriend. After he broke up with Amodio, Kovari headed for London, where he ended up sleeping in the spare bedroom of his friend John Pape in Southern London.

Within a couple of weeks in London, he found a job and decided that he wanted to get an apartment, even though his friend Pape told him that he could stay for as long as he wanted. Kovari wished to have his own place to meet men and have a private place to invite them back. About six weeks later, he told Pape that he had found a great place to live in the Barking area of London and was very excited to move there.

On August 23, 2014, he moved out of his friend John Pape's south London apartment. He texted Pape the Google Maps location of his new apartment, which was located on Cooke Street. A few days later, Pape texted Kovari to see how it was going in his new place. Pape received no answer from him. Two days later, Pape received a text message from Kovari saying things were good. That would be the last text sent from Kovari's phone.

On August 24, Ryan Edwards, who also lived at 62 Cooke Street and was a neighbor and acquaintance of Stephen Port, received a text message from Port inviting him over to meet his new "Slovakian Twink Flatmate." Edwards went to Port's place and partied with the two men all night.

The next afternoon, Edwards received a text from Kovari, telling him that Port was not a very lovely person and that the two of them had had a big fight. Kovari didn't know what he would do as he couldn't live with Port anymore.

Later that same evening, Edwards texted Port and asked him how his new roommate, Kovari, was doing. Port said that Kovari had decided to move out and stay with some military guy he had met online on one of those gay dating apps.

Barking is a small town in East London, United Kingdom, with about 187,000 people. It's primarily a fishing and farming community. Barking came from the English slang for "Barking Mad," attributed to the alleged insane asylum attached to the Barking Abbey, which was part of St. Margaret's Church, dating back to the 13th century.

On August 28th, the Summer of 2014 was winding down, and East London resident Barbara Denham, 67, leashed her border collie named Max to take him for his daily walk. She always took the same route through the quiet and grassy property of St. Catherine's Church. It was the perfect place to walk as she could unleash her dog and not worry about car traffic or many people being around. This daily walk was something she had done for the 28 years she had lived in the area, and only this time would things be different.

When Barbara entered the Church grounds, things were as expected, only the sky was dark and grey, and the grass was damp from the rain that had fallen earlier that morning. She unleashed Max to let him run free and do his business as always. She started to saunter towards the church, admired the architecture, and thought about how amazing it would have been to live in such an impressive building or castle. As she approached the Abbey on the Church grounds, she noticed a young man sitting upright with his back against the stone wall. Barbara thought she would approach the man and say hi, but as she got close enough to talk with him, she noticed he didn't move.

> "I saw what I thought was a man sitting down on the grass, with his head slightly down and his back against the wall. He was wearing dark glasses slanted over his face, and although I have seen a lot of homeless people sleeping in the area, I just knew something wasn't right."

Barbara clapped her hands and shouted out, "WooHoo." There was no response or movement from the young man. "He has a bluish pallor, and when I saw his eyes glassed over, I knew he was dead. There was no blood, and he looked very peaceful." Ms. Denham said she remained calm when she realized she had found a dead body. "I don't know whether it is watching horror programs or murder mysteries, but I was pretty calm. I took out my phone and called the emergency services, and they came pretty quickly."

This victim, too, had his shirt pulled up towards his chest, exposing his stomach, and was wearing sunglasses. His bags with all of his possessions were placed beside his body.

Two days later, her local paper announced that the young man she had found in the park, Gabriel Kovari, 21, had died of a drug overdose. East London was an area known for drug use and petty crime, so though it was a big shock to have found a dead body in the park, it wasn't a total surprise for there to have been a drug overdose in the area.

Police first contacted Kovari's friend, John Pape, by going to his apartment. They connected the two men as Pape allowed Kovari to use his address when he opened a bank account. The four officers told Pape that Kovari's body had been found in the park at the St. Margaret Church in Barking. Pape was able to give the police Kovari's parents' information so they could contact them and let them know about their son's death.

Gabriel's mother, a pharmacist, described

Gabriel as a gifted artist who wanted to make a difference. "He was full of love and cared for others and loved the company of his friends, and he was a very inquisitive and special child, gifted in arts."

After the police left Pape's apartment, he searched online for information about his friend's death. He learned online about another mysterious death in the same churchyard just a couple of months earlier, in June. Pape couldn't stop thinking about the coincidence of the two young gay men both found dead in the same park at about the same time, so he contacted Kovari's ex-boyfriend in Spain to chat with him about it. "I wanted Amodio to mention it to the police and make sure that they put the two deaths together."

Meanwhile, Anthony Walgate's mother was still following up with the detectives almost daily, wanting answers to her son's death. They often didn't respond or tell her they had no replies yet. When she, too, heard the news about another young man also found dead in the same park of an apparent overdose, she knew something was going on.

Around the same time, Stephen friended Gabriel Kovari's Spanish ex-boyfriend, Thierry Amodio, on Facebook, pretending to be an American student in London, Jon Luck. He did this to keep tabs on whether the police told him of any suspects and who they were.

Port told Amondo that he had spent a couple of nights with Kovari sometime around August 22nd and wondered if the police might want to talk to him, as his DNA might be found on Kovari's body. Port also claimed Kovari was with Tony, an older Irish man who drove a Green Toyota. Amodio kept asking Port if he had more information about this Tony guy, and on September 19, Port told Amodio that he had found this Tony man who had been with Kovari. Tony texted Luck/Port, so Luck/Port asked him what had happened to Gabriel. Tony told him they were at a party somewhere in Barking and that Gabriel had left with a young guy named Daniel, who was tall, thin, and had light brown hair. That was the last time he saw Gabriel. Luck/Port told Tony that Gabriel was found dead, and Tony said he knew nothing about it and told Luck not to contact him again.

Shortly after this, the Coroner's Court reviewed Kovari's death. It was established that there were no signs of a struggle or any bruising or cuts to Kovari's body. Therefore, he wasn't in a fight or forced to take drugs. It was also revealed that there was no camera footage of the churchyard when Kovari went to the park and died. They also had no evidence from any of Kovari's clothing, as it was sent along with his body back to his home country so that his parents could bury him.

Kovari's landlord and friend, John Pape, was the only person to show up to the court, as his parents didn't want to travel to London. He brought up three young gay males found in the exact location, all dead from apparent overdoses, and asked if the detectives had ever tried to investigate the possibility that all three deaths were connected. The inquest finished with an open verdict.

Two days later, Amodio texted Luck/Port back to tell him that the police had found another dead man's body in the same park at the St. Margaret Church in Barking. The man's name was Daniel Whitworth—a young gay man who overdosed and had a suicide note on him.

4

DANIEL WHITWORTH

About three weeks after Barbara Denham found the body of Gabriel Kovari, she was walking her collie Max again in the same park. She noticed another young man sitting in the same place where she had found Gabriel. "This man was sitting the same way, with his head down as if he was sleeping." Right away, Barbara thought, "Please God, no, not another one. Please let him be a boy who is just drunk or something."

"I suppose I knew before I went over that he was dead. I just knew. " Barbara exclaimed. "But I touched his ankle where his skin was exposed and felt it was cold." She took her cell phone from her purse and called the police. "I'm the lady that found the first body. I have found another young boy."

"To have found two young men in the same position upset me. I was concerned about my reaction because I was trying to control myself. I did feel sorry for both, for the families. Someone else found a third body on the other side of the wall. I don't know how soon after I saw the second one." Barbara said with shakiness in her voice. "It was lucky I didn't find that one as well."

The second body she found was Daniel Whitworth, 21, from Gravesend in Kent, where he lived with his boyfriend, Ricky Waumsley, and worked as a chef, becoming very well known in the area for his cooking skills.

Both men were found dead in the same place in the same park, but Whitworth's body had a suicide note placed beside him. The suicide note suggested that he was responsible for the death of the first body found (Kovari) by overdosing on the party drug GHB during a sexual encounter. Whitworth committed suicide as he could not deal with the guilt of what happened.

The note should have connected the two deaths for the police detectives, though, for some reason, it didn't. The police took the note at face value, and no further attempts were made to investigate his death.

Whitworth was sitting against the graveyard wall on top of a blue bedsheet, probably dragged like the previous two dead men found in the park. His shirt was also pulled up around his chest, exposing his stomach. Police could not find his cell phone on his body or anywhere in the park. They also found a little bottle containing some liquid, which was later tested and found to be GBH.

The police went to Whitworth's home to inform his boyfriend, Waumsley, that they had found Whitworth's body in the park. When the detectives asked Waumsley if the two were friends, Waumsley told them they were in a long-term committed relationship. Detectives then asked him if he knew that Whitworth was seeing other men. Police also suggested that Whitworth was using gay sex apps and GHB.

After the police left, Waumsley went online, looked through the gay dating apps, and found that Whitworth had profiles in several places. It came as a surprise because it was not in his character or behavior in any way. Both Waumsley and several of his coworkers and friends didn't believe the story that he had committed suicide after killing another young man with an overdose during sex.

After their investigation, the Barking Police would deem the death as non-suspicious and rule it a suicide since they believed the note found on his body. Whitworth's stepmother claimed the police came to her and told her that her son had died of a drug overdose, despite no investigation and no explanation of the bruises found under both of his arms.

Suicide Note:

> "I am sorry to everyone, mainly my family, but I can't go on anymore. I took the life of my friend Gabriel Kline. We were having some fun at a mate's place, and I got carried away and gave him another shot of G. I didn't notice while we were having sex that he had stopped breathing. I tried everything to get him to live again, but it was too late. It was an accident, but I blamed myself for what happened, and I didn't tell my family I went out. I know I would go to prison if I went to the police, and I can't do that to my

family, and at least this way, I can least be with Gabriel again. I hope he will forgive me.

BTW, Please do not blame the guy I was with last night. We only had sex, and then I left. He knows nothing of what I have done. I have taken what G I have gone with sleeping pills, so it's what I deserve if it does kill me. I feel dizzy (misspelled on purpose) now as I took 10 minutes ago, so I hope you understand my writing. I dropped my phone on my way here, so it should be in the grass somewhere. Sorry to everyone. Love always, Daniel P.W."

I am Sorry to everyone, mainly my family but I can't go on anymore, I took the life of my friend Gabriel Kline, we was just having some fun at a mates place and I got carried away and gave him another shot of G, I didnt notice while we was having sex that he had stopped breathing, I tried everything to get him to breath again but it was too late, it was an accident but I blame my self for what happened and I didnt tell my family I went out, I know I would go to prison if I go to police and I cant do that to my family and at least this way I can at least be with Gabriel again, I hope he will forgive me.

BTW. Please do not blame the guy I was with last night, we only had sex then I left, he knows nothing of what I have done. I have taken what G I had left with sleeping pills so if does kill me its what I deserve. Feeling dizzy now as took 10 min ago so hoping you understand my writing.

I dropped my phone on way here so should be in the grass somewhere

Sorry to everyone

Love always

Daniel P W

Suicide Note

The police never questioned the suicide note and sent copies of a small part of the note to Whitworth's parents, asking them if they could verify that the handwriting belonged to their son. Even though both parents agreed that the handwriting looked like it belonged to their son, the written words were not how their son talked or wrote. That was good enough for the Dagenham Police. They accepted it as verification that it was an actual suicide note written by Whitworth and therefore never sought any further analysis of the suicide note. Later, when Whitworth's parents saw the whole suicide note, they knew their son hadn't written it. They immediately told the police this and asked whether they had investigated anybody mentioned in the note. According to them, the response from the police was, "It is what it is, and you just have to deal with it."

The parents brought another issue to the police: the note said, "not to blame the guy that he [Whitworth] was with last night." They wanted to know who this person was. The police told them that it would be impossible to investigate the note in such detail and that they needed to accept that it was what it was, an overdose by a prostitute. The police would never search for the guy mentioned in the note or even try to trace Whitworth's movements during his last night alive. If the police had researched this mystery man, the investigation would have easily led to Stephen Port.

Around this time, Stephen Port appeared in court for the death of Anthony Walgate. He was being tried for the charges of perverting justice during the police investigation into Walgate's death. During the trial, the defense attorney told the court that Port had always been a law-abiding citizen who maintained employment regularly and was not a threat to re-offend. The judge in the case questioned why Port had just not called for help when the original overdose occurred. Port's lawyer said that it was Port's fear of his sexuality being discovered by the public. He feared for his job as a bus station cook and that being gay would surely get him fired.

Port ended up with only an eight-month sentence, and when the Walgate family found out, they were outraged. Walgate's mother already believed that Port had murdered her son by this time.

Shortly after Port's conviction, the Coroner held court for the Daniel Whitworth death case. During this hearing, the court heard that Whitworth's suicide note was assumed to be written by Daniel, even though the parents said otherwise. There was a discrepancy in the investigation with the bruising discovered under his armpits and on his chest. The detectives claimed that it raised no concern or suspicion, yet the Coroner stated that the injuries would have had to have happened before his death.

Another discrepancy in the investigation was when the police didn't test for DNA on the blue sheet on which Daniel Whitworth's body was found. The court asked about the DNA results from the blue sheet. There were none. Detectives hadn't even run basic tests on the sheet. This fact was pivotal in proving that, at the very least, detectives didn't thoroughly investigate. Especially since they already had Port's DNA. We know Port's DNA was later found on the blue bedsheet that Whitworth's body was placed on at the church gravesite. Port's DNA was also found on Whitworth's body, clothes, and even the suicide note. Since Port had previously been convicted of a crime, his DNA was in police files.

Despite this, like the Walgate court hearing, there would be an open verdict. There were too many unanswered questions for the court to conclude.

Later, some communications between Port and Whitworth were also found. The two men had met on the *Fitlads* website in August that same year. On September 3rd, Port suggested that the two of them go for a drink before having dinner at Port's apartment so that Whitworth knew he wasn't some psycho. About two weeks later, on September 18th, Whitworth was seen leaving his job, telling his coworkers he was meeting a friend in Barking. It was the last time he would be seen.

Even in February 2015, after Port pleaded guilty to perverting the course of justice in Anthony Walgate's death, the police still never connected the murders of the other two young men. Actually, the prosecutor said there was no suggestion that Port bore any responsibility for these young men's deaths.

After Port's conviction, some of Walgate's friends spoke to the police again. They said he knew he was responsible for their friend's death. But the police responded by telling them that only two people knew what happened that night, one of them dead, and the other wasn't talking—a rather flippant and uncaring response from the police.

5

JACK TAYLOR

Port served his eight months and was released on parole. He had to wear an ankle bracelet. When he returned to his apartment in Barking, he had to face his friends and neighbors, as he didn't tell any of them about his crime, trial, or conviction. Port said to them that he was sent away for selling drugs. He knew they wouldn't believe he would get eight months for simple possession. Port now had to find a new job since they fired him after his conviction.

Initially, the first three victims were deemed not to have died in suspicious circumstances. Despite the local police force's LGBT advisory group reporting that there was a serial killer at large, the police told the families of the victims and the public that the crimes were not linked.

The fourth victim, Jack Taylor, was a 25-year-old forklift operator from Hull. He was applying to be a police officer. On the surface, Taylor lived a straight lifestyle and had several girlfriends. Only he knew his secret of being gay. He usually used the *Grindr* app to meet men on the side to fulfill his urges so that nobody he worked with would know.

Jack was partying with friends at a local nightclub until about 10 p.m. on Friday, September 13th, and decided to go home. Once he was home, he started cruising the Gay meeting apps, and somewhere around 2 a.m., he met and started chatting with Stephen Port.

During their conversation, Stephen asked Jack, "Do you take T?" "T" is a street name for crystal meth. This question became relevant in future court cases. Jack answered no; he had never done it. "The two decided to meet at the Barking Rail Station at 3 a.m.

After they met, Stephen walked Jack back to his one-bedroom apartment, where Stephen was thought to have spiked Jack's drink with GHB. After Jack passed out, he injected him with poppers and raped him. Later, Jack's body was left at St. Margaret's Church, leaning against the same fence where the two previous bodies were found, only this time, it was on the opposite side.

When the police arrived, they found Taylor leaning against the brick fence, just as the previous two bodies. And his shirt had been pulled up and rested around his chest. Taylor had a syringe in one of his pockets, a little bottle filled with liquid, and a couple of pills in another. It looked as if he had been dragged to where he lay.

Again, after a brief inquiry, the police ruled that Jack had died of an overdose—a self-inflicted overdose. And there was no connection between Taylor's death and the other bodies found at the park earlier.

However, Jack's two sisters, Jenny and Donna Taylor, knew that their brother never used drugs and thought his overdosing wasn't right. Even weirder was that Jack was supposed to have overdosed by injection. Yet, the needle found on him had never been used. The sisters did not understand why the police had not tested any evidence for DNA or tried to find out what Jack was doing in that area of town. He didn't live there.

After not learning anything from the police, except that their brother's death was an overdose and it was not connected to any other body found in the park, the sisters decided to investigate what happened to their brother. First, they searched the internet to see if anything was mentioned about their brother's death. They were surprised to find out about three other young men who had been found dead from an overdose in the same churchyard.

They started to go through the details of Taylor's last weekend alive. They wanted to find out everyone who he was with and go to all the locations he had been to that weekend. They found out that the area where Taylor went was known for drugs and male prostitution. But they both knew that he was not a drug user. In fact, he often spoke out against others who used drugs. It didn't fit that he would walk into a churchyard, sit down, and shoot up.

Taylor's two sisters went to the police about two weeks later to find out if they had discovered any new information about the case. They were shocked to learn that not only did the Dagenham Police have nothing new, but they weren't even investigating his murder. The detectives told them they just had to accept that their brother had overdosed. Since they discovered a syringe in his pocket, some white powder in a baggie in his wallet, and several needle marks on both of his arms, to them, it was an overdose. The police told the sisters they wouldn't help them with any investigation or information.

Frustrated, the sisters decided they would go to the press with the knowledge that there had been other suspicious deaths in the same area. The media attention created a lot of pressure on the police to do more.

About two weeks later, the police agreed to take the sisters to where they had found their dead brother's body. While the sisters were at the Barking Train Station, they discovered a CCTV camera looking over the area. They asked if the footage was available for them to view. When they all sat down to watch the footage, the sisters were shocked to see their brother walking from the train station with another man. They asked the detectives why nobody had told them about the film footage of their brother. Instead of answering them, the police took offense that they were even questioning the police investigation.

The sisters took the footage to the media. After they reported that it was Taylor's sisters who found the footage and not the police, and that the police did not investigate the other man seen with their brother on the last night of his life, the detectives decided to reopen the mysterious death case.

About two weeks later, a sergeant from the Barking Police contacted the sisters to let them know that they had also found footage that showed their brother entering the churchyard grounds with another man. The sisters requested that the images of the man filmed with their brother that night be released to the press. But the police refused. Detectives told them they didn't feel that Jack's death was suspicious, so it wasn't possible to show someone's image on the news.

Again, after the two sisters went to the press and more pressure mounted, the police released pictures to the media of Jack Taylor walking with a tall blonde man at Barking Station on October 13th. They asked for the public's help in identifying the man. It took only two days for the police to find out that the man was Stephen Port. Surprisingly, it wasn't the public who identified Port but a police officer who already knew him.

Donna Taylor, Jack's mother, said the police should be held accountable for all the men's deaths. She accused the police of "class, gender, and sexual bias" and has suggested that lives may have been saved had they acted sooner.

After forensic psychologist Nadia Persaud examined each of the four bodies, the inquest returned an open verdict. A forthcoming ruling means that there is a need for more questions to be answered to determine the reason for the deaths. Nadia said, "The most concerning are the findings by the pathologist of manual handling before the deaths. One of the bodies was wrapped in a bedsheet, sunglasses on another body's face, and bottles of GHB were on or near all four of the bodies, and none were tested for fingerprints or DNA."

On the morning of October 15th, Stephen Port was arrested at his apartment on suspicion of administering poison to four men, causing their deaths. DCI Tim Duffield interviewed Port from the Met's Homicide and Major Crimes Unit over the next four days.

6

ARREST, INTERROGATION, AND PRISON

During the interview, Port repeated his previous story about Anthony Walgate and finding him on the sidewalk outside his apartment. Port claimed that he met Whitworth at a sex party at an East London drug dealer he knew, but said he knew nothing about the man or his death. He claimed to know nothing about the other two men. But as the interrogation continued over the four days, he changed his story and slowly admitted to his involvement with all four dead men found in the churchyard park.

The following are the transcripts of Stephen Port's interrogation.

INTERROGATION OF STEPHEN PORT

Police Interviewer (PI) Tim Duffield: "So, did you have any involvement in the death of the male that we spoke about just a short while ago, Gabrielle Guevara or Gabrielle Kline?"
STEPHEN PORT (SP): "No, I did not, no."
PI: "Were you involved in administering any drugs, poison, or noxious substances to him?"
SP: "No, I don't administer drugs to anyone or give drugs to anyone. Um, that's done at the party by someone of the name organized."
PI: "Who is that, sorry?"
SP: "Daniel. He organized it. Sometimes he is the dude that hands out the drugs to the guests."
PI: "Daniel?"
SP: "Yeah."

The detective moved a picture across the table face up towards Port.

PI: "Daniel, this is the man that you spoke of earlier?"
SP: "I don't know. I mean, it might be the same guy, I don't know, but he's the only Daniel I know."

There was a short pause as Port continued to look down at the detective's papers in front of him.

SP: "Like he does what I did, he'd pick up guys and bring them to the party."
PI: "Yes."
SP: "But he would stay longer and would administer drugs, hand out drugs, or whatever, but I would leave, and he would stay."
PI: "And did you go with Daniel to meet people?"
SP: "No, No. I knew he was doing the same as I was, but I would see him at the party, and I had a brief conversation about it, but I never actually engaged with him outside of that."
PI: "Outside of the party?"
SP: "That's right."
PI: "Which parties were these?"
SP: "All sorts, Frat parties."
PI: "Frat parties."

Another pause in the conversation occurred until Port covered his mouth and coughed a few times.

PI: "So when was the first time you met the person you are talking about, the man you know as Daniel?"

SP: "It was on the first few occasions I was there with Rafa Scott. Daniel was there. I don't even know if it's the same Daniel that we are even talking about. He is the only Daniel I can recall as such; he's the only one that rings a bell."
PI: "You think his name was Whitford?"
SP: "He was tall, almost as tall as me, brown hair."
PI: "It might help you if I showed you a picture. We call this CRT."

The investigator started directing Port's attention to the pictures he had placed on the table in front of him.

PI: "You see, this is Jack Taylor."

Port slid the picture of Jack Taylor towards himself and took a long, quiet stare at it.

SP: "I don't pay full attention to the guy's faces when I have been to the parties, but I don't recognize his face."
PI: "So you don't recognize his face?"
SP: "No, I do not, no."
PI: "That's Jack Taylor, so you don't recognize Jack Taylor?"
SP: "No, I do not."

PI: "So, have you ever slept with this man?"
SP: "No."
PI: "Or had sexual intercourse with him?"
SP: "He doesn't look like the type I would go for myself."
PI: "He's not the sort of person you would go for?"
SP: "No, I don't want, he's more yoga-drinking boys, and he looks older. He doesn't look like some of the boys I've taken to parties, and he's not one of them."
PI: "So you don't recognize him as being one of them?"
SP: "No."
PI: "No? Okay."

The detective then picked up the photo of Jack Taylor and put it away amongst the other papers and photos on the table.

PI: "Again, Jack was found dead on September 14, 2015. Stephen, did you have any involvement in his death?"
SP: "I did not, no...no."
PI: "Did you kill Jack Taylor?"
SP: "I did not, no.... no."
PI: "Did you administer any drugs or noxious substances to him?"
SP: "No, no."

PI: "To cause him harm?"
SP: "No....no, I did not, no."
PI: "And you say you've never seen him before, is that right?"
SP: "That's right."
PI: "That's right."

The detective left the room for a short break. When he returned this time, he had several maps with him. He sat down and started placing the maps around the table.

PI: "What I've got right here is several maps. It's not easy to get it all on one piece of paper. Just so we're clear here, again, it shows your home address, and it shows you the church, St. Margaret's, and then behind it, you've got the Abbey and the primary school. The walls around the Abbey, have you ever had any reason to go into that area?"
SP: "No."
PI: "Have you ever been through into the Abbey?"
SP: "Ahh, no, I haven't, no. Those are touchy areas. I once went to the church with my ex Danny on Christmas day, went to the church, but that's as far as I got."
PI: "You've not been into the grounds behind

it, where you've got the old Abbey, the walls, or the grounds there?"
SP: "No, it looks spooky, so that I won't go there."
PI: "You've never been?"
SP: "No."
PI: "In all the eight years that you've lived across the road from that park?"
SP: "No, that's all private, so I wouldn't go there. It's a private area. It belongs to the church."
PI: "This is fairly open when you go past. Would you agree with that or not?"
SP: "At the field, yeah, the field is, but the church is behind the walls. I won't go past there."
PI: "Because three of the four people that have been found dead were found there. Slumped up against the wall near the Abbey."
SP: Softly mumbled, "Yeah."
PI: "What was that?"
SP: "I didn't know that."
PI: "You didn't know that? So that's news to you, is it?"

Stephen then remained quiet, folded his hands on his lap, and looked down at the church map on the table. What sounded like short sighs kept coming from him as he started to rock back and forth.

PI: "Did you put them there?"
SP: "No."
PI: "You see, Anthony (Walgate) was found outside your address with a large amount of GHB in his system. The other three men we've discussed were all found over by the wall area."

The detective then took his pen and circled the places where the bodies were found.

PI: "On the Abbey, you can see on this map again that they were slumped against the wall with a large amount of GHB in their body. Can you account for that at all?"
SP: "No, I don't."

The detective then flipped the map over and brought out another page. The detective now had a suicide note retrieved from the third victim, Daniel Whitworth's hand.

PI: "Did you write this letter here?"

The detective then pushed the page over towards Stephen.

SP: "No, I did not."
PI: "This letter was found with Daniel (Whitworth)."
SP: "No."
PI: "Are you telling me the truth, Stephen?"
SP: "I am telling you the truth, yes."
PI: "Now all of these boys, young boys, all found dead, Stephen, in the early stages of their youth and their early twenties."
SP: "What do you want me to tell you?"
PI: "Close to your house. One of them had been in your house, either just before the time when he died and was found to have large quantities of drugs in his system. The other three were found just over the road in the churchyard, or just beside the churchyard in the area that we've discussed, propped up against the wall, a short distance from your house, all again with high levels of GBH in them. Enough to kill them is a highly unusual way to die for one person. This is four."
SP: "Right."
PI: "All found very close to where you live, all men, young me, the type of men you say that you find attractive, all now dead, Stephen."

Stephen remained very quiet, still with his hands in his lap and looking downwards, not facing the detective.

SP: "As far as Anthony I know, the other three, I don't know how they come to be."
PI: "Stephen, this is serious, okay?"
SP: "Yes, I know."
PI: "You must tell us the absolute truth."
SP: "What I've said was true."

Analysis of Interrogation

Stephen Port showed many signs of anxiety in police interviews which helped officers convict him of the four murders and several rapes. Port scratched his nose while being questioned. His voice had a shallow volume, indicating that his words did not match the confidence levels behind them. Port's body language showed constant signs of anxiety when the volume of his voice dropped with every answer.

Dawn Archer, a professor of Linguistics, argues that there are indicators that Port was lying. "Guilty speakers will use more negation. His volume drops, which suggests that a level of confidence doesn't match the words he's saying. In other words, he does not believe what he's saying."

Experts also tell us that it's a sign of anxiety when your volume is meager during interviews. When we tell lies, we distance ourselves from our lies with our volume.

Port said "No" forty times out of forty-seven questions asked by the police. He kept closing his lips to ensure he didn't say too much and crossed his arms to avoid leaking information. Port clenched his right fist and squeezed his hands. His body language showed us his tension and his feelings of being under pressure.

By the time the questions were more challenging for Port to answer, he was almost inaudible. For example, the interviewer asked Port if he was telling the truth about the boys, "The type of men you say you find attractive, all dead now, Stephen." Port replied in an almost inaudible low tone, "Apart from Anthony, I know nothing about the other three or how they came to be." Port squirmed his body around the chair and clenched his hands, telling us he was hiding something. He then told the detective that everything he had told him up to this point was valid.

Stephen Port was charged with four counts of murder. Once the press reported on Port's arrest for the murders of the four young men found in the park, another eight men came forward and said that they too were drugged and raped by Port in his apartment. All of them had met him on a gay hookup app online. Many described Port spiking their drinks and injecting them with a small syringe usually meant for children when they were sick.

Eventually, Port was charged with eight more sexual offenses against the men who came forward to the police. He was convicted on seven of those charges but acquitted on one. In four of those cases, he was also convicted of rape.

Trial

Stephen Port's trial began on October 9, 2015, at the Central Criminal Court of England and Wales, commonly known as the "Old Bailey." Part of the prison stands on the road named after the Old Bailey. It is on the site of the medieval Newgate Gaol, which has been around since the sixteenth century. Old Bailey Street follows the line of the city of London's ancient wall, which was part of the bailey, or castle. The actual court building on this property was built in 1902. This crown court deals with major criminal cases within the Greater London area. The trials held in the Old Bailey are open to the public but are subject to stringent security procedures.

The first day Stephen Port was brought into the courthouse, the grounds were full of screaming people, some crying and calling him names. Port just looked up at the Lady Justice statue on the top of the court building.

A series of references, some from the Bible, are placed around the walls of the entire hall. Port read parts of these phrases repeatedly while he was trying not to pay attention to any of the people yelling outside the courthouse, and especially to avoid catching the eye of one of the victim's family members.

The law of the wise is a fountain of life."

The welfare of the people is supreme."

Right lives by the law, and law subsists by power."

Poise the cause in justice's equal scales."

Moses gave unto the people the laws of God."

London shall have all its ancient rights."

Most people were shocked at Port's appearance. He no longer had the hairpiece he had worn on his head for over ten years. His drug-induced party life had taken its toll on him, and he looked way beyond the 41 years he had lived on Earth. He would not once look at any of the victim's families or friends throughout the whole trial.

Prosecutor Jonathan Rees QC started by telling the Court that Stephen Port would meet men through websites and phone apps such as *Grindr*. He informed that the case would feature graphic evidence of a sexual nature and that they should approach it calmly, dispassionately, and analytically. The prosecution said, "This is a case about a man, the defendant, who in the pursuit of nothing more than his sexual gratification, variously drugged, sexually assaulted and in four instances killed the young gay men he had invited back to his flat."

Rees continued,

> "Port described himself as 70% gayer than straight with a preference for young, smaller boyish type men often referred to as 'twinks'. His appetite for penetrating drugged young men was reflected in the drug-rape pornography he watched, and he occasionally

> filmed himself having sexual intercourse with the unconscious males. He had the propensity to render young gay men unconscious with drugs without their consent, so he could have sex with them in that state. That was his inclination, his fetish, and what turned him on."

Rees then listed the drugs that Port had used on these young men as "Poppers or bottles of Amyl Nitrite, Viagra, M, also referred to as Meow Meow, T or Tina, the name for crystal Meth, and G, which was either GHB or GBL in its liquid form." Rees continued by saying that "GHB is of significance in this case. The postmortem examinations on the four young men who died revealed that each had died from a drug overdose featuring higher levels of GHB."

Rees finished by saying, "Each of the victims was found outside, very close to Port's apartment—three of them in the St. Margaret's churchyard." Rees said that the three victims found in the churchyard were propped up against the brick fence in the same position and with their shirts pulled up as if they had been dragged to their resting spots.

Rees then reminded the jury of Port's first arrest, "It was after the death of Anthony Walgate that Port was arrested and convicted for perverting the course of justice after he made false claims to the police. He had falsely denied ever having met Gabriel Kovari and Jack Taylor. Port also denied writing the wrong suicide note found in Daniel Whitworth's left hand."

Rees continued by stating, "The defendant allegedly met with Walgate, a fashion student and male escort, through the website *Sleepy Boys*, offering him £800 for an overnight. He met him at the Barking Train Station at 10 p.m. on June 17, 2014, using the name "Joe Dean." Rees said, "Port was a male escort. According to one of his former partners. Port described himself as having a big sexual appetite and particularly liked men in their late teens. Walgate had sent a friend a text giving this friend full details of who he was meeting, just in case he got killed."

Rees stopped and looked at the jury members one by one slowly before continuing, "Around 30 hours later, at 4 a.m. on June 19, 2014, Port called the emergency services to report a young boy was collapsed or had had a seizure or was drunk on the street outside his flat. Port did not give his name and claimed he was just driving by and saw the man."

"Police and ambulance attended, and a doctor pronounced Walgate dead shortly before 8 a.m., although clearly, he had been dead for some hours. The body contained a bottle containing GHB, and the postmortem revealed high levels of GHB in Walgate's blood and urine within the range at which deaths from GHB intoxication have been reported," said Rees.

Rees continued his story, but now looked like he didn't believe what he was about to say. "Port was discovered by police, who rung him back on his phone, asleep in his bed. Port then told the officers that he had found the man lying unconscious and had propped him up against the wall as he thought the boy had had a seizure, and then went into his flat and fell asleep."

The Court then heard about the eight living victims who were allegedly drugged and sexually assaulted by Port. The prosecution said, "It offends common sense to suggest that it was just an unfortunate coincidence that all of these men happened to either die or be sexually assaulted from an overdose featuring high levels of GHB, shortly after meeting with Stephen Port."

The first victim of Port that the police could find was only 19 years old, who met Port in February of 2012 through the app *Grindr* and was invited to his flat. The man claimed to have suddenly passed out and awoke to find Port having sex with him, to which he didn't consent. The victim later conveyed to a counselor that his drink must have been spiked, and he had been date-raped by Port. The victim also told some of his friends about the attack.

Rees explained to the jury, "There are similarities in these circumstances with the case of another man who, three weeks earlier, had been seen with Port at Barking Station in a state of distress and unsteady on his feet, incoherent, and vomiting. Port had told the station ambulance and police he had found the 23-year-old under the influence outside his home. The prosecution explained that Port drugged him at his flat after the two men met through the *Fit-Lads* website by giving him a clear liquid, which he thought was water, that caused him to fall unconscious.

Rees said, "He was deliberately drugged so the defendant could engage in sexual activity with him while he was unconscious." When the man woke up, he found himself naked and lying on the floor. Port then helped him get dressed and walked him to the Barking Station. "There is a common factor underlying the explanation of why each victim suffered an overdose, and that common factor is the defendant. The considerable efforts to cover up his connection with each deceased indicate that he, rather than the deceased themselves, was responsible for the fatal overdoses." Rees continued by saying that Port also tried to cover up his connections to each of his victims. "Each victim's mobile telephone was missing, and in each case, the defendant lied to the police about his knowledge of and involvement with the deceased."

Port pleaded not guilty to the four murders, the four counts of administering poison with the intent to endanger life or inflict grievous bodily harm, or the seven counts of rape.

When Port took the stand, he constantly mumbled his answers and often had to be asked to repeat what he said. Most of his replies were just one or two-word answers and often weren't relevant to the question he was asked. The prosecutor began to look like an angry schoolteacher trying to get one of their students to recite something from a book. "Speak up, please!" "What did you say?" or "Please state your answers more clearly." Throughout the cross-examination, he kept a blank, unemotional look on his face. His eyes appeared dead.

Prosecutors asked Port about the videos they found on his phone and why the men appeared unconscious. He responded by saying that the police were showing you the last part of the videos and that there were several hours of him with the person he was having sex with within the video, having regular sex.

A critical point during Port's questioning in Court was when he was asked why he lied about knowing or meeting the four dead men. He said he only lied because the truth sounded unbelievable, and he knew the police wouldn't accept it.

The Court heard that when detectives finally searched through Port's computer, thcy found evidence that Port pretended to be Jon Luck while chatting with Kovari's Spanish ex-boyfriend. It was divulged to the Court that Port did this to try to keep tabs on the investigation of Kovari's death. The police also checked through Port's cell phone and found 83 homemade movies of him having sex with other men. More incriminating was the fact that several of those men were unconscious during the video.

In the case of Daniel Whitworth, a handwriting expert testified that the suicide note found on his body was absolutely not written by Whitworth and was very similar to Port's handwriting. Even more damning was the Court hearing how the paper on which the note was written came from Port's apartment. The police also tested the blue sheet on which Whitworth's body was left and found Port's DNA. It was proven to be from the bed in his apartment.

On the stand, Port eventually admitted to writing Whitworth's suicide note but claimed that Whitworth actually dictated to him and he just wrote out what he said. Port also admitted to having met Jack Taylor in the same church park where he was found dead and that they had had a two-hour drug-induced sex session. He said Taylor was really into using drugs.

On November 23, 2016, after the seven-week trial, Stephen Port, 41, was convicted of the murders and rapes of Anthony Walgate, Gabriel Kovari, Daniel Whitworth, and Jack Taylor. He was also convicted of the rapes of three other unnamed men whom he had drugged and ten counts of drugging men without their knowledge or permission.

Port was sentenced to life imprisonment with a whole life order, meaning he will never be released on parole. During the sentencing, the judge commented, "I do not doubt that the seriousness of the offense is so exceptional that a whole life order is justified. I decline to set a minimum term, and the defendant will die in prison."

The police had problems keeping order in the halls surrounding the courtroom when Port was sentenced. The cheers and screams were loud, with several people shouting that they wanted Port to die.

After the trial was over, Malcolm McHaffie, Deputy Chief Prosecutor for CPS London, told the press,

---

> "Stephen Port committed many murders and rapes against young men. Port would control these men through the calculated use of the drug GHB, which he administered without them being aware. This was a complicated and challenging case, but assisted by the large amount of evidence found on Port's many social media sites. The details of each of the deaths were strikingly similar, as each of the victims was aged between 21 and 25 and had died within a short time of meeting Port. Port had engaged in sexual activities with all of them, and they had

> been killed of toxicity from drugs, and in three cases, a bottle of GHB was found in the circumstances with being planted."

Port's family still maintains that he is innocent. Port's mother has told the press that she knows her son is a kind boy and did not murder anyone.

Port was sent to HMP Belmarsh prison, a Category A prison that holds some of Britain's worst killers. He would meet Richard Huckle, Britain's worst pedophile, during his stay there. The two of them struck a friendship and eventually a sexual relationship. When asked by the press how the two men could have had a sexual relationship in prison, the HMP Belmarsh replied that though both men resided in the maximum part of the prison, their cell doors were left open for the inmates to mix. The free time for the prisoners to mingle lasts about 90 minutes daily, and because they only have three guards to watch over them, things could happen. There was far too much for the guards to see everything that happens all the time. Both

Port and Huckle have been moved but are probably still in contact by letters through the mail.

Port has openly expressed to several people that he hopes Hollywood makes a movie about him and that he gets someone like Kevin Bacon to play him in the film. There is a *BBC* TV series called *Four Lives*, and actor Stephen Merchant plays Port. The series was originally named *The Barking Murders* but was renamed to honor the victims. Port is unhappy with the choice because he believes Merchant looks nothing like him. He is also apprehensive about the movie blackening his name and making him a target for attacks or even being killed by other prisoners.

Port's sister, Sharon, told the Sun newspaper that the movie would make him look bad and that the movie makers wouldn't know the truth. Therefore, it'll all be lies. "This will only make my brother look evil, but he's not evil."

STEPHEN PORT APPEALS

On Thursday, August 30, 2018, Stephen Port appealed his convictions for the murders of four young men. Still, he did not appeal the several other convictions of sexual offenses against seven other living victims. A judge had to review Port's documentation to the court and decide whether to give the applicant permission to proceed.

After lodging his appeal, Port sought legal advice. He thought the charges were too high and untrue. Port figured that, if anything, he should have been convicted of manslaughter, as these deaths were a series of self-inflicted drug overdoses. He also claimed that it was proven in court that each victim had other drugs in their system, including alcohol, before they even met Port.

Part of the claim said that Port should have been more mature and assertive with the men when they took the GHB, but most people who know Port claim that he is very young in the head, but not a murderer.

The families of the victim's spokeswoman immediately responded that it changed nothing and that Daniel Whitworth, 21, Anthony Walgate, 23, Gabriel Kovari, 22, and Jack Taylor, 25, were all drugged and raped by Port. Also, after killing the men, Port tried to cover up his crimes by disposing of their mobile phones, lying to the police, and planting the fake suicide note on the third victim's body.

On November 16, 2018, the judge dismissed Port's application to appeal at the first stage, ruling out the need for a panel of judges to hear his case. Jack Taylor's sisters, his fourth victim, said they were glad the appeal was dismissed because of the worry it caused them. It was quite a shock to them to learn that he had appealed the case in August.

INQUESTS OF THE DEATHS OF STEPHEN PORT'S VICTIMS

In October 2018, it was decided that a judge would be appointed to conduct the inquest into all four of the deaths related to Stephen Port's conviction in 2016. It followed a request by the current coroner, Dr. Shirley Radcliffe, to allow the inquest to be held in a different area or for her to step aside in favor of a judge. The results are expected to be in the hands of the victims' families sometime in 2019.

There has been genuine public interest in the outcomes of these inquests, especially since the original 2015 inquests into the deaths of both Gabriel Kovari and Daniel Whitworth were quashed. Those earlier open conclusions were reached when police had not connected the four men.

The victims' families were required to cover

the legal costs of the inquests being conducted for their murdered family member. Jack Taylor's sister Donna told the *BBC* in September 2018, "We are trying to raise as much money as we can to have the best legal representation possible during the inquests because we think that, with what's happened, with the way we've been let down by the police, that we feel that we are going to need that." But she thinks it's unjust that the police are assured of public funding for their legal representation while the families are not. "It's ridiculous after everything we've already had to go through, especially from our point of view, to fight for this from the very beginning, to then find yourself in a position of having to do this now. It's just ridiculous. The boys were murdered, there's a huge amount of police failings, and under these circumstances, it shouldn't be like this," Donna said.

Mandy Pearson, Daniel Whitworth's stepmother, agreed. "The police are dipping into public money. They can do it, no problem, and we've got to fight for what we need. A lot of this should be funded for us because, in the first place, the police didn't do their job. Otherwise, Stephen Port would have gone to prison, we would have felt justice had prevailed, and we would have left it at that."

Mandy also thinks that much more significant changes are needed. "There are so many families in our position that can't afford the legal costs, so there should be something there for bereaved families. We're not just fighting for us; we're fighting for changes in this law, where we should be funded. We're looking for changes all along the line."

The families also applied for legal aid under the "Exceptional Case Funding Scheme," but it's uncertain if they qualify for assistance. The government revised the legal assistance so that caseworkers consider when granting legal aid with the intention that funding would be more likely for those whose loved ones kill themselves or suffer an unnatural death while in the state's custody, such as in prison or a mental health unit.

The families raised over 10,000 GBP from donations from over 300 people on a successful crowdfunding campaign on social media.

In another twist to the case, newly disclosed documents from August 2018 revealed that Stephen Port was awarded 135,383 GBP of taxpayers' money to cover the appeal of his four murder convictions. It is deplorable considering the victims' families were left to their own devices to raise funds for their costs surrounding the trial and legal fees.

Police Misconduct

BBC One broadcast a documentary in March 2017 that suggested a catalog of police failings in the Metropolitan police's response to the deaths in this case. Crucial witnesses, such as Port's neighbor, who claimed Port would show up at his house with a large amount of a white powdery substance and liquor bottles, were not questioned. That neighbor claimed he received weird text messages from Port about Gabriel Kovari.

After Gabriel Kovari was found dead, his previous roommate, John Pape, searched the internet and was surprised to find several other unexplained overdose deaths in the Barking area. Pape found it strange that the Barking Dagenham Police did not link the cases. Pape found that peculiar, especially in the Anthony Walgate case, because their bodies were found in the exact location. The cases also had many similarities to the Kovari case.

It wasn't until Daniel Whitworth was found dead in the same park that John Pape called the police and demanded to know if the police thought the cases were connected and could be the result of murder. Pape was also very concerned for his safety, but the police told him not only were the cases not linked, but there was no killer out on the loose. So, not to worry.

John Pape offered to come into the station to be interviewed by the police if he had some relevant information about Kovari's death. He knew about all the places and things that Kovari had done before his death, but the police showed no interest.

The neighborhood's widespread belief was that the police had no idea what they were doing by not connecting the two cases. The dog walker who found the two bodies in the park, Barbara Denham, couldn't understand why they wouldn't link the two murders. Even the local gay organization, the *Pink News*, reported a serial killer in the area and urged people to be aware.

On Friday, May 12, 2017, the seventeen family members of the victims of Stephen Port filed a lawsuit against Scotland Yard, claiming that the officers discriminated against their relatives because they were gay. The High Court action was over "breaches of duty and inaction" and accused the police of breaching the Equality Act 2010. The families also claimed that the police were negligent and misused or abused their power by failing to investigate properly. Court documents revealed they sought "aggravated and exemplary damages" of over £200,000. The detectives admitted to missing the opportunity to spot similarities between the killings.

The misconduct started when Port was jailed for perverting the course of justice in the death of Anthony Walgate, who ended up being his first victim. He was only given an eight-month sentence. Port claimed that Walgate overdosed in his flat and that he panicked and left the body out front of his apartment in June 2014. But then Port went on to kill three others after his release in September 2015. The families of the murdered men say they are insulted and distressed over the lack of police answers about the mistakes they made and wonder why Port was not caught sooner. Some seventeen officers faced misconduct probes after the case was referred to the Independent Police Complaints Commission.

The police admitted to catching Port due to missed opportunities, leaving the families with new hope that an end was in sight. The Commission compiled over 7,000 pages of material on the cases and has completed its first draft.

During Port's trial, we discovered that he became obsessed with pornography that focused on both men and women being raped while they were out of control on drugs. Port went to dating websites or apps to meet his victims. It wasn't until after Port's trial that the police introduced new guidance to deal with allegations involving "Chemsex" incidents. And now, they must review 58 cases where people died from GHB poisoning in London during the years that Port was active in the community. The police are unaware of the total number of victims since Port also drugged and raped seven other victims in separate incidents, where the victims didn't die.

Mandy Pearson, Daniel Whitworth's stepmother, said, "We continue to seek answers and accountability from the police about how, for a whole year, they let us believe that Daniel had committed suicide, in which time Port went on to kill again. We hoped that the police would be held to account for their activities, with Port now behind bars. It won't bring any of the boys back, but we've been determined to get to the bottom of what happened, so we hope this will help with that. We won't rest until we get the truth."

In January of 2021, a formal inquest was held into the police conduct during the deaths of the four men. The final verdict was reached, saying that the police's failings probably contributed to the deaths of the victims. They also found that the local police did not conduct a background check on Port, leading to omissions and failures during the Walgate investigation.

Even though police claimed that the lack of resources caused their failings, the victims' families all claimed that it was prejudice because the victims were gay. Assistant Commissioner Helen Ball would formally apologize to the victim's families on behalf of the metropolitan police, but claimed that the police were not homophobic.

THE LETTERS

LETTER 1

I'M INNOCENT

One of the more intriguing parts of this case is the information we can get from Stephen Port's letters from prison. Throughout his letters, he professed his innocence without hesitation, but so do most convicts in prison. He often claimed that the victims had taken the drugs themselves throughout many samples I have placed here, and he hadn't administered them. He claimed he might have sold the drugs or given the drugs to them, but he didn't inject any of the victims. So, at best, he should only be charged and convicted of selling or supplying illegal drugs.

Port also claimed that the drugs found in the bodies of the dead men were only used to enhance their sexual performance. They all took the drugs willingly to have a "great sexual session." So, in his mind, there was no rape.

"I am trying not to think about my trial yet as I am not looking forward to how many people and press will be there. I don't like being the center of attention, and not under these circumstances. I have told my legal team not to waste time trying to get me bail, which would not be allowed anyway, and to focus on my case. Yes, of course, my plea will not be guilty. I haven't and would never harm anyone, of that I am sure."

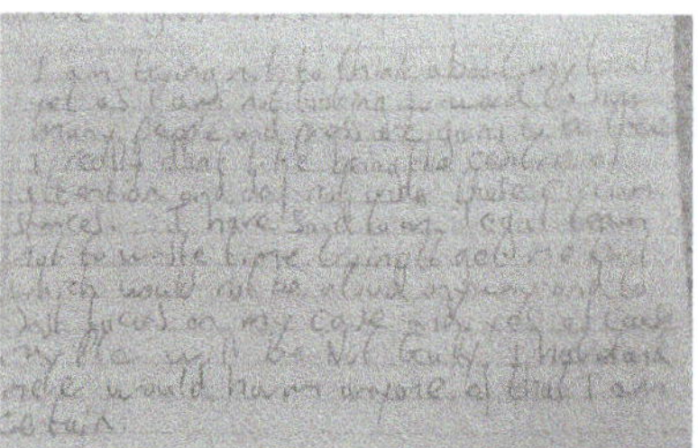

"I know I never killed anyone with drugs, but I feel sad that guys have died from taking drugs, and guys still are dying every week from drug-related problems or end up in prison like me. I will make it my life goal to campaign against drugs and make people more aware of the horrific effects of the ones they say are not addictive."

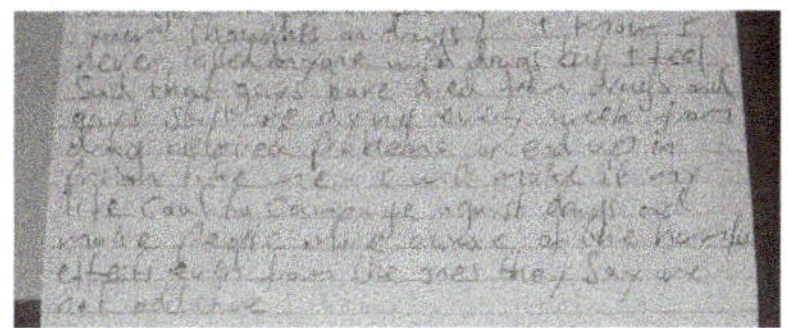

"My pleas and case management hearing will be on the 7th. Of January, and if it goes to trial, that will be in April 2016, but I believe the charges will be dropped by then when the evidence proves that it's an accidental death, not murder, and that I did not administer GHB to anyone."

> "Of course, I cannot do this until I am found not guilty, which I am certain they will, as I know I am innocent, and God will be with me as he knows I could never kill anyone. I do have a good heart, and I have always tried to help others, and I treat everyone with respect."

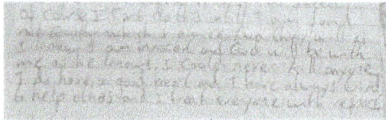

Stephen Port's statement appears to be an attempt to shift blame away from himself while acknowledging that deaths occurred. By saying he never killed anyone with drugs, he denies direct responsibility despite overwhelming evidence to the contrary. His wording suggests that he sees the victims' deaths as a result of drug use in general rather than his actions, deflecting attention from his role in administering the fatal doses.

By expressing sadness over drug-related deaths and pledging to campaign against drug use, he positions himself as someone concerned about the issue rather than a perpetrator of murder. The statement could be an attempt to reshape his public image, portraying himself as someone who regrets the broader consequences of drug use rather than admitting to intentionally drugging and killing his victims.

His choice of words subtly places responsibility on the victims, implying that they made choices that led to their deaths. Instead of acknowledging that he deliberately drugged them without their consent, he frames the situation as if they were just unfortunate casualties of drug culture. This kind of statement is not uncommon among criminals who seek to distance themselves from their crimes, either as a way to cope with their guilt or to manipulate public perception.

LETTER 2

WHO WILL PLAY ME IN A MOVIE

It's amusing that Port mentions how the media is talking about him and making up several stories about him, most of which are invalid. Later in the same letter, he talked about selling his report to the press or newspapers, but only for a lot of money. He also wonders who could play him best in a movie.

> "Not sure who could play me in a film. I have been told I look like a younger version of Kevin Bacon. So, maybe he or Eddie Redmayne (*The Theory of Everything*) and maybe the guy who played Captain America? Lol. My friend here looks like Ben Whishaw (*Q in the James Bond movie*).

I would like to say that he could play me, but he's got dark hair, and he's short, so probably not. Who would you choose for you? Who is your favorite actor?"

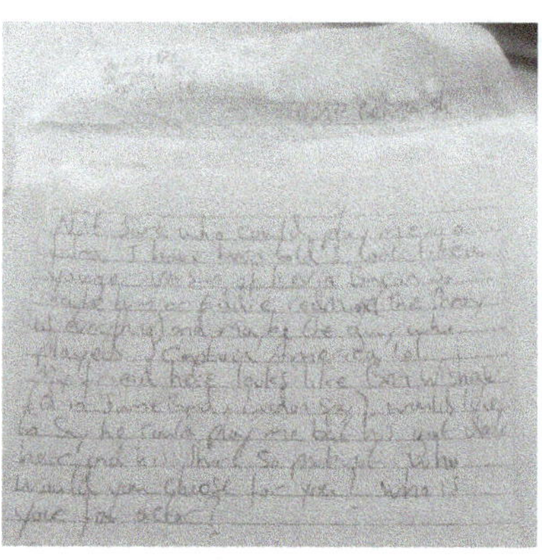

"When I do get released, there's going to be loads of media, but I won't talk to the press unless they offer me loads of money for my story. Lol."

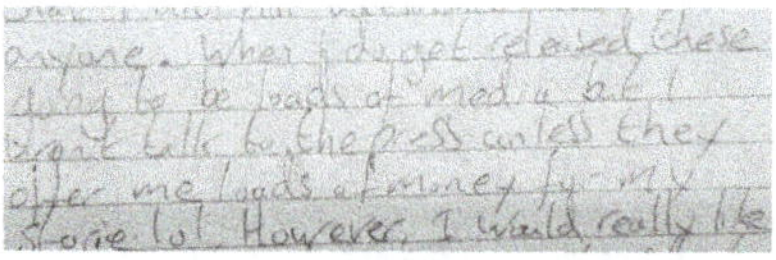

anyone. When i do get released these
going to be loads of media but I
won't talk to the press unless they
offer me loads of money for my
storie lol. However, I would really like

“I’m not certain I could write more than two pages as there’s not really that much of a k, but I would sell a story to the paper though. I won’t profit from it, though. I would use every penny to make certain to make sure this never happens.”

LETTER 3

HOW TO BE A MALE HOOKER

Another part of Port's letters I find fascinating is when he tried to explain how to protect yourself from harm while being a male escort. One of his warnings was never to take a drink from a client since it could be drugged and make you pass out. You wouldn't want to be stuck alone in a client's apartment high on drugs, as you could get raped or murdered.

The second point Port brought up was to make sure that you know the address you are going to and tell your friends where you are going, the name of the person you are supposed to meet, and the time you plan to return home. If you go missing afterward, they can report it to the police.

I guess it's pretty good advice to take when

it's coming from a man who has been convicted of raping and murdering four men he had bought for sexual encounters, all on the same nights he had met with them. They all showed a high drug content in their bloodstreams, having been raped and murdered by Port. So, if anybody would know what to watch out for, it would be Port.

> "Have you slept with any of the famous guys you met? I did have a couple of famous clients when [I] was escorting, but of course, I can't mention names, but they were generally MPS [Minister of Parliament – Government leaders equivalent to Senators in America]. Why do you want to be an escort? The money is good, but be certain to check the client's details first. Most never give their real name. So, always take a PayPal deposit first. Normally so to make certain they are not wasting your time. Never do anything for less than 150 [pounds], and do not work alone. Give your partner the client's phone number, photo, address, etc. Use your own lube and condoms, and ask what they want to

do first. Don't do anything extreme, like being tied up."

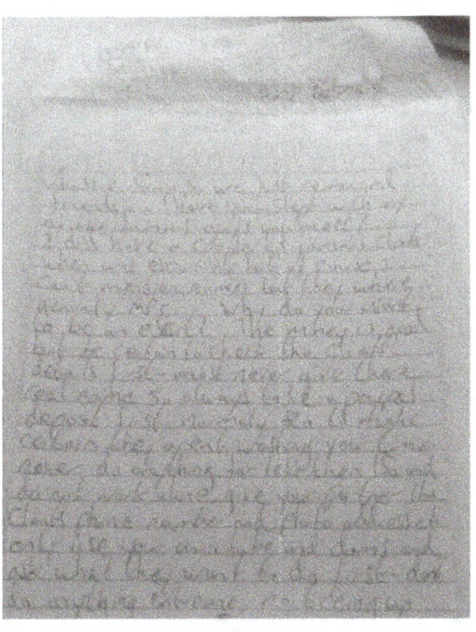

"Don't go to public places or any kind of restaurant, as that's for a different type of escort, which I would never do. Always take your own drink and never accept any drink or food from clients. Take money first once he's happy with you and before you start anything. It's also advisable to go with your friend so the client can give the money to him and then he leaves. I know you're big enough to look after yourself, but never assume anything, and always keep alert. Most escorts take their own drugs with them to make it more bearable, but don't take them in front of the client and only use your stuff and only a small amount so that you're still in complete control. Never mention money and sex in the same email or text."

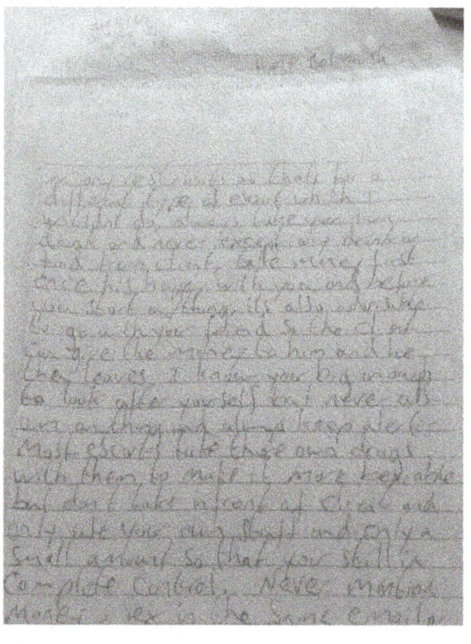

"Never mention money and sex in the same email or text. Always best to speak to the client on the phone first before arranging to meet. A couple of my older friends I first met when they were clients of mine, and one even became my flat mate when he was going through a divorce from his wife, which I believe I have mentioned before. Anyway, if you want to wait until I am out of here, I will give you some tips on how to make the client happy quicker, but I won't mention here as sure the person who has to read this letter first doesn't want to know those details. Lol."

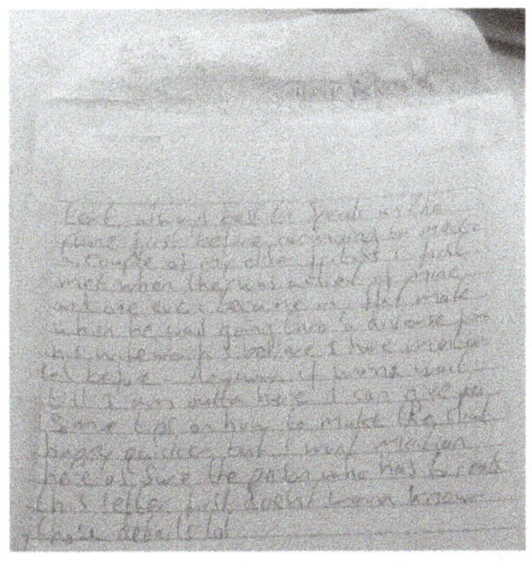

LETTER 4

TOYS & MOVIES

Another note was how frequently Port talked about his excitement in getting different toys and movies. His favorites were science fiction and fantasy stories like *Star Wars* and the *Transformers*. He even mentioned once having an ex-boyfriend leave him because he collected toys. Port often asked if Cody would send him different toys and movies, as he couldn't access them in prison. You would think he would be focused on his trial and what everyone in the country was saying about him.

"Buy me the BB8 toy from Star Wars or the remote control flying Millennium Falcon and, of course, Yoda and

Darth Vader fare. Yep, I know I am a big kid. I once had a boyfriend who left me because I liked going into Toys R Us. He couldn't accept me still like collecting Transformer and Star Wars at my age. Lol. But we are still very close friends and had some mega amazing sessions together."

"Do you have an American account? Instead of sending me a postal order, would you be able to order me some books/comics of Transformers Robots in disguise, please? Has to be sent directly from Amazon, though also a Pucca jigsaw with no more than 500 pieces, though. As I don't have a big enough table, I don't think they will let me have and Transformers or Star Wars, though, which is a shame."

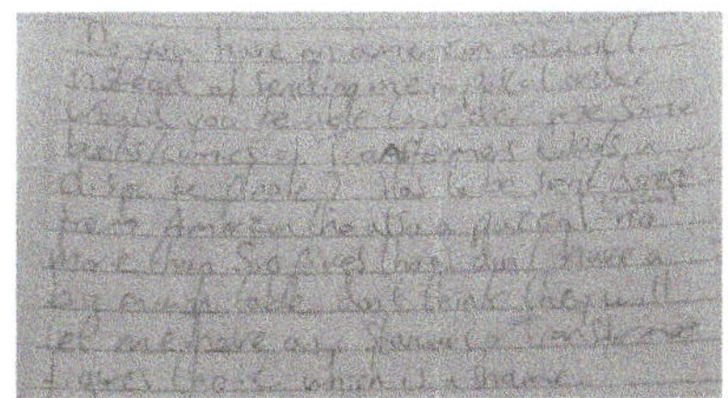

BB8 Star Wars

Pucca Jigsaw Puzzle

LETTER 5

I SHOULD BE A NURSE

Throughout Port's letters, he expressed the desire to dedicate the rest of his life to working for charities. Often, he would say that his dream job would be to work for places like the Red Cross. Port also wanted to warn younger people about the evils and dangers of doing drugs. He would do this once he was found not guilty and released from prison.

I got the feeling that Port was saying these things as more of trying to prove his innocence, because now he had friends and partners who had died of drug overdoses. He felt it was his place to go out in the world to help others who found themselves in the same place he had been. He often attached these desires to help others with the expression "he would never want to hurt anyone," and that "drugs were just a way of enhancing his sex life."

"My dream job would be to work for the Princess Trust, Red Cross, or any charity where I could make a difference and help others."

"When I do get released, there's going to be loads of media, but I won't talk to the press unless they offer me loads of money for my story. Lol. However, I would really like to use the media coverage to start a campaign to make people aware of the dangers of some drugs and educate people that drugs can kill."

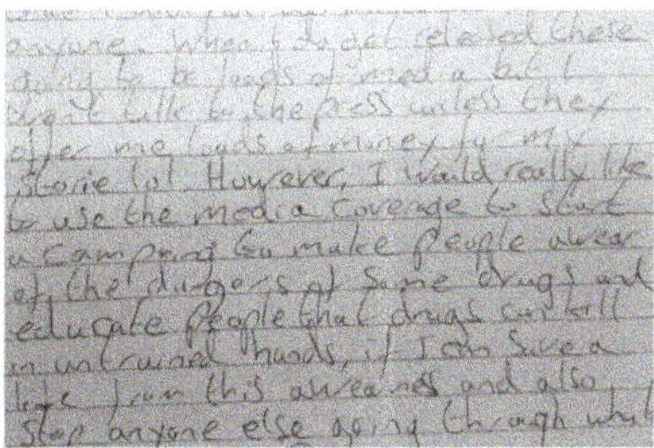

anyone. When I do get released these
going to be loads of [illegible] a bit I
won't talk to the press unless they
offer me loads of money for my
storie lol. However, I would really like
to use the media coverage to start
a campaing to make people awear
of the dangers of some drugs and
educate people that drugs can kill
in untrained hands, if I can save a
life from this awearness and also
stop anyone else going through what

"I never knew the dangers of GHB, and I don't believe many people really understand it could be lethal if mixed with alcohol or even prescription drugs and if you don't drink enough water when high. I just wanna get the message out there and also the dangers of doing drugs with strangers from online sites like Grindr."

LETTER 6

PLEASE SEND ME

"Dear Cody,

Sorry for my rushed letters over the weekend. I just wanted to let you know I received your letters and didn't want you to think I returned the items. I still don't know if they will let me have the Star Wars Annual. Well, fingers crossed they will let me. [Cody had sent the Star Wars annual to Port after the first letter].

I know I can receive magazines if sent directly from W.H. Smith [U.K. Bookstore chain], but not certain about other items from suppliers. I was told that you could call the prison to find out the numbers at the top of the page.

Not sure if they will allow me to have a watch or radio. I feel bad asking for cash, but if you could please post ten pounds, I can buy a pen of biscuits and order a magazine, as hunger and boredom are getting me down. I will ask my dad to post the money back to you as soon as the bank will allow him access to my account.

I had asked the Governor [Prison Warden] to write to my bank to give my dad full permission to access my bank account. He will have to cancel my direct debits like phone and internet, that will probably take a few weeks.

How was your weekend? What did you do? I hope I will be able to take lessons or work soon so I can at least have some money in my canteen and get off the wing, as I'm feeling really, really depressed at the moment. I'm just so glad I have you to write to, and I look forward to your reply.

I have a good legal team, and my QC is one of the best in the country. He's amazing, and he's confident he can prove my innocence. I have told my parents not to speak to the press after all the lies after they twisted everything to make it look certain I did it when there's only evidence to link me to two of them. Which I mentioned before, but I would never harm anyone. I would sooner kill myself than take another's life.

I've been watching Big Bang Theory, and glad there are new episodes on Thursday nights, as I've seen all the repeats over and over. I don't follow my soaps, but started to watch Neighbors and Home & Away here. I also watch Star Gate and Star Trek when it's on. I can't wait for the new Top Gear when Chris Evans takes over, but it won't be the same without Clarkson. But I love supercars, so I'll be happy if I can get to see something like the new Aston Martin DB10 that's in the new Bond movie. Wished I could see that.

Hopefully, I will be out of here when the DVD comes out. So much more I want to write, but I have to give this pen back to the insider as it's dinner time now, and will get locked

up after. I will post this on the way.
All the best.

Stephen Port"

This letter was primarily sent to ask for more things, including money, to be sent to him. Port did throw in that he was innocent again, as well. Sometimes, it felt like Port was only a teenager with a constant fascination with movies like Star Wars and other science fiction.

LETTER 7

GETTING TO KNOW ME

“Dear Cody,

Thank you so much for the money. I finally bought a pen and paper from the canteen. So, I can now write you many more letters. This is just a brief letter to let you know I received the money, so that you don’t have to worry.

I will write a longer letter today and try to answer as many of your questions as I can. I have to write in your letters a number next to your questions 1,2, 3, etc., so I can look back and remember what you asked as

I tend to ramble on and forget what you asked, LOL.

They won't let me have the Star Wars Annual until I leave. So, I have asked my solicitor to write to the Governor, so I have not shown any aggression towards anyone, and I have no history of violence of any kind. So, they have no reason not to give me the Star Wars book. But luckily, I got a Star Wars book from the library which had big print as I can see it as I have not got my glasses yet. Just there's no pictures in the book, though. I can now order a Saturday-Sunday newspaper thanks to your money so that I can have a TV guide, and they sometimes have a magazine with it.

I won't yet order a Top Gear magazine as I need the money to last, as I've spent 14 pounds already. I bought toothpaste and Imperial leather soap, as the prison stuff is crap. I got some coffee, digestives, caustic caramels, chocolate spread, porridge, and some Jaffa cakes, which is not nice I ate them all at once, the whole packet on Saturday night while watching Doctor Who.

I have been watching I'm a Celebrity Get Me out of here. I like George [George Shelley is a boy-band pop music singer in the UK], and I'm certain that he will most likely win. Not just because he's cute, but he seems to be able to do any of the challenges that he's faced with.

I would love to come stay with you in Manchester when I get out of here. Are you certain that would be okay? It's likely I will not be allowed back to Barking, for my own safety, after what was said in the press. But I think I will sell the flat before I am released. Anyway, my friend Mike can take care of removing and storing my things, but I'm not allowed to contact him for three months. My sister is in contact with him, though and says he's doing alright and living back with his family until he's allowed back to my flat.

He's been a good friend to me. We first met ten years ago when I was an escort. He was a client, and we became really close as friends, not boyfriends, as he was married with three kids. He helped me when I was in prison back in March. He looked after my flat and, checked the post, and paid the bills so that I still had a flat when I got released on an HDC tag. [You have probably noticed that Port contradicts himself by in one letter saying that he owned his flat and would sell it before he gets out, while in another letter, his friend pays his bills for the flat as if he rents it].

He's going through a divorce, so I let him move into the flat as he wasn't happy in the family home. It helped me, and it helped him. He got on really well with my family, and he became like a dad to my boyfriend. He didn't have parents, as they disowned him for being gay, and he had autism. He used to help him with his college work and cook him dinner when I was at work when I was doing a late shift. That was a few years ago, though.

He got a job as a steward on the cruise liner, and he's doing really well now, the ex-boyfriend, not Mike.

Being an escort is really dangerous. It's vital you never accept a drink from a client. Always take your own drink, take money first, and be alert. I had a friend who was also an escort, and we would tell each other where we were going and always gave the client's name and address or room number if it was a hotel. I would text him every hour to update him. He used to take some methadone before he went, so that it made being with older men all the more bearable. But I preferred not to, as I just wanted to get it done with, get paid and go home.

I never saw it as pleasure, just work which helped me save up a deposit for my flat. I only got into doing it when my friend said you're a good-looking lad with a nice body. Why not make some money from it? And he told me what he did. At first, I was a bit nervous about having sex with all the guys for money. But it wasn't that bad. Most of the clients I had just wanted some company or to just touched me. Some had the odd fetish and just wanted to dress me up in uniforms and take pictures of me, etc. Some just paid me to go out for dinner with them. Would I be able to get a job on the doors or bar work in Manchester? As I want to get back into work as soon as possible when I am released.

To answer what I miss, I miss my home, my family, and my friends. Good food, DVDs, toys [Not sex toys; Port actually liked to play with kid's toys], a comfortable sofa, going shopping and drinking, driving, and my last boyfriend and his beautiful smile, the way he kissed me and would rest his head on my shoulder and kiss my neck. He had an amazing blue eyes and short ginger hair. He loved Minions, and I used to buy him the toys. For his 23rd birthday, I bought him a massive cuddly "King Bob" from the movie. I liked them a lot as they are so funny. I love the humor.

Are you dating anyone at the moment? I only started using Grindr when a friend and dealer had offered me free bags of methadone if I found him guys for his parties and to use my pictures, etc., and I did a few times. And I never stayed long at his parties as he was into some heavy stuff I didn't get involved with.

I have a varying taste in music. I like the one by Nightwish, Adele, and

Will Young. I wished I could get his new album called "Joy." I heard it on CFL Friday's show.

Next letter to follow, all the best.

Stephen Port"

Like in several of his letters, Port prioritizes his favorite movies or what's happening on television series before mentioning his situation of being in prison and going to trial for murders and sexual assaults. It's like his legal battles were low on his list of priorities. Perhaps he was in denial.

LETTER 8

YOU CAN'T INTENTIONALLY KILL WITH GHB

This is another letter from Stephen Port where the first page or two is about science fiction movies, magazines, food, and lighter subjects. Eventually, he finally started to discuss why he was arrested and how he couldn't possibly have killed any of the men that he was with, as several drugs were found in their blood. Port also mentioned how he couldn't have raped any of them.

"Dear Cody,

Thank you so much for writing to me. It's the first letter I have had since my arrest, and I have not been allowed calls to my family, and I have no idea how they are coping. I have written them a couple of letters and asked if they could top up my canteen money as I only have seven-pound left after buying my essentials, coffee, biscuits, and some white chocolate.

The food here is alright but not enough. I was constantly hungry last week as after dinner at 4 p.m., there is nothing to eat until the following morning, and you only get a kid-sized breakfast pack. If possible, could you send me an A4 writing pad and a pen in a sealed packet? [according to Cody, that's for security] Please, as this pen is running out already, and I only got it on Friday.

Also, I know I'm being cheeky to ask, but it gets so boring just watching TV in my cell most of the day. I would be very grateful if you could send me a magazine. I like Top Gear films or Star Wars, but anything would be nice. Hopefully, some magazine will have a picture that I can put up on my wall.

I like Star Wars and feel sad I won't get to the new film next month. I will pay you back when I get access to my account. I have a single cell as I am a VP prisoner. [VP prisoners are vulnerable prisoners – they would probably be attacked if they were put into the general population].

Everyone here has been alright with me, just the normal questions like did I do it or not, etc., and I've been asked a few times to sign a picture of me in the paper, which is the only article I have read describing me as a serial killer which is so ridiculous, as a serial killer has intent to kill, and you can't intentionally kill someone with GHB.

How would it even be possible to give someone a high amount without them knowing [it], as it tastes vile? There's no way to disguise the taste, so the guy must know what he's taking and wants to be getting high on it. In the first place, it has a slow effect, so some guys take more before it's even kicked in and end up with a double hit.

However, some gays can take a large amount if they're used to it. My ex once drank a thirty-milliliter bottle full bottle of GHB when he was a wee bit high on M [methadone]. He was then rampant for a few hours but then took some more M, and he was back to normal, just with a sore throat as he didn't dilute it, so it burns his throat just a little bit. He was fine in the end. It's also quite addictive, so wanting more is natural. If I wanted to kill someone, I would use an easier method, like hitting over the head with a rolling pin.

I have been advised not to discuss my case with anyone as I am being monitored, but it's common knowledge that I knew two of the guys. The first one I met online, and when he came around, he took his own G (GHB). I wasn't watching how much he was taking as he seemed to know what he was doing and measuring his own dosage, but I am certain he was on other pills. Maybe prescription drugs which acted bad with the GHB, which mixed any system.

They didn't mention that in the papers, anyway, I did call an ambulance when I saw he wasn't right, and I helped him outside to get some fresh air. He then sat down against the wall outside. I then saw the police arrive with an ambulance, so I panicked and went back inside.

A couple of hours later, the police came and questioned me and said he was dead.

I thought they were going to blame me and arrest me, so I lied and said I just saw him outside looking in and called an ambulance. But a few days later, they arrested me as they checked his phone and saw that he had arranged to meet me.

So, I got charged with perverting the course of justice, and I was sentenced to two months as a cut D prisoner in Brixton Prison and two months on psych.

The other boy I met at a sex party I got invited to from Grinder. I can't remember too much about it due to the number of free drugs on offer out of the party. I did overdo it a bit and remembered feeling sick. He and another guy asked where I lived and helped me home.

I just fell onto my bed and passed out. I woke up after hearing a loud bang and a glass smash. I could also hear voices and shouting, but I couldn't move. I couldn't even turn my head. It was as if my body wasn't there, so I closed my eyes and slept until I woke up the following afternoon.

The flat was empty, just a broken glass and a spilled drink on the coffee table. I cleaned up and thought no more of it. Please excuse my bad handwriting. I don't have my reading glasses. I have told the nurse, and she said that she would make an appointment with the optician, but it could take three to four weeks and then it will be another couple of weeks to wait for the glasses to be made.

Why were you in prison? How long did you get? I was a head chef for a catering company but got dismissed when I was convicted [earlier for perverting the course of justice] back in March of 2015. I have been to Manchester a few times. I worked in Leeds for a short while a few years back and used to take day trips to Manchester with my boyfriend, who lived in York. [Cody Lachey had told Stephen Port in his letter that he lived in Manchester and used to be in prison] My trial is not until April next year, so I have a long wait here. I do hope that you will write to me again, and I will answer more of your questions when certain you receive this letter.

Many thanks.

Stephen Port"

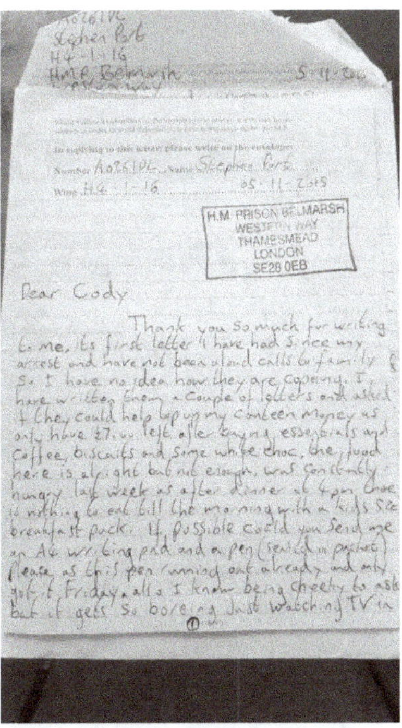

Stephen Port
H4-1-16
HMP Belmarsh 5-11-2015

In replying to this letter please write on the envelope:

Number A0261DC Name Stephen Port

Wing H4-1-16 05-11-2015

H.M. PRISON BELMARSH
WESTERN WAY
THAMESMEAD
LONDON
SE28 0EB

Dear Cody

Thank you so much for writing to me, its first letter I have had since my arrest and have not been alowd calls to family so I have no idea how they are copeing. I have written them a couple of letters and asked if they could help top up my canteen money as only have £7.[illegible] left after buying essentials and coffee, biscuits and some white choc. the food here is alright but not enough, was constantly hungry last week as after dinner at 4pm there is nothing to eat till the morning with a kids size breakfast pack. If possible could you send me an A4 writing pad and a pen (sealed in packet) please as this pen running out already and only got it Friday. also I know being cheeky to ask but it gets so boreing just watching TV in

①

[illegible]
Stephen Port
H4-1-16
HMP Belmarsh
Western Way
5-11

cell most of the day I would be very grat-
ful if you Could Send a Magazine, I'like
Topgear, Film or Star wars but anything
would be nice and hopefully Some Mag will
have a picture I can put up on wall, I like
Star wars and feel Sad I wont get to see
the new Film next month. I will pay you
back when I get access to my account.
I have a Single cell as am a VP prisoner
everyone here has been alright with me
Just the normal qustions if I did it or not
etc and was asked a few times to sign a
picture of me in papper which is the only
artical I have read disquibing me as a
Serial killer which is So rediculose as
a Serial killer has intent to kill and you
cant intent, only kill Someone with GHB.
How would it even be posible to give
Someone a high amount without them
knowing as it tastes Vile there no way to
disguise that taste so the guy must know
what his taking and wants to be getting
high on it in first place, it has a slow
effect so some guys take more before
its even kicked in and end up with a
double hit, However, Some guys can
take a large amount if used to it. My
ex once drank a 30ml full bottle when
②

5-11-2015

he was a wee bit high on it, he was
then [illegible] for a few hours but then
took some more of it and he was back to
normal, Just with a Sore throat as he
didnt dilute it so burnt his throat a
bit but he was fine, its also quite addi-
tive So wanting more is natural. If I
wanted to kill I would use an easier
method like hitting over head with rolling
pin or Sumthing. I have been advised
not to discuss my case with anyone as
I am being Monitored but its Common
knowledge I knew two of the guys, the
first one I met online and when he came
round he took his own G, I wasnt watching
how much he was taking as he seemed
to know what he was doing and measuring
his own dossage but I am certain he
was on other pills maybe presciption drugs
which acted badly with the G when mixed
in his System, they didnt mention that
in pappers. Anyway, I did call an ambulance
when Saw he wasnt right and I helped him
outside to get Some air and he sat down
up against wall outside, I then Saw police
arrive with ambulance so I panicked and
went back inside, a couple hours later
the police came to question me and Said
③

Stephen Port
H4-1-16
HMP Belmarsh
5. 11. 20[illegible]

he was dead. I thought they was going
blame me and arrest me so I lied and
said I just saw him outside looking
ill and called an ambulance, but a
few days later they arrested me as they
checked his phone and saw he had arranged
to meet me so I got charged with perverting
the course of justice and I did 12
months as a Cat D in Brixton and 2
months on tag. The other boy I met
at a sex party I got invited too from
Grindr. I can't remember too much
about it due to the amount of free drugs
on offer at the party. I did over do it a
bit. I remember feeling sick and he and
some other guy asked where I lived and
helped me home, I just fell onto my bed
and passed out. I woke up after hearing
a loud bang and a glass smash, I also
could hear voices and shouting but I could
not move, couldn't even turn my head, it
was as if my body wasn't there so I closed
my eyes and slept till woke up following
afternoon, the flat was empty just a
broken glass and spilt drink on coffee table.
I cleared up and thought no more of it.
Please excuse my bad writing as I don't
have my reading glasses, have told the nurse
(4)

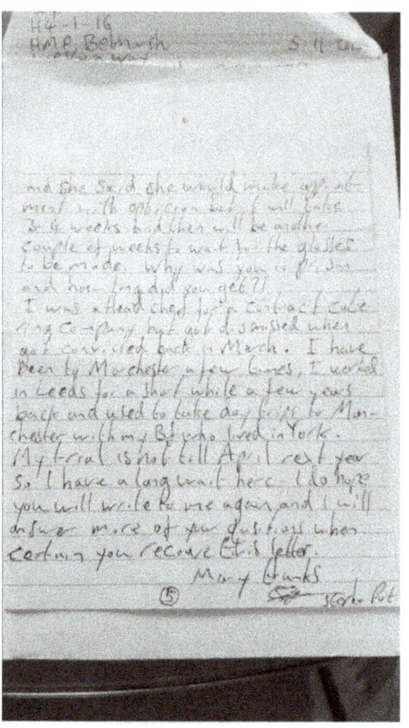

H4-1-16
HMP Belmarsh 5-11-[illegible]
[illegible] Way

and she said she would make appointment with optician but it will take 3-4 weeks and then will be another couple of weeks to wait for the glasses to be made. Why was you in prison and how long did you get??
I was a Head chef for a Contract Catering Company but got dismissed when got convicted back in March. I have been to Manchester a few times, I worked in Leeds for a short while a few years back and used to take day trips to Manchester with my Bf who lived in York. My trial is not till April next year so I have a long wait here. I do hope you will write to me again and I will answer more of your questions when certain you receive this letter.

Many thanks

(5) Stephen Port

LETTER 9

FAMILY LIFE

"Dear Cody,

Just received your letter dated the 19th of November. This week has been slightly better as I just started working in the ink shop, just filling up cartridges for printers, but time goes fast. So, the day goes a bit quicker, and the guys speak to me now, and they don't seem to be bothered about why I am here.

They just take me at face value. One guy I've been working with said he thinks I'm a nice, polite guy and said you don't seem like a murderer. And I told him I was not and that I would sooner kill myself than take another's life.

Anyway, I only get two pounds, sixty a day Monday to Thursday, but at least it helps me buy essentials, but no luxuries though as just a pack of coffee is three pounds, ninety-nine and Jaffa cakes are pound. They're gone in one go, as I love them, LOL. I finally have an optician appointment for Monday.

So, I should have my glasses soon, and my writing will become more readable, I hope. So, what have you been doing this week? I have lots of memories from my life. While being in here, I remembered a lot of things I hadn't thought about in ages.

My childhood was quite normal. My dad was strict but never abused me. My mum is quiet but speaks her mind when she wants to. I always had what I wanted within reason. At school, I wasn't really bullied, but I used to get called stretch because I was tall and skinny. But at 16, I started going to the gym after reading some books on bodybuilding. After a few months, my arms and shoulders started to get a bit bigger, so I didn't look like a beanpole anymore. I became better at sports, and no one would bully me. [This is another contradiction as he just said he wasn't bullied, but when he worked out and became more muscular, nobody would bully him anymore?] I was quite shy, but I had plenty of friends as I was more of a jock because I was good at basketball.

My ex-boyfriend was disowned when he came out as gay at 14, put into care by his foster parents, and sexually abused and ran away until he was put into the care of his granddad's, who was 76. He did his best, but with him having autism and ADHD, he was very difficult with his moods. He could become very aggressive.

However, at 18, he met me online, and at first, he would just stay a week at a time. His grandfather used to drive him down until I taught him to drive, and he got his own car. After two months, he moved in with me for the first year we had a normal relationship with normal sex. I know you are probably thinking that I am the older guy, but I never had to supply him with a drink and didn't know about drugs back then.

He was always horny and very loving, and we did everything together. He had his moods at times, and I had to call his grandfather to come down and help me as he would run out shouting and screaming in the street a few times. The neighbors would call the police, but it wasn't from anything I did; it could be from one of his friends online, or I got a text from a friend that would upset him. He would get jealous very quickly, as he wanted my full attention. Nobody else could have me. He didn't like change, and everything would have to be as he wanted.

During the second year, he met a friend online that was his age. It wasn't anything sexual between them, so I didn't worry. But he gave me methadone and said try it with Steven, your boyfriend. So, we did it to give it a try. It was amazing, but after a while, he would want me to try other stuff, so his friend game him GHB. He was sick at first, but he kept wanting more.

Then, after a while, he started getting into the habit of taking GHB and being very submissive. He said do what you want to me. I trust you. He wanted me to have control over him, and he wanted me to tie him to the bed.

Also, I can only guess, as he was abused when he was young, that now it became a part of him. But instead of being forced to do it, he wanted it to be completely submissive. Sorry, I am rambling again. I know you want to know more about me and not my ex-boyfriend, but he was such a big part of my life for four years, that was back in 2013.

When we split up, we didn't remain friends, but he didn't get on that well with my new boyfriend. They would clash and argue, and they would both fight for my attention, so he went back to live with his grandfather, and the new boyfriend moved in with me."

[In Cody's previous letter, he told Port that he had been drugged and sexually abused.]

Did you report this guy who

drugged you? I could never do that because what's the point of sex if you're both not enjoying it? I do prefer one one-on-one sex rather than group sex. I liked his full attention, and I want to give him mine. It's so much better with kissing and cuddling. Also, which you don't do in a group orgy, it's just about getting in and coming, etc. I prefer the real love.

I am being charged with administering a drug with intent to cause harm, which is murder times four. I was just charged with perverting the cause of justice as when my friend had a bad effect, I took him outside and left him there. When the police arrived, and I said that I didn't know him, as I was scared. They then accused me of taking drugs with him. Now, they accused me of giving him the drugs to intentionally kill him, which is so ridiculous. He was my friend, and I would never do that, and I certainly didn't do that to my other friends.

It's most likely these guys had too much G at a party, and these guys took him to a park to avoid being done for drugs, etc., or even maybe the guys enjoyed sex outside. I have done it in the past, and it's quite exciting in the fresh air.

Anyway, I am not allowed to discuss my case as these letters could be used as evidence. But I have nothing to hide. I have told the police everything I've just mentioned to you. My role models used to be Van Damme, Arnold Schwarzenegger and, Chuck Norris, and Sly Stallone. I took up martial arts and became a senior grade in Taekwondo-Do. I won five silvers in the British Nationals and a Bronze at the English Championships.

But as you've seen from my pics, I've never really gained big muscles, just slim and toned because I had a really good six-pack. I got a job as an underwear model for Jordan Conrad [British Fashion designer] and Debenhams Range [a high-end department store], and I used to have long blonde hair, so I looked like a surfer. I did swimwear too.

I'm just looking back at your letter and trying to answer as many of your questions as I can.

I like Doctor Who, and I wish I had a Tardis, LOL. [A fictional time machine or spacecraft in the Dr. Who series] I like the stories and adventures. Matt Smith was my favorite, but after watching a few episodes with the new guy, I think he's amazing. He fits the part as he looks older. It makes more sense, as he's supposed to be 2000 years old.

I did like David Tenant, though. I do like Family Guy and Futurama, but the main cartoons I like are Transformers and Marvel Avengers.

I have been to Manchester's gay village. I was in a club there on New Year's Eve/New Year's Day back in 2007. I think I was with a boyfriend who lived in York. I was overseeing an opening of a restaurant in Leeds. I was helping train the staff and managers. I was living in a Travel Lodge [hotel] paid for by my company. I used to take the boyfriend out for dinner and charge it to the company, and they never did know they were paying for two, LOL.

I will get my canteen ordered tomorrow morning. More Jaffa cakes are yummy. Thanks again for sending the 25 pounds. I won't say no if you want to send me more HeHeHe. I really do appreciate your loyalty and friendship, and I wished you were my boyfriend. Can't wait to meet you when I get out of here.

Have a great weekend,

Best regards.

Stephen Port

kiss kiss kiss."

LETTER 10

IF I WERE FREE NOW

"Dear Cody,

Thank you so much for the 25 pounds. I can order some shoes and some Christmas sweets. I only just received your letter dated the 8th. [December] I don't know why it's taken nine days to get to me, but yes, they must be busy coming up to be Christmas. I finally have reading glasses so I can see to write better now and it's so nice wearing my own clothes.

If I were free now, I would go to the cinema to see the new Star Wars film and then go to Pizza Hut for a large ham and pineapple pizza. How was your birthday? What did you do? My favorite meals here is the cheese and macaroni, steak, and kidney pie. I like the chicken Tikka Baguette also. I don't like any of their mince dishes. The lasagna or minced beef pies are awful. It's a shame, as lasagna was my favorite meal on the outside. I can make an awesome lasagna. I wish I were the chef here. I would definitely make some changes. I would improve the menu with better tasting food and do it within their budget or less as I can see they must waste a lot.

I am well and healthy, lost some weight, though, I was 84 kilograms and now 80 kilograms. I try to keep fit. I do my abs at night before bed and use the gym Friday and Saturday, but now [that] I am working, I can't go outside for exercise. I used to run around the yard. Now, I only get air on Friday and Saturday when I go to the gym. I miss that. So, it's just Sunday I get outside, which makes sleeping more difficult as the fresh air and exercise would help make me tired.

I am enjoying the work. It's good

to be doing something. I chat with the other guys here. I have made a good friend here. We work together, and we sit in my cell and chat when we get some time. He was feeling really depressed as he wasn't getting on with his cellmates, and not many others would speak to him. He said he didn't speak to me at first because he read in the papers that I hated gay guys and killed homosexuals, lol.

I told him no, I am gay myself, and my friend died of a drug overdose after a sex session, and that I am being accused of giving him the drugs which led to his death, but I certainly didn't kill anyone. Anyway, he told me he was thinking about ending it all, but now we are friends, he's a lot happier. He's been here a year already and is still on remand until April. Same as me. There are also a couple of other older guys we have started getting on well with and planning a card game at Christmas with some Quality Street [chocolate candies] for the winner.

My mum and dad are a lot better now as the police and media are leaving them alone now. They sent me

10 pounds, and Dad has bought me some more new clothes, which I hope I will get once the prison checks them over. Still not been allowed a visit yet, though, which is quite depressing as I was hoping to see my sister before Christmas.

I am not sure about writing a book. I'm not certain I could write more than two pages as there's not really that much to fill a book, but I would sell my story to a paper. I would not profit from it, though. I would use every penny to make certain this never happens to anyone again. So, no other families have to lose a loved one to drugs or being imprisoned for administering GHB. Just more awareness is needed.

I know it's impossible to stop people from trying drugs, but if they are educated in the correct use of them, I believe lives can be saved. Of course, I can't do this until I am found not guilty, which I am certain they will, as I know I could never kill anyone. I do have a good heart, and I have always tried to help others, and I treat everyone with respect.

What have you got planned for Christmas? I look forward to spending next Christmas with you in Manchester, what will we do? There are no Christmas cards on the canteen list, so I can't send you one, but I will write another letter, and I will try to answer your other questions. They still won't let me have the boots you sent. My sister sent me the Star Wars Annual and the Minions book direct from Amazon. That really cheered me up!

Chat Soon

Stephen XXX."

[illegible] Belmarsh

[illegible]

In replying to this letter, please write on the envelope:

Number A0[illegible] Name Stephen Park

Wing [illegible] 17-12-15

HMP [illegible] BELMARSH
WESTERN WAY
THAMESMEAD
LONDON
SE28 0EB

Dear Cody

Thank you so much for the £25 I can order some [illegible] and some Christmas sweets. [illegible] Only just [illegible] [illegible] don't know why it takes 19 days to get to me but yes [illegible] they must be [illegible] for the [illegible]. I finally have reading glasses so I can see to write better now and its so nice wearing my own clothes.

If I was free now I would go to the cinema to see the new Starwars film and then go to Pizza Hut for a large ham + pineapple pizza.

How was your Birthday? what did you do?

My favorite meals here is the cheese

(1)

Macaroni [illegible] [illegible] I like the chicken [illegible] [illegible] also. I don't like any of there [illegible] dishes like lasagne [illegible] [illegible] beef pie [illegible] [illegible] on the outside lasagne was my [illegible] meal [illegible] [illegible] lasagne. I wish I was the chef here I would [illegible] make some changes I would improve the menu with [illegible] food and do it within there budget at least as can see they must waste a lot.

I am well and healthy, lost some weight [illegible] I was [illegible] now [illegible] [illegible]. I try to keep fit I do my abs at night before bed and use the gym [illegible] but now I am working I can't get outside for exercise. I used to run round the yard but now I only get [illegible] on a [illegible] but [illegible] [illegible] [illegible] [illegible] its just Sunday I get outside, which makes sleeping more difficult as the fresh air + exercise would help make me tired. I am enjoying [illegible] work tho its good to be doing something [illegible] chat to the other guys here. I have [illegible] a good friend here we work together and we sit in my cell and chat when we get [illegible] time he was feeling really depressed he

(2)

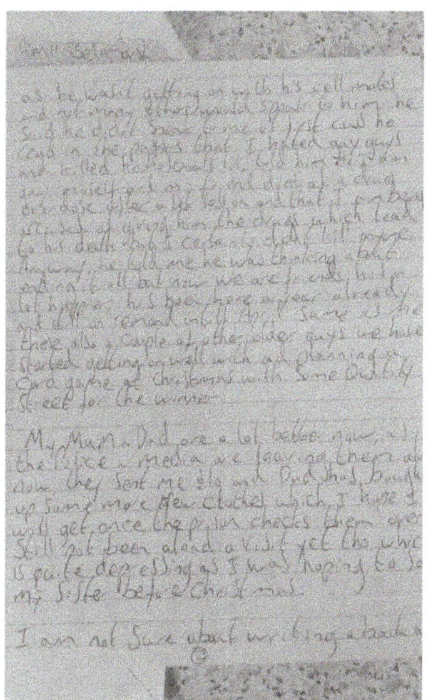

[illegible]

My Mum & Dad are a lot better now, [illegible] the police & media are [illegible] them [illegible] now they sent me £10 and Dad has bought up some more new clothes which I hope I will get once the prison checks them [illegible]. Still not been allowed a visit yet tho which is quite depressing as I was hoping to see my sister before Christmas.

I am not sure about writing a book [illegible]

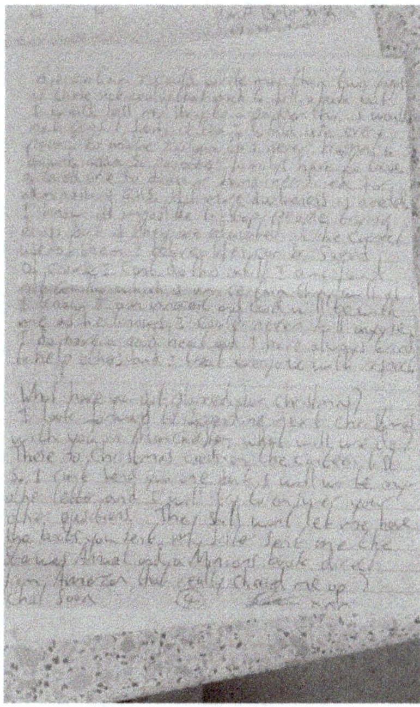

[illegible]

LETTER 11

TOYS R' US

"Dear Cody,

Thanks again for the 25 pounds. I have just one of my canteen orders for Thursday. I ordered some mince pies and a Christmas cake, Maltesers, Cadbury eclairs, and, yep, my favorite Jaffa cakes. So, I will have a good munch while watching Dr. Who on Christmas Day, and Mrs. Brown Boys should be fun. On Boxing Day, I will be watching Shaun the Sheep and after that, Dickenson and Top Gear. What will you be watching?

How was your birthday? Get any nice pressies? Any plans for Christmas? If you could have any present for Christmas, what would it be? Do you collect anything? If I were out now, I would buy myself the BB8 from Star Wars or the remote-controlled flying Millennium Falcon and, of course, a Yoda and Darth Vader figure. Yep, I know I am a big kid.

I once had a boyfriend who left me because I liked going into Toys R Us. He couldn't accept that I still liked collecting Transformers and Star Wars at my age, Lol, but we are still very close friends and had some mega amazing sessions together. I miss speaking to him, but not allowed to as he was questioned by police as a witness. But he did write a really good witness statement and said I have always treated him well, and he always consented when we had a drug sex session together with the occasional threesome. He really enjoyed watching porn where a sub boy (over 18) was being used by older guys while he was high and enjoying ourselves.

This time last year, we were planning a Christmas session with a good friend of mine. We became boyfriends on New Year's Day. Going to be difficult this New Year's as I remember what an awesome time we had last year from Christmas Day to New Year's Day. It was amazing. I wish I could go back in time to then.

Anyway, I just have to look forward to next Christmas, but I will definitely be more idle and just stick to alcohol and avoid other stimulants. What's your best memory of past Christmas' and New Year's? When I was younger, living with the parents, I remember unwrapping my presents on Christmas morning. I used to get Star Wars and transformer toys, etc., and console games. I know you said your childhood wasn't good, so when did you first have a good Christmas?

I am trying not to think about my trial yet as I am so not looking forward to how many people and press are going to be there. I really don't like being the center of attention, and definitely not under these circumstances. I have said to my legal team not to waste time trying to get me bail which would not be allowed anyway, and to just focus on my case, and yes, of course, my plea will be not guilty. I haven't and never would harm anyone, of that I am certain.

The lads here are fine. I have had no trouble from anyone, and I get on well with most of them. Just a couple I avoid. There's one guy who just comes into my cell and cuddles me from behind and rubs me so much. He did the same to my friend. We had to ask him to leave us alone. He is harmless and obviously gay. He's a lot bigger than me and shouts if annoyed, so we treat him carefully. He really should be in healthcare under supervision.

I am not on a Cat A-wing. There's a mixture on this VP wing and even a couple of Cat D who are being released shortly. My friend doesn't know what Cat he is but said he wasn't given one yet. Have a fantastic Christmas and New Year's. I look forward to hearing from you in 2016. All the best wishes.

Stephen Port xxx."

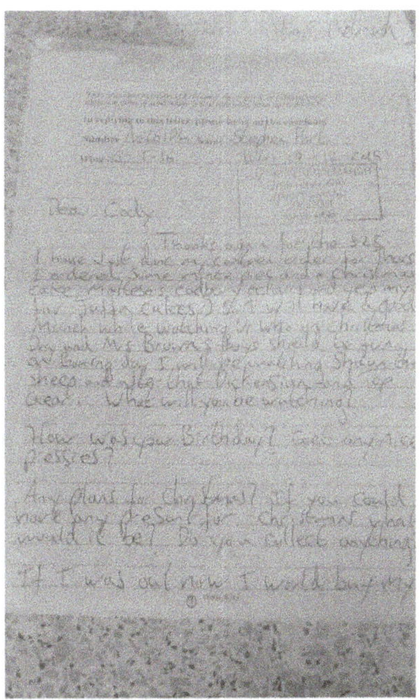

Dear Cody

Thanks again for the $25

I have just done my canteen order for Thurs[illegible] I ordered some mince pies and a Christmas cake, Maltesers, [illegible] (my fav Jaffa Cakes) so I will have a good munch while watching [illegible] Christmas day and Mrs Brown's Boys should be good. on Boxing day I will be watching [illegible] great. What will you be watching?

How was your Birthday? Get any nice pressies?

Any plans for Christmas? If you could have any present for Christmas what would it be? Do you collect anything?

If I was out now I would buy my

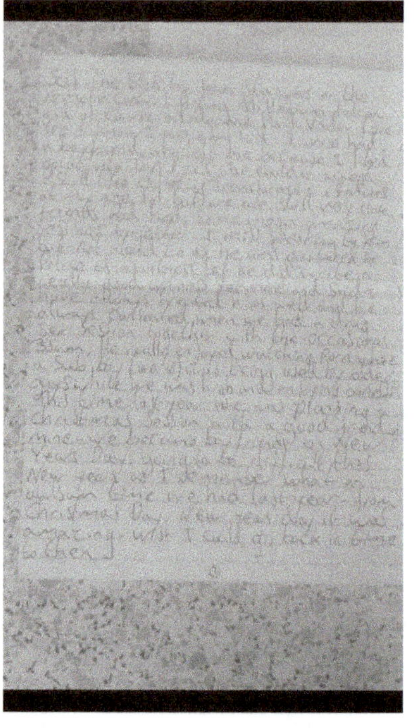

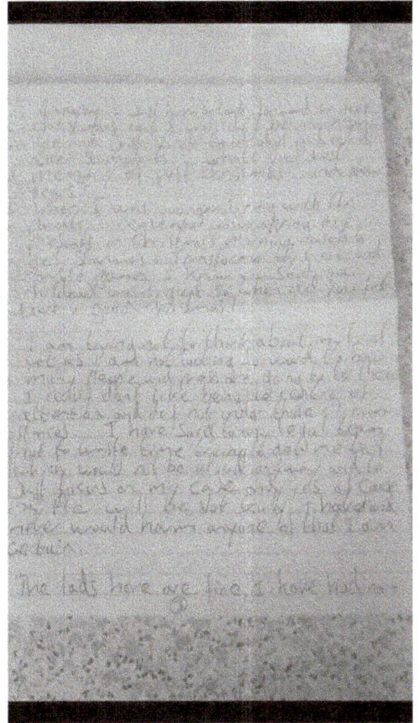

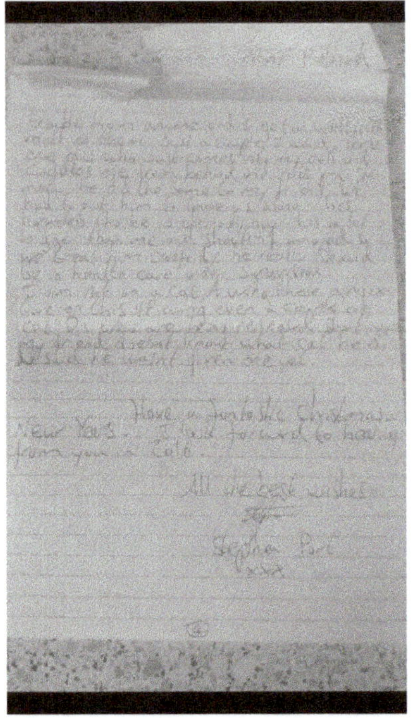

[illegible]

Have a fantastic Christmas [illegible] New Years. I look forward to hearing from you [illegible].

All the best wishes

Stephen Port
xxx

LETTER 12

I AM THE ONLY CELEBRITY HERE

"Dear Cody,

Thank you so much for the Darth Vader card. I love it. I got the Christmas canteen list today with Christmas specials on like Quality Street [chocolate candies] 3 for 99, but my favorite Dan Cake Xmas Log 1.79 and Galaxy bar 1.39. So, if you want to send me an Xmas present postal order, I can order some as I got to do a two-week canteen order next Friday, but please only send it if you are certain you can afford it as I felt bad asking as you're not working and I am sure you have enough bills of your own.

I am a Cat A but not on a Cat A wing. There are all Cats on this VP wing, including Cat D. I am on remand with charges of administrating a drug with intent and working as an escort, but it is not true, as you have to keep alert as a client could drug you, have sex and not pay, that's why I never worked alone or accepted drinks and only used my own condoms and lube, etc.

I think I am the only celebrity on this wing as there is no one I recognize from TV. One guy is doing the coke with the guy who he kept his daughter as a slave, which has been on the news lately. The guys here are all really nice and more talk to me, but there are a couple I stay clear of. They have been in fights, and when a couple of them kicked off when we were socializing, they locked us all back in our cells for the rest of the day. Everyone got punished, and it was just over a TV remote.

My solicitor, QC, and Barrister are coming to see me in the morning as the CPS papers have been served. I will make a longer letter to follow with more about me and the sex pictures, etc. It's 11 p.m. now off to bed.

Regards

Stephen Port x."

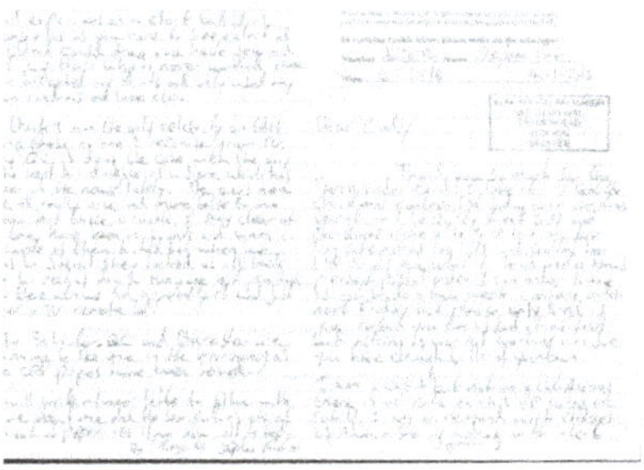

LETTER 13

MY DREAM JOB WORKING FOR RED CROSS

"Dear Cody,

It's Really nice to get your letter tonight. It's 10:30 p.m. now. I was just watching Deutschland 83. Have you been watching it? The main guy is really cute. When it first started last Sunday, an agent drugged his coffee and knocked him out for a few hours. I don't think they should show things like that on TV as it could have given the wrong side to people as he woke up wearing new clothes, and he didn't even complain and ask why they did that.

Anyway, Happy New Year to you.

I had a good Christmas, but New Year was a bit depressing as I was alone when it struck midnight. I kept thinking about the year before when it struck midnight. I was spooning my boyfriend on the bed while fireworks were going off outside. It was so romantic and loving. He said it was his best high ever. It was for me, too.

I am doing all right. It is nice having a close friend here. We cuddle often but nothing else as we never get any privacy together with other friends and officers walking in and out of my cell, but I am not that bothered by it as he is more like my little brother. I enjoy his company, and it's just nice to have that body contact when I hold him close. He's shy like me and tells me everything about himself and his case, not as major as mine, just some indecent images on his laptop, etc.

But he is facing 91 charges, and his trial is also in April. I don't share his preferences, but I am not judging him as he's a decent guy, and he doesn't believe I did what I am accused of. Two new prisoners moved into his cell, so I didn't get a chance to put an app in to share with him. He asked me to ask you if you could please send him some airmail stickers, they are free from the post office as he wants to write to his friends abroad.

Would you be comfortable to write to him directly if I give you his details, or would you prefer not to? I understand if you feel it could be awkward. He wanted to see my Grindr profile pictures. Do you have any from the papers? Could you send them to me, please? They might not let me have them, but you can try if possible.

Just would like to show him pics of me with blonde hair. Talking about hair, I don't think they would let me have my piece sent in, which is just against my human rights, but uncertain what the law is regarding that. Maybe you could check online and find out what the law is, but guessing as it's not medical, it won't be seen as relevant. If you do campaign for better treatment of prisoners, you could mention about being in a three-person cell. My bro barely gets any space or privacy and spends lock-up time just lying on his top bunk watching TV and reading papers.

Also, there's only three working showers between 75 prisoners on this wing. I never get a chance to get a shower. There's not enough social time to wait for one to be free, so at night, I just wash down in the sink with shower gel and sponge. It's easier for me as in a single cell. I keep looking back at your letter to find which question to answer next.

My dream job would be to work for the Princess Trust, Red Cross, or any charity where I could make a difference and help others. The church area is a known guy cruising area and a place for those who enjoy outside jiggy jiggy, but I personally prefer it with a boyfriend inside unless on a private beach in the Grand Canary Islands, lol.

I don't gotta that area at night. It's spooky, but there's lots of homeless guys and druggies who sleep around there. When I get outta here, the first thing I am going to do is go to the pub for a pint of Guinness, then take my family and friends out for dinner to thank them for all their support and you so when I come to Manchester.

I only just sent my canteen sheet up this morning. I ordered Hariboloo, cookies 69, Jaffe's, coffee 3.99, peanut butter, lemonade. I only have a few quid left as spent most of it over Christmas as sharing all my sweets and cakes with friends. I would be grateful if you could send a postal order as I would like to buy a duvet cover and pillow to help me sleep better. My plea hearing is via video link on the 15th.

The strange gut who cuddles me and my friend is still here. My friend is a bit scared of him as he cuddles too tightly. I can take it as I am quite solid, but he's really skinny, so when this guy comes in, I sit in the middle of the bed so he can't get behind him. He's as big as both of us put together, lol. He doesn't say much. He sits there just looking at us. Sometimes, he will comment on whatever I'm talking about with a friend/bro. Luckily, he doesn't stay long, which is a relief.

What are your New Year's resolutions? Have you met any new guys recently? Off to bed now. It's 12:30

a.m. Please write again soon, look forward to hearing from you.

Best wishes,

Stephen XXX."

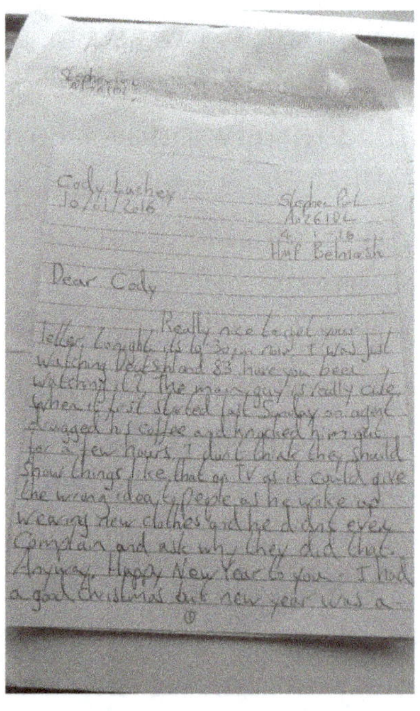

Cody [illegible]
10/01/2016

Stephen Port
[illegible]
4-1-16
HMP Belmarsh

Dear Cody

Really nice to get your letter. [illegible] its 10:30pm now. I was just watching Deutschland 83 have you been watching it? The main guy is really cute. When it first started last Sunday an agent drugged his coffee and knocked him out for a few hours. I don't think they should show things like that on TV as it could give the wrong idea to people as he woke up wearing new clothes and he didn't even complain and ask why they did that. Anyway, Happy New Year to you. I had a good Christmas but new year was a

①

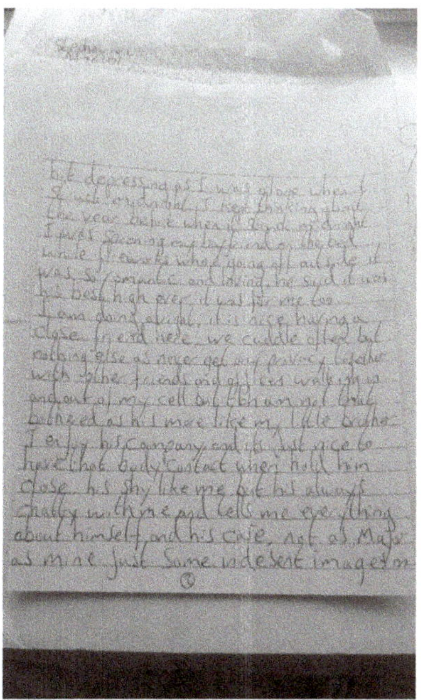

bit depressing as I was alone when I
[illegible] I kept thinking about
the year before when [illegible]
I was spooning my boyfriend, she had
[illegible] going off outside it
was so romantic and loving, he said it was
his best high ever it was for me too
I am doing alright, it's nice having a
close friend here, we cuddle often but
nothing else as never get any privacy together
with other friends and officers walking in
and out of my cell but Ethan and I [illegible]
bothered as he's more like my little brother
I enjoy his company and it's just nice to
have that body contact when I hold him
close. he's shy like me but he's always
chatty with me and tells me everything
about himself and his case, not as major
as mine just some indecent images on

his laptop etc but he's facing 9 charges
his trial's also in April. I don't share
his preferences but am not judging him
as he's a decent guy and he doesn't believe
I did what I'm accused of. Two
new prisoners moved into his cell so I didn't
get a chance to [illegible] to share with
him. He asked me to ask you if you could
please send him some air mail stickers,
they are free from the Post Office as he
wants to write to his friends abroad —
Would you be comfortable to write to him
directly if I give you his details or you
prefer not to? I understand if you
feel it could be [illegible]. He wanted
to see my Grindr profile pictures, do
you have any from the papers? Could
you send them to me please? They
might not let me have them but you can

try if possible. Just would like to
show him pics of me with blond hair
talking about hair. I don't think they would
let me have my piece set in which is [illegible]
against my human rights but not certain what
the law is regarding that, maybe you could
check online and find out what the law is
but guessing as its not medical it won't be
seen as relevant. If you do campaigning
for better treatment of prisoners you could
mention about being in a 3 man cell,
my one barely gets any space or privacy
and spends lock up time just laying on his
top bunk watching TV and reading papers.
also there's only 3 working showers between
75 prisoners on this wing, I never get a
chance to get a shower there's not enough
social time to wait for one to be free
So at night I just wash down in the

(6)

Sink with shower gel and sponge its
easier for me as I'm in a single cell.
I keep looking back at your letter to find
which questions to answer next. My dream
job would be to work for the Prince's
Trust, Red Cross or any charity where
I could make a difference and help
others.
The church area is a known gay cruising
area and a place for those who enjoy
outside jiggy jiggy but I personally
prefer it with a boyfriend inside or
unless on a private beach in Grand
Canary Islands lol. I don't go to that
area at night its spooky but there's lots
of homeless guys and druggies who sleep
around there.
When I get outta here the first thing I
am going to do is go to the pub for a

(5)

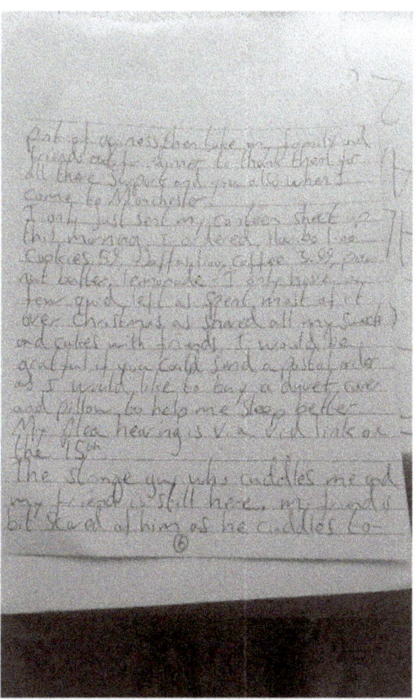

part of Guinness then take my family and
friends out for dinner to thank them for
all there support and you also when I
come to Manchester.
I only just sent my canteen sheet up
this morning I ordered [illegible]
Cookies 5? [illegible] Coffee 3.99 [illegible]
nut butter, lemonade. I only have a
few quid left as spent most of it
over Christmas as shared all my snacks
and cakes with friends. I would be
grateful if you could send a postal order
as I would like to buy a duvet cover
and pillow to help me sleep better.
My plea hearing is via video link on
the 15th
The strange guy who cuddles me and
my friend is still here. my friend is
bit scared of him as he cuddles to-
(6)

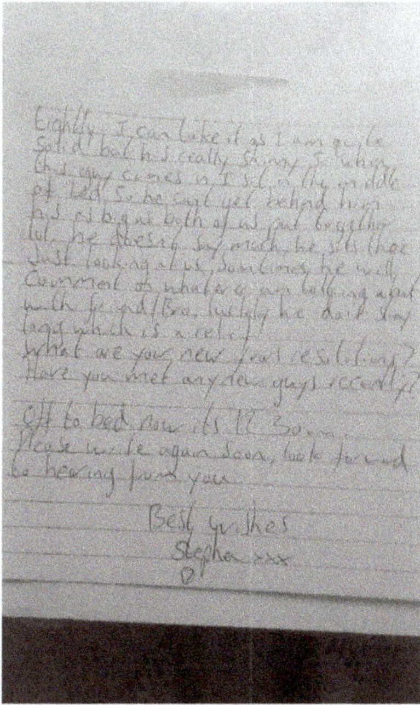

tightly. I can take it as I am quite
solid but his really skinny. So when
this guy comes in I sit in the middle
of bed so he can't get behind him
his as big as both of us put together
lol. he doesn't say much he sits there
just looking at us, sometimes he will
comment on whatever we're talking about
with friend/Bro. luckily he don't stay
long which is a relief!
What are your new years resolutions?
Have you met any new guys recently?

Off to bed now its 12.30 a.m.
Please write again soon, look forward
to hearing from you.

Best wishes
Stephen xxx
(7)

LETTER 14

WILL YOU BE MY NEW BOYFRIEND?

"Dear Cody,

I hope you are well. I have not heard from you in a while. I do hope you haven't given up on me, or I hope I haven't said anything to upset you. I miss hearing from you. I still have had no visits yet as my sister is still waiting for the forms. Not even be able to phone anyone either. It's all taking so long. I am sure you have heard that the trial won't be until October now as they don't even have enough evidence yet to go to trial in April, so my plea will be in April instead.

What have you been doing? Are

you working now? After my ten-week trial, I look forward to starting afresh. And my mortgage has been frozen, so at least I won't be in arrears when I go home after the trial. However, I will probably sell it and move to Manchester and maybe stay with you if you still would like me to but will depend on what restrictions they put on me. [The Court]

I can't wait to see my friends and hopefully get back with my ex-boyfriend or find a new boyfriend. But for certain, I never ever want to touch another drug as long as I live. I just want a normal, loving relationship like I used to have before. I didn't realize how much harm drugs really did to my brain. It's been over three months now since I have had any stimulants, and for the first time in over a year, my mind looks clear, and my brain seems to be healing, but still so much I can't remember, lots of blanks.

I wish I could go back in time to September 2013, which was the first time I ever tried real drugs when a friend Jake gave my ex-Danny a bunch of meth to try with me. Now I wish I didn't give into him. I just did not want him to do it alone or with some strange guy as I thought by doing it together, it would be safer. It was a lot of fun at. First, I admitted to that, but after six months, the effects were more minor, so we started taking more and adding E to make it stronger. It got to a point when I only saw him when he wanted to come around for a session. He would drive me back to Kent on the Monday or Tuesday, depending on if we had anything left.

If I had known the damage it would do to my brain. I wouldn't have ever been tempted to try it. I hope when I leave here, I can get the message out to stop anyone being tempted into drugs. I now know how it destroys lives, even though I was never addicted to it. It just became routine to do it with the boyfriends. I only ever did it when they wanted to, though, with their consent. He was autistic, not stupid, not like Down syndrome. He was more than capable of telling me exactly what he wanted, and he loved sex and being high; otherwise, he would not have kept coming back to me again and again.

Anyway, sorry, just a rant there as police using the "that he had some sort of emotional problems and saying I took advantage of him," which is so untrue. I loved and cared for him like any other boyfriend. Do you still take drugs, and do you go to orgies or saunas? What are your thoughts on drugs?

I know I never killed anyone with drugs, but I feel sad that guys have died from drugs and guys are still dying every week from drug-related problems or end up in prison like me. I will make it my life goal to campaign against drugs and make people more aware of the harmful effects, even from the ones they say are not addictive.

I am doing all right here at the moment, although I only seem to be working in the mornings now. At lunchtime, I got locked back up and left for the rest of the day. I only get exercise and socialize on Fridays and weekends when I go to the gym with my friend, and we play backgammon and table tennis, which is good fun, but wish we could have more time together. Look forward to hearing from you.

Best wishes,

Stephen Port XXX"

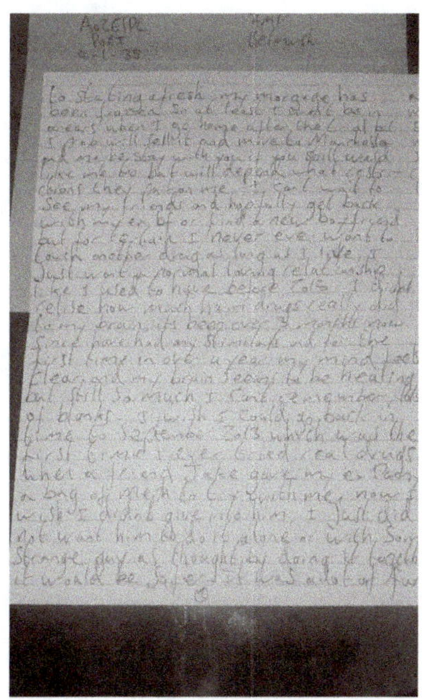

[illegible] PORT [illegible] HMP [illegible]

to starting afresh my mortgage has
been frozen so at least [illegible] be in
arrears when I go home after the [illegible]
I [illegible] will sell it and move to Manchester
and [illegible] stay with you if you still would
like me to but will depend what [illegible]
[illegible] they [illegible] me. I can't wait to
see my friends and hopefully get back
with my ex bf or find a new boyfriend
but for [illegible] I never ever want to
touch another drug as long as I live. I
just want a normal loving relationship
like I used to have before 2013. I didn't
realise how much [illegible] drugs really did
to my brain. it's been over 3 months now
since [illegible] had any [illegible] and for the
first time in over a year my mind feels
clear and my brain seems to be healing
but still so much I can't remember, lots
of blanks. I wish I could go back in
time to September 2013 which was the
first time I ever tried real drugs
when a friend [illegible] gave me [illegible]
a bag of meth to try with me, now I
wish I didn't give into him. I just did
not want him to do it alone or with some
strange guy as thought by doing it togeth[illegible]
it would be safe. It was a lot of fu[illegible]

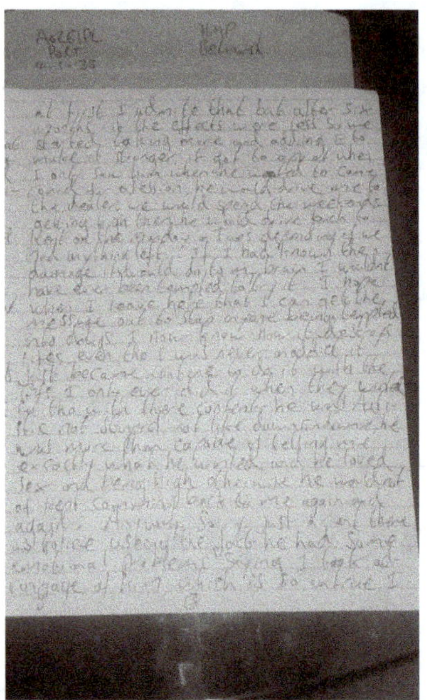

A0261PL
Port
4-1-25

HMP
Belmarsh

at first I admit to that but after six months of the effects wore off so we started taking more and adding E to make it stronger. It got to a point where I only saw him when he wanted to come round for a session, he would drive me to the dealer, we would spend the weekends getting high then he would drive back to [illegible] on the Sunday or Tues depending if we had anything left. If I had known the damage it would do to my brain I wouldn't have ever been tempted to try it. I hope when I leave here that I can get the message out to stop anyone being tempted into drugs. I now know how it destroys lives even tho I was never addicted it. [illegible] became [illegible] to do [illegible] I only ever did it when they would [illegible] for there company he was [illegible] the [illegible] he was more than capable of telling me exactly what he wanted and he loved sex and being high otherwise he wouldn't of kept coming back to me again and again. Anyway so [illegible] of them [illegible] using the fact he had some emotional problems saying I took advantage of him which is so untrue I

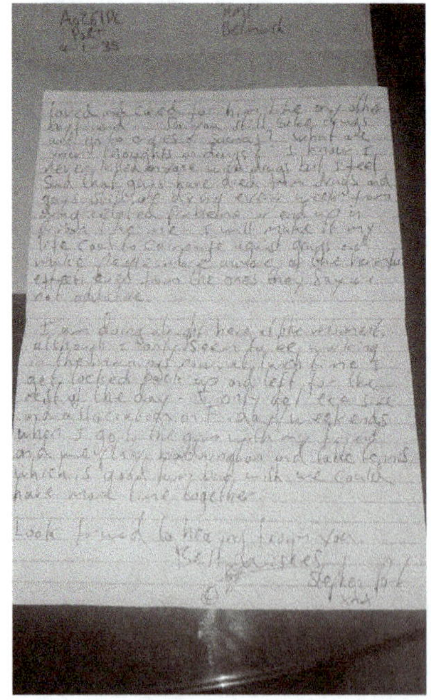

A0261PL
Port
4-1-25

HMP
Belmarsh

loved and cared for him like any other boyfriend. Do you still take drugs and go to a gay sauna? What are your thoughts on drugs? I know I never forced anyone into drugs but I feel sad that guys have died from drugs and guys still are dying every week from drug related problems or end up in prison like me. I will make it my life goal to campaign against drugs and make people more aware of the harmful effects even from the ones they say are not addictive.

I am doing alright here at the moment although I only seem to be [illegible] in the [illegible] for lunch time. I get locked back up and left for the rest of the day. I only get exercise and association on Friday plus weekends when I go to the gym with my friend and play badminton and table tennis which is good but I wish we could have more time together.

Look forward to hearing from you.

Best wishes,

Stephen Port

LETTER 15

I NO LONGER TAKE STIMULANTS

"Dear Cody,

So nice to hear from you again. I thought you had given up on me. What did you do with your time in Ireland? I have never been, maybe you can take me with you next time? I am doing alright, and time goes by a bit quicker now that I have more things to do. I am still working in the ink shop. My friend is in the ink shop as well now, so it's nice to chat while working, but he has lessons on a Tuesday. I have applied for lessons as well, but I got no response.

I get 11 pounds a week, which

doesn't go far, but I buy a few biscuits. My family and friends sent me some birthday money, so I bought a nice watch from the canteen and ordered a DVD player, radio, and a chessboard from Argos. I just haven't got any CDs or DVDs to play. Would love to see the Minions movie, Terminator Genisys, and Years and Years on CD. Hint Hint!

I am still in a single cell, but my friend keeps his stuff in my cell as he's been having food stolen. He doesn't trust one of his cellmates. I am still going to the gym. I have put on more muscle, defined my six-pack better now, and gone back to being 84 kilograms. My friend weighs 57 kilograms, and I have started training him with lifting weights. He is working to get stronger, and he's lifting 5 kilograms in each arm now, so he's improving. We train for 45 minutes then we go play badminton, we are not very good, but we have a good laugh.

I have more energy now that I no longer take any stimulants, which used to make me feel tired all the time. There's been no movement with my case. Still waiting for the CPS to send their final evidence, which is a three-week slate. My solicitor believes that they can't decide what to charge me with as it's now obviously clear that the guys died from a mixture of drugs and not just from GHB, and this proves that rape was not the intention; otherwise, they would have only had GHB in their system and not meph, etc. Also, as meph keeps you awake for hours and, GHB would only add to the high but wouldn't knock you out, and you can't force someone to snort it.

It's clear there was consent, so the murder charges should be dropped, and as I didn't administer the drugs, it's not manslaughter either. Also, they had poppers in their system, and as you know, you can only sniff this yourself, and you only take it during sex. It proves they weren't being raped, and when they drug tested me, I had GHB in my system, so I didn't use it to rape unless I can rape myself.

Anyway, my plea hearing is next month, and the trial is in October, if it even goes to trial. I am not really missing sex. Trying not to think about it. I just draw pictures of my last boyfriend, which helps ease the tension, but I do miss the kissing and cuddling and waking up in the mornings with the boyfriend next to me and his smile and watching movies together and going bowling together etc.

My family are alright, but mum has been a bit unwell. I phone her on Sunday morning, and this cheers her up a lot. My sister has started visiting me now once a month, and she brings me new clothes. I have to arrange a clothes exchange for her next visit as I am at my limit of what I am allowed. When she visits, she buys me a lot of chocolate from the visitors' canteen, has two dairy milk, a Cadbury cream egg, and a Twix with a couple of coffees.

It's nice to know what is going on out there. She says my ex-partner is doing alright but suffering a bit with his depression, as all this has been a lot for him to take in. I can't wait till this nightmare is over and I can get back to a normal life (without drugs). I would still love to come and stay with you, but it depends on what restrictions they put on me. I possibly won't be allowed to use my social sites again, which is fine with me. I have had a few letters from close friends, and my friend Mike has now been cleared to visit me, so he's just waiting to book a date.

Do you go out on the scene much? Anyway, I look forward to hearing from you again soon. Please give my regards to your mum.

All the best,

love from

Stephen XXX."

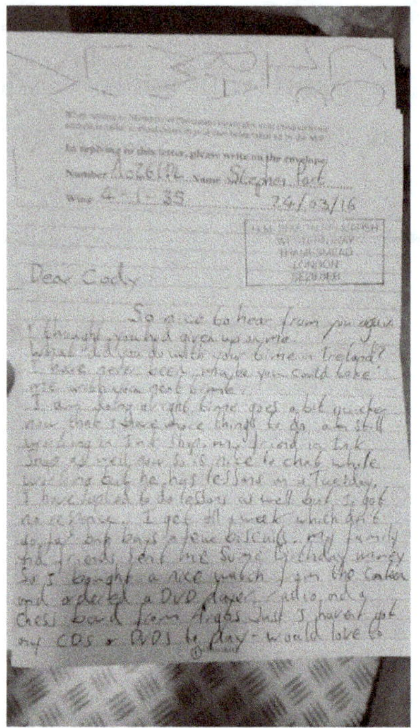

In replying to this letter, please write on the envelope:
Number [illegible] Name Stephen Port
Wing 4-1-35 24/03/16

Dear Cody

So nice to hear from you again
I thought you had given up on me.
What did you do with your time in Ireland?
[illegible] maybe you could take
[illegible] with you next time.
I am doing alright time goes a bit quicker
now that I have more things to do. I am still
working in [illegible] shop, my friend is [illegible]
[illegible] so it's nice to chat while
working but he has lessons on a Tuesday.
I have applied to do lessons as well but I got
no response. I get [illegible] a week which don't
go far but buys a few biscuits. My family
and friends sent me some birthday money
so I bought a nice watch from the canteen
and ordered a DVD player, radio and a
chess board from Argos but I haven't got
my CDs or DVDs to play - would love to

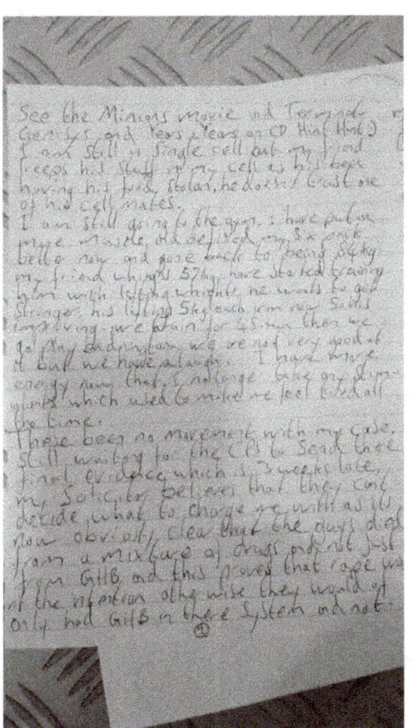

See the Minions movie and Terminator
Genisys and Years & Years on CD that [illegible]
I am still in single cell but my friend
keeps his stuff in my cell as he's been
having his food stolen, he doesn't trust one
of his cell mates.
I am still going to the gym, I have put on
more muscle and defined my six pack
belly now and gone back to being 56kg
my friend who weighs 57kg have started training
him with lifting weights, he wants to get
stronger, he's lifting 5kg each arm now. [illegible]
[illegible] we train for 45 min then we
go play badminton, we are not very good at
it but we have a laugh. I have more
energy now that I no longer take my sleeping
pills which used to make me feel tired all
the time.
There been no movement with my case,
still waiting for the CPS to send their
final evidence which is 3 weeks late,
my solicitor believes that they can't
decide what to charge me with as it's
now obviously clear that the guys died
from a mixture of drugs and not just
from GHB and this proves that rape was
not the intention otherwise they would of
only had GHB in there system and not
①

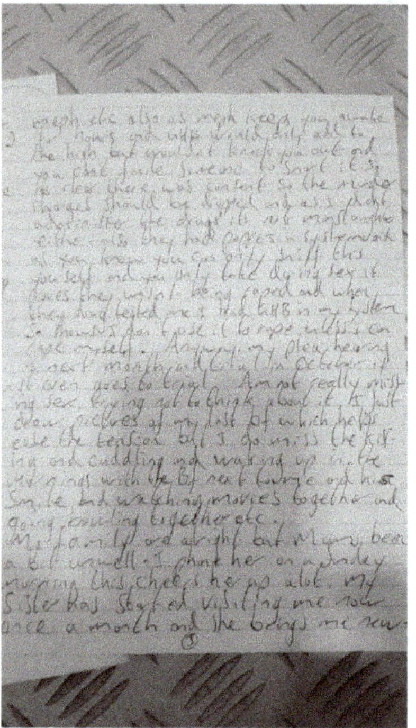

meph etc also as meph keeps you awake
for hours and [illegible] would only add to
the high but [illegible] knocks you out and
you [illegible] [illegible] to [illegible] it so
[illegible] there was content so the murder
charges should be dropped and as I didn't
administer the drugs it's not manslaughter
either [illegible] they had [illegible] in system [illegible]
as you know you can only sniff this
yourself and you only take [illegible]
[illegible] they weren't being raped and when
they [illegible] tested me I had GHB in my system
so [illegible] [illegible] to [illegible]
[illegible] myself. Anyway, my plea hearing
is next month and [illegible] in October if
it even goes to trial. Am not really missing sex, trying not to think about it. I just
draw pictures of my last bf which helps
ease the tension but I do miss the kissing and cuddling and waking up in the
mornings with the bf next to me and his
smile and watching movies together and
going [illegible] together etc.
My family are alright but Mum's been
a bit unwell. I phone her on a Sunday
morning this cheers her up alot. My
sister has started visiting me now
once a month and she brings me news
(8)

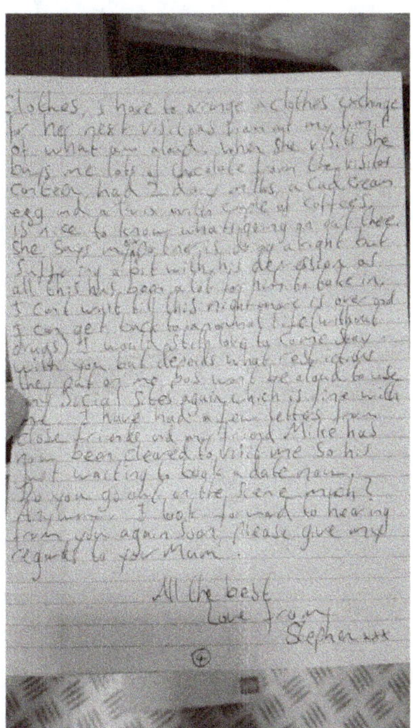

clothes, I have to arrange a clothes exchange for her next visit as [illegible] my [illegible] of what I'm allowed. When she visits she buys me lots of chocolate from the visitor canteen, had 2 dairy milks, a Cadbury's Cream egg and a twix with couple of coffees. Is nice to know what's going on out there. She says my dad is doing alright but suffering a bit with his depression as all this has been a lot for him to take in. I can't wait till this nightmare is over and I can get back to a normal life (without drugs) I would still like to come stay with you but depends what restrictions they put on me, but won't be allowed to use my social sites again which is fine with me. I have had a few letters from close friends and my friend Mike has now been cleared to visit me So he's just waiting to book a date now. Do you go out on the scene much? Anyway I look forward to hearing from you again soon, please give my regards to your Mum.

All the best
Love from
Stephen xxx

(4)

BOOK 3

DAVID SHEARING - THE WELLS GRAY PARK MURDERS

1

THE CRIME

THE WELLS GRAY PARK MURDERS

The "Wells Gray Park Murders" were unlike anything seen in British Columbia, Canada. The horror of the crime, more than forty years ago, transcends decades.

On August 2, 1982, three generations of a family set out on a camping trip to Wells Gray Park, located in the interior of B.C. The park is located about 300 miles northeast of Vancouver and 465 miles northwest of Calgary and has a total area of 5,250 square kilometers. The family included Bob and Jackie Johnson, their two daughters, Janet, 13, and Karen, 11, and Jackie's parents, George and Edith Bentley. They were all set to meet at the Old Bear Creek Prison site.

When the Johnsons arrived in their car, they set up a tent for their two daughters to sleep in. The Bentleys were bringing their new camper for the adults to sleep in. The last time they would be heard from was on August 6th, when Edith called another of her daughters.

On August 16th, Bob was scheduled to return to his job at Gorman Brother's Lumber in West Kelowna, but he didn't show up. Since this was very unusual behavior for him, Bob's supervisor tried calling his house several times. There was no answer. About a week later, his boss called the police and reported Bob missing, and the search for the family began.

About a month later, a man out picking mushrooms called to report seeing a burnt-out Chrysler in the woods just off Battle Mountain Road, a logging road near Wells Gray Park. Authorities descended on the area. The car turned out to be the Johnson family car. The camper was nowhere to be seen.

In the back seat of the car were the incinerated remains of four adults, and in the trunk, the two girls. Autopsies revealed that they had been shot in the head, execution style, with a .22 caliber weapon. They were identified as the missing Bentley-Johnson family.

2

MISSING FAMILY

On August 23, 1982, Al Bonar, manager of the Gorman's Lumber Mill in West Kelowna, B.C., called the RCMP detachment in Kelowna. He reported that a long-term employee, Bob Johnson, was missing. "Bob hasn't taken a sick day, let alone missed a day's work by just not showing up in 20 years," he explained to the officer. "They had gone on a camping vacation with his family to Wells Gray Park about two weeks ago and haven't returned. He has missed almost a week of work now. The family was scheduled to return on the 16th of August."

The missing person's report was forwarded to Sergeant Baruta of the Clearwater detachment. Baruta checked around the local park and businesses to see if he could find out anything. The Bentleys (Bob's in-laws) had also given them photos to pass around. The report was sent to the Kamloops detachment, where Sergeant Mike Eastham headed up the Serious Crime Unit for the interior of B.C. Never in his life did Eastham expect to be in charge of one of the most expensive missing person investigations in Canadian history.

"There was a lot of speculation as to what really happened to them. Anything from they had run away to join a cult, they were lost, joined a commune, or something like that. Everybody had their fingers crossed, hoping that they were going to be found safe and sound. And as it was, it didn't turn out that way. Six innocent lives gone, like that," Eastham said.

The first tip they received came from a local gas station located about 40 miles east of Clearwater. The attendant, Reg Bedard, remembered seeing the grandparents, George and Jackie, traveling with their two grandchildren. They had stopped at the Avola PetroCan to refuel their truck and asked the attendant if she knew of a good place to pick berries.

The police led a search that included help from the community, including private pilots and Clearwater residents. The search went on for weeks to no avail.

Finally, on September 13, 1982, an Abbotsford man, Kurt Krack, remembered seeing the Johnson vehicle while picking mushrooms in Wells Gray Park sometime in late August. He claimed he had seen a burnt-out Chrysler in the woods off Battle Mountain Road.

Sergeant Baruta headed up to the location that Krack had described to him. It was basically a horseback riding trail, almost too rough for an average car or truck. From the road, Baruta could see tire marks running off the road into the bush. He stopped his vehicle and got out to follow the tire marks. It wasn't long before he saw the outline of what looked like a burnt-out car.

Once they reached about 150 feet away, he could see the license plate enough to read the numbers. "Yes, this is the one," he said with an anguished sigh. When the officers approached the vehicle, they glanced inside. What they saw caused them to rope it off and call the homicide team immediately.

Sergeant Baruta did a great job keeping everyone else from the crime scene. The press had somehow already found out about the missing car being found and its location. Several media helicopters were flying overhead, trying to get pictures. Even more media crawled all over the area in vehicles, trying to find the correct location.

When Sergeant Eastham arrived, he approached Baruta and asked him what they were dealing with. Baruta removed his sunglasses and started to explain. "Well, Mike, what it appears to be is a burnt-out vehicle. There's absolutely nothing left inside. It's completely burnt out. The shell appears to be intact, and it looks like there's human skeletal remains in the back."

Eastham said, "Walking towards that car, you could feel it. I don't want to say that you could smell a death. But you could smell the death. And you just knew what you were going to walk into." Eastham approached the car with the forensic identification team. "You know you're going to be looking at something that you don't want to see. You know it's going to be smelly; you know it's going to be somebody's life that's been snuffed out."

The team had to remove the remains without damaging any of them. "When I looked into that car, into the back seat, you could see some bone fragments, and it was evident that it had been a person. At that point in time, we didn't know if it was one or two people in the back of that car."

The Johnson vehicle was a 1979 cream-colored Plymouth. What should have been a fairly new car now looked like an old, burnt-out, rust bucket that had been in a field for twenty years. There was broken glass all around the car, probably pieces from the headlights, taillights, or a missing back window. The ground was scorched for about 20 feet all around the car. It had burned so hotly that the door handles and all four tires had melted away. The car doors were all closed except for the driver-side door, which had been left open. On top of the car was a carrier that the family probably used to carry their camping supplies. What remained were just burnt-out cans and bottles. They figured whoever burned the car like this was probably storing gasoline or some other accelerant.

The trunk was closed, but a key ring with five keys attached to it was in the lock. When Eastham got close enough to the trunk to look at the keys and lock mechanism, he noticed a dusty smell. At first, he figured the smell was coming from the four dead bodies piled into the back seat. But it was now time to see what was in the trunk.

The trunk's mechanism was useless from

the fire, so Eastham grabbed a crowbar and pried it open. The skulls of two children were facing upwards — one of them looking directly at the detective. The skulls rested on what looked like a pile of charred bones. There was a prominent hole just over the left eye area of one of the skulls, possibly an exit wound from being shot in the back of the head. "The sight that we had to look at was indescribable. Two little skeletons, what was left of them. These two little skulls looking at us with their hollow eyes. One of them had what looked to be a bullet exit wound above one of the eye sockets. And it was quite evident at that time that it was the two children, Karen and Janet," Eastham explained.

The detectives had to positively identify the bodies that were burned in the car. Initially, it was thought that only two adult bodies were in the back seat: Bob and Jackie Johnson. It seemed obvious that the bodies of their two daughters, Janet and Karen Johnson, were in the trunk.

Thoughts about what happened here swarmed Eastham's mind. He heard the grandfather, George Bentley, carried a 410/.22 over/under rifle in the cab of his truck. Was the family shot and killed with his own rifle? Did they pick up a hitchhiker, or were they approached at the park? It wasn't in the police's minds that this crime would have been just one culprit. A few people must have done this much killing and destruction, maybe three. Was everyone killed at the same time? What was the reason for the slaughter?

Many key questions needed to be answered, but first, they had to find out where the grandparents were and what happened to their truck and camper. It should have been the first vehicle found. After all, it was much bigger than the car and had an aluminum boat on the top.

Eventually, the forensics team ended up with about fifty plastic bags, which contained the remains of whoever was killed and burned in the car. There were also a lot of their personal effects, such as jewelry, a belt buckle, and a woman's wristwatch.

It wasn't long before the forensics team came to Sergeant Eastham to inform him there were six skulls, not four. So, more than likely, they were already looking at all six bodies of the family that were missing. As well, forensics confirmed one of the skulls from the car's back seat also had a bullet hole through it.

Eastham arranged for the Johnsons' and Bentley's homes to be searched to find hair or blood samples or anything that could be used to match what they found in the car. This murder happened before DNA exploded onto the scene and became law enforcement's most effective crime-solving tool. But eventually, the dental records confirmed that the bodies belonged to the missing family.

3

INVESTIGATION

While the family held funerals and mourned the deaths of their family members, the police started work on solving the murders. For the police, the next priority was to search for the truck and camper. The grandparents had a 1981 red and grey Ford pick-up truck carrying a 10½ foot Vanguard camper. It had a picture of an orange sunset painted on the front window. They were also carrying an aluminum boat with a small Evinrude motor on top of the camper.

At first, the police decided to put out an APB on the truck and camper with the license plate number on the off chance the killers were driving it around the local area, in B.C., or even in the nearby U.S. Soon enough, the media got word of the search for the truck and camper and released it to the public. After that, the police were inundated with calls and tips about sightings of the missing truck. Most were throughout Canada, all the way to Quebec, even.

The RCMP's Clearwater detachment set up a large-scale search for any information on the family with help from federal and provincial services, civilian volunteers, and even private pilots. They knocked on every door in the area with pictures of the Johnsons, Bentleys, the car they were driving, and the truck and camper.

The search led to the first tip on the missing truck and camper. A resident of B.C. on vacation in Saskatchewan recognized the pictures and called the hotline. The witness reported that they had actually followed the truck and camper, which still had the boat on top of it, into a gas station and saw two men get out, not a family. The witness also said that the two men ended up in the same restaurant he was in, and he believed he heard them speaking French.

The two men were described as being in their late twenties, quite shabbily dressed, rugged, with long, unkempt hair. The smaller of the two men was blond, and the larger had dark hair. Police decided to interview the servers and other workers from the gas station/restaurant in Saskatchewan. After that, they had sketches made up for the two suspects.

Another tip came in from one of the Wells Gray Park attendants, who remembered seeing the truck and camper parked at the area known as the "Old Bear Creek Prison site." The prison site was an old mobile prison that had long since been removed. It had taken up about a 3-acre area of the park.

Eastham and his partner looked around the old prison site and found a few things, such as three canning lids matching the canned goods on top of the Johnson's burned Plymouth. There were also Extra Old Stock beer bottle caps, which were the kind of beer Bob Johnson always drank. They decided it would be best to bring in a search team to have a closer look.

The searchers later discovered Extra Old Stock beer placed in a nearby riverbed, probably to keep it cool. They also found six spent .22 shell cartridges. The campfire pit had seats set up for six people, and there were sharpened sticks, probably used for roasting marshmallows at the fire. Four-level blocks were laid out at the same site that could have been used to place the camper. It seemed likely that this was not only the place the family had been camping but also the place where they were murdered.

The rest of 1982 passed without any further movement on the case. By January of 1983, several cash rewards were being offered. $7,500 was offered for information leading to the missing truck, and $35,000 was offered for information leading to the arrest and conviction of the person(s) responsible for the deaths of the Johnson and Bentley families.

By the end of April 1983, the case started to go cold. There were almost no new tips or calls coming in about the murders or the missing truck. So, the police came up with a new approach – a publicity campaign lasting one month. It involved driving across Canada with a truck and camper that were the same as the one owned by the Bentleys. This drive happened at the same time as a reenactment of the crime was televised. Eastham explained, "When you come to a dead-end, you gotta come up with some pretty creative ideas on how the hell you are going to move forward. How are you going to keep this in the public's mind? People care about what happens in their own homes, in their backyards. But if you live in Manitoba, you don't pay attention to the B.C. news."

RCMP Constable Gerald Dalen and Constable DeWitt were the officers chosen to drive the truck across Canada. "We had to make it personal, and we needed to make it local all across the country." The trip started on May 9, 1983. They were going to drive from Kamloops to Montreal in about three weeks. At each stop, they handed out sketches of the two French-speaking male suspects that had been identified the year before.

The road trip started to become extremely popular throughout the country. Crowds of people waited for their arrival in many of the cities where they stopped. It became the most crucial part, as it put the unsolved murders in the spotlight and kept people talking about them. After the 15-day trip ended, the police were again receiving tips and calls like they had received when the murders first happened. Over 1,300 tips came in from people who seemed to have had their memories jogged from seeing the truck and camper replica drive through their towns.

One, in particular, caught the ear of Eastham. It came from a mechanic out of Windsor, Ontario. He claimed that two men drove up to his shop in the middle of the night. They had just unloaded their camper and were looking for a quick paint job for their truck, so they offered him cash to do it.

The men waited at the shop while the mechanic painted their truck. During their conversations with the mechanic, they showed him a .22 caliber rifle and a Saturday Night Special handgun. They told him they needed to get rid of them. The mechanic told them he wanted nothing to do with it as he had had trouble with the law before and wanted to stay straight. The two men became very standoffish with him and asked him if he knew where they could go and get rid of the rifle. The mechanic sent them to someone across the U.S. border in South Detroit, Michigan.

Eastham said, "This guy described the truck as having modifications to the front and rear bumpers. George Bentley had modified his truck similarly before his trip to Wells Gray Park. Nobody knew this, and so this mechanic's information looked good, and he had to be telling the truth."

Eastham, wanting a quick answer, called the Detroit Homicide unit directly, avoiding the red tape that would arise if he went through the proper channels, including Interpol and the FBI. Detroit Homicide verified the information he had received from the mechanic, so Eastham decided it was time to go to Detroit.

While making his trip plans to Detroit, Eastham received a phone call from Sergeant Baruta of the Clearwater detachment. "Mike, we found it! The truck and camper."

Eastham was in shock, "Where?"

"A couple of forest rangers. They were aware of it because of the press coverage," replied Baruta.

"There's no way! We've been following them across the country and just got a tip that they were in Detroit," said Eastham.

"Yeah, well, I'm looking at it right now. It's here. The license plate is the only thing not burned, and it reads 4836FY. You need to come home!" Eastham and Leibel immediately flew back to Kamloops to speak with the forestry workers who had discovered the truck and looked over the area where it had been found.

On Tuesday, October 18, 1983, two forestry workers, Douglas Kehler, 33, and Peter Miller, 31, walked into the RCMP's Clearwater detachment and said they had found the burnt-out Bentley truck and camper up Trophy Mountain. It was at about the 4,700-foot level.

During the interview with one of the workers, Sergeant Eastham asked, "So, when exactly did you see the truck and camper?"

The worker replied, "A few weeks ago."

"A few weeks ago, why did you wait so long for? It's been all over the news."

He replied, "I was staying in a ranger cabin deep in the park. I hadn't been near a TV in a while. I came in as soon as I heard."

When the police first flew over the location, there was only the truck, and it appeared that no camper or boat was there. Eastham could see why the truck was never spotted. Somehow, the fire had changed the truck from the original red and grey to an earth-like color. Once the police unit landed the helicopter and was at the site, they could see what was left of the camper as well. A few feet down from the truck was a large canyon, so it was more than likely that the killers wanted to drive it off the cliff. The only thing was that they high-centered it and got stuck, so they did not make it to the cliff.

Where the truck was located was a clue in itself. It was a good indication that whoever the killers were, they knew the area well enough to plan this. It could mean that the killer was from the Clearwater area or had some family that lived there.

The most significant finding on or around

the burnt-out truck was that somebody had recently planted tree seeds near the truck. This fact was interesting because the truck had a $7,500 reward. That would be motivation enough for anyone who merely stumbled across the vehicle to turn it in—motivation enough for anyone but the murderer, that is. Eastham and Baruta also found a bullet hole in the passenger side door of the truck. "I'd say we keep this to ourselves," Eastham told Baruta, "That way, we weed out any false confessions or bad tips." The bullet hole was only known to the police and whoever killed the family. The police kept it from the press and the public.

The find pumped some new energy into the investigation, and 20 more officers were assigned to do another door-to-door canvassing of the Clearwater and Wells Gray areas. Only this time, they were going to contact every single house.

During this more thorough interview phase of the investigation, the name David Shearing was first brought to the police's attention. An informant decided to call once they heard a story about Shearing running over a man on the Wells Gray Highway a few years before this case.

The following day, David Shearing's name came up again. This time, during one of the door-to-door police canvassings of the houses in Clearwater. The detective knocked on the door of an older, one-story ranch-style home, and a gruff-looking man came to the door.

"Yeah!" the man said aggressively.

"I'm Officer Haslett."

Then, a woman's voice behind the door could be heard, "Who is it?"

"Nobody!" The man shouted out his answer while looking behind his front door.

He looked back at the cop and asked, "What do you want?"

"You may have heard that we recently found the truck that belonged to the Bentleys?"

"Yeah, I heard about that."

Just then, the woman's face peeked out from behind her husband's body, "Is that the one up by Trophy Mountain?" she asked.

The man quickly turned his head towards his wife and scolded her, "He's talking to me!" Then, he whipped his head back towards Officer Haslett. "What about it?"

"Well, we're wondering if maybe you remember seeing anything suspicious. Anything that might help us find out who put the truck there?"

"I already told you guys. I haven't seen anything like that."

"What about you, ma'am?"

The man answers for her. "No, there's nothing."

The woman then looks towards the man and says. "You're not going to tell him about David and the truck that got shot up?"

"This isn't our business!" the man answered angrily.

"I told you everything we're going to tell you."

The officer changed his line of questioning to calm the situation and learn something more. "Alright, sir, I will leave you my card, and if you can think of anything else, please contact us. Thanks."

The officer told Eastham and Leibel when he returned to the station. "We had investigative two-man teams that would follow up on these types of specific tips. We couldn't really use the polygraph test much as there was the privacy act thing in our way," Leibel explained. "And it couldn't be used in court anyway."

They set up surveillance at the house so they would know when the husband left. And as soon as he did, they picked up the wife and brought her in for questioning. She confirmed the story. "She told us Shearing wanted to know how he could register a stolen vehicle and fix a bullet hole in the door," Leibel confirmed.

Eastham added, “She told us that there’s a guy by the name of David Shearing and that he lives on a ranch out in the Wells Gray Park Road, and he made mention of finding a vehicle up in the mountain with a bullet hole in the door. All of a sudden, we’ve got a name, David Shearing, and we need to know who the hell is David Shearing?”

4

WHO WAS DAVID SHEARING?

David Shearing had lived on his father's 160-acre hobby farm, located just two miles away from where the bodies of the Johnsons and Bentleys were discovered. He had lived there his whole life until about four months before his arrest on November 19, 1983, when he moved to the Tumbler Ridge area to find some work as a laborer.

Shearing's father, William, worked at Bear Creek Prison, a minimum-security prison, and raised cattle on his farm for extra income for most of his life. David, the youngest of three children, was born in 1959. His teachers and school friends considered him a quiet boy and a good student.

Marvin Tremblay, who was the same age as David, went through elementary and secondary school at the same time as him. Tremblay claimed that Shearing was prolific in mathematics and mechanics, and when he set his mind to it, he could do almost anything he tried. "But he was very shy," Tremblay remembered. "You'd have to get very close to him before he would talk to you. He didn't get involved in any of the school activities much. Once in a while, he would show up at a school dance or go to a drive-in movie with him. I heard that he liked to drink beer a lot, but I had never seen him get into any trouble when he drank with me."

Shearing graduated from Clearwater High School in 1977 and enrolled in a heavy-duty mechanics course at Caribou College in Kamloops. He planned to get a job working in Kamloops, a major stop for big rig trucks traveling from Calgary to Vancouver. However, after completing his course in heavy mechanics, he could not find any work. His mother, Rose, 66 at the time, said that her son did odd labor jobs around the town and area. He even made the ski trails for Wells Gray Park one year.

Jack Vogels was the bar manager of the Wells Gray Hotel in Clearwater, and he remembered Shearing coming into the bar: "He was a real loner. He came in now and again for a few beers, but he never had any girlfriends.

He didn't even hang around with any of the guys that were in the bar regularly."

In the spring of 1982, Shearing was still living on his father's farm when his father died of a heart attack. His sister married and remained in the area, but his brother became a Deputy Sheriff with the Provincial Government, doing prisoner escorts and court security duties in Prince George. In the early Fall of 1983, Shearing moved up to the Tumbler Ridge area.

In 1983, Tumbler Ridge was still a town under construction, so he figured there would be plenty of jobs to do there. If you hadn't been there during this time, it would be hard to imagine the sheer amount of work going on there. Quintette was a major coal company set to open in November 1983. There were over 1,800 people there to work on their building alone. Other workers were frantically trying to finish houses to live in before the winter hit.

Tumbler Ridge was just one of many rapidly developing towns in the northern parts of B.C. and Alberta, usually around some sort of industry mill, such as coal or oil. The towns attracted people who were unable to find work for different reasons. Ex-cons accounted for a large percentage of these workers. Because of their social status, it was a good place to earn money and stay off law enforcement's radar.

Many construction workers lived outside the town in a series of work camps, just small old trailers placed in roughly cleared lots. Some construction workers and laborers didn't want to pay dues to these camps. So they went out into the bush, cleared some land, and made a makeshift cabin in which to live. Shearing was one of these workers who built a small cabin on someone else's land. It was made almost entirely of stolen building supplies from around Tumbler Ridge. He lived there with some recently acquired friends.

Shearing soon found himself unable to keep a regular job in Tumbler Ridge. It's hard to say whether it was his attitude, quality of workmanship, or inability to get along with the others. He soon fell into a group with similar work behaviors to his own. But it's hard to eat or drink much with a group of men who aren't working. So, they began to steal tools and work equipment from the construction sites at night to survive.

THE CONVERSATIONS

OFFICER GERMAN

(AROUND THE TIME OF THE MURDERS)

In early September 1982, a large yellow Ford pickup truck passed RCMP Officer Ron German on a road in Tumbler Ridge, BC. The truck had a missing headlight, which wasn't worth much more than a second glance in Tumbler Ridge. Most trucks driven by construction workers were missing headlights and taillights or had a cracked windshield. After a long day, the last thing Officer German was interested in doing was a routine vehicle check at 1:25 a.m. But as the truck passed, his eye caught the two passengers quickly moving their heads up and down. He then spotted lots of tools loaded into the bed of the truck. The truck turned onto Quadra Camp Road, heading towards a trailer park. His suspicions got the better of him, and he turned his vehicle around and decided to follow.

When German got behind the truck, he turned on his blue and red dome lights to signal the driver to pull over. The Ford gently pulled to the side of the dirt road and stopped. As German pulled in behind the truck, the driver exited and headed towards him. He quickly opened his door, stood up, and told the driver to stay where he was. It was never a good sign when a driver leaped out of his truck and headed for an officer who was still parking their vehicle. It could have been that the driver was inexperienced and had never been pulled over before. But it also could have been something sinister. German quickly powered on his off-road lights, which helped stop the driver's approach and blind the passengers seated in the truck.

"Hey there, how are you doing tonight?" German asked politely.

The driver answered nervously and shakily, "Not too bad, Officer."

"Could I see your driver's license?" German asked.

The driver shrieked, "Sure," and quickly pulled his license out and gave it to German.

German read over the license and returned

it to the driver, "David William Shearing, so where are you headed tonight?"

"Just back to Quadra Camp from work." Shearing continued, "Going to go there for a bit, then head back home." Shearing was very fidgety and looked around everywhere to avoid making eye contact with German.

"Okay," German answered while he started looking the truck over more closely. "So, what's in the back of the truck?"

Shearing answered slowly, "Well, we got some impact tools here, a compressor, some wrenches, and stuff." German looked over the tools as Shearing listed off the items, and they all matched up pretty well. In all, he figured there was somewhere around $40,000 worth of tools there.

During this exchange, German also noticed the two passengers did not move once, not even to turn around to see what was happening, which gave him a strange feeling. Almost always, passengers tried to see what was going on between a driver and a cop at a road stop like this. To top things off, what were construction workers working on this late at night? The workers often came in from Dawson Creek, a good hour and a half away, and would have left for home already.

German asked Shearing to get into his police vehicle's back seat, which Shearing did without hesitation. German didn't cuff Shearing but thoroughly searched him with Shearing's consent. He just locked the doors so Shearing couldn't be any threat to him while he checked out the passengers still in the truck, who still hadn't made any moves. He noticed the passenger seated on the far right had his right shoulder lowered, a good indication he was hiding something.

German walked around the back of his car and moved along a ditch towards the truck on its right. He knew his vehicle's bright lights would prevent the occupants in the truck from seeing him. He slowly inched his way, taking slow, deliberate steps, hoping he would see what the two men were hiding.

Suspecting they had some sort of firearm on them and wanting to retain the element of surprise, German slowly drew his firearm as he approached the truck window. By now, both passengers were focused on trying to see what was going on behind them. They squinted into the rear-view mirrors but were only blinding themselves from staring into the bright fire lights blaring from German's car. Before they knew it, German was practically on top of them.

He immediately noticed a 30/30 rifle,

cocked and lying across their laps facing towards the driver's door. The passenger on the far right had both his knees bent forward, ready to fire if he approached from that side of the car.

Very carefully, German slowly moved his firearm, placing it right behind the passenger's ear through the open window. "Don't even think about moving," he said sharply. "Get your hands on the dash!" Both passengers placed their hands on the dashboard without hesitation.

German slowly reached around with his free hand to open the truck door without taking his eyes off both passengers. He quickly grabbed the 30/30 from the truck and uncocked the hammer to make the rifle safe. Walking back to his vehicle, he found a round in the spout upon inspection of the firearm. He placed the rifle in his car.

German walked back towards the rear of the truck with his weapon still drawn and commanded the middle passenger to get out with his hands above his head slowly. The dirty, messed up man responded as asked and backed toward him. German cuffed him and placed him in the backseat of his squad car beside Shearing.

Now, he had to take the third passenger,

who probably would have fired at German if he had approached the truck from the driver's side. This guy had the most attitude in the group and showed enough confidence that German figured he might not come easily.

The officer approached the truck from the driver's side before ordering the man out of the vehicle. The man turned his head away from German, so he holstered his weapon. The last thing a cop wants to do is start grappling with a suspect while his gun is in his hand.

At first, there seemed to be a quiet standoff between the two. Every second felt like an hour. German slowly approached the truck and, with a lightning-quick jump, leaped forward, grabbed hold of the suspect, forced him out the door, bent him over, and cuffed him. The rapid succession of movements surprised the suspect so much that he did not even have a chance to struggle.

German took the two passengers' information and ran a check on them. The first passenger he cuffed gave a fake name, but eventually, he figured out he was Wyman Laitenan. Once German retrieved some of the serial numbers from the tools in the truck's back, he let Shearing and Wyman go. No tool theft was reported, and no warrants were outstanding for those two men. But he arrested the third passenger for the attempted murder of a peace officer. Before leaving for Dawson Creek, German discovered that Shearing lived in a homemade shack about five miles out of town.

The following morning, German received a phone call from one of the engineer trailers in camp, reporting a break-in the previous night, where a lot of their tools had been stolen. The Dawson Creek detachment only had three RCMP members working there, and German had been alone for the last few days. This lack of police resources kept him close to town and following his standard routine instead of keeping his eyes on that yellow Ford pickup truck he had pulled over the night before. Mike Johnson, one of the other officers who worked there, returned the next day. After German explained what had happened when he was off, the two decided to find Shearing and, hopefully, the stolen tools.

Officers German and Johnson split up in two vehicles to cover more area and drove through the bush on the rough gravel roads that lined the work camps. It was a few hours before they spotted a homemade shack. They stopped, parked just out of sight, and got out of their suburban truck to get a closer look. They came upon two men digging a hole in the ground, including Shearing and Fred White, the same guy German had booked for attempted murder two nights before. How did he get out and back here so quickly, German wondered? Beside them was the yellow Ford pickup truck.

The officers returned to their truck and headed toward the shack at full speed, with sirens and lights blaring. The men dropped their shovels and made a run for it. Johnson quickly came to a stop, skidding his suburban sideways. They both jumped out of their vehicles and started in pursuit.

The two men led the officers on a lengthy and frantic chase that didn't end until both officers fired a warning round from their weapons through the woods. Seconds later, German tackled Shearing, and Johnson caught White.

After the two were cuffed, the officers started to drag them back to the suburban, asking them questions on the way. "Where's your friend, Dave?" German shouted out.

"Fuck you!" Shearing returned at him.

"Is he in the house?"

"No!"

"Let's go check," German responded sarcastically.

"You can't force me to go in there!" Shearing yelled back at him.

That was just what German needed to hear. He grabbed Shearing by the cuffs and forced him in through the shack's front door. Only, Shearing started calling out, "Willie! It's me, Willie!"

German then saw Wyman Laitenan sitting in the corner under a wooden bunk, pointing a .303 at them. Once Wyman noticed German, he threw his weapon out onto the floor in front of them, shouting, "I'm unarmed!"

Johnson returned from putting White into the suburban and grabbed Shearing, so German could get Wyman cuffed. They took the two back to the suburban, and placed them in it. Then, they took the three men on the two-hour trip back to Dawson Creek and booked them for possession of stolen property.

German discovered that White was released because the corporal on duty disagreed German had the right to book him on attempted murder just because he had a rifle lying across his lap, cocked and pointed at the driver's side car door, while German was conducting a stop.

While German was chatting with Jesse Harrison, the Quadra Camp trailer park manager, one day, he heard some interesting things about David Shearing. So he decided to make a note. Shearing had been behind in rent, and the last few times Jesse had gone to him to collect the money, Shearing told him that he was not only going to burn down the camp but was going to kill the owner of the trailer park, Joseph LeBlanc. The threat actually scared LeBlanc into taking a stress leave from the camp. Shearing had also bragged about derailing a train, but German had never heard of it. Even stranger were the many stories going around from some of the women in the camp about Shearing and his unnatural sexual behaviors.

After the theft in Dawson Creek, Shearing was set free since he did not have a criminal record. He had to appear once a week at the RCMP detachment, though. He maintained a good record by always showing up on time. During one of Shearing's regular weekly visits to the detachment, news broke about the police finding the Johnson family's missing truck. German commented as Shearing signed his papers, "Look at that. They finally found the truck and camper!"

After Shearing finished his paperwork, he responded, "Really! Where?"

"Oh, right in the park. Imagine that, after all that looking, it just sort of popped up on a mountainside. Pretty amazing!"

"Yup, bushes are pretty thick over there, hard to see down on the ground. I used to live near there."

"Really?" German answered, sounding like he was looking for an answer.

"Yeah, those murders happened a couple of miles away from my house. Really, a shock to everyone there." Shearing answered as he left the office.

In the meantime, on November 21st, Shearing was scheduled to appear in court for the possession of stolen property charges. His two friends, who were arrested at the same time as he was, were both in prison for other charges unrelated to this case.

On November 17th, German received more information on a stolen 3000-watt home light generator. He and his corporal headed out to make a visit to Shearing. Not only to see if they could find the generator, but also to make sure he was still around and planning on coming in for his court date.

When they arrived around 9:30 that morning, the officers pounded on the door. One of Shearing's friends, Jason Hill, answered.

"Sorry to get you guys up so early," German said to him with a smile in his voice.

"No problem," came from the voice of Shearing from within the house. He had been sitting on his bed, smoking a cigarette, before getting up and coming to the door.

"You've got court coming up on Monday!" German continued with enthusiasm.

"Yeah," Shearing mumbled back at him.

"What are you going to do?"

"Well, I am going to plead guilty to the possession charge."

"You have a lawyer?"

"Sort of. I've got legal aid."

As German and his corporal left, they checked in the back of Shearing's truck, where they spotted the stolen generator. The two of them decided not to say or do anything about it. Sergeant Eastham had stayed in contact with them and let them know that Shearing was now a suspect in the Johnson-Bentley murders. It was probably better to leave it there for now and use it later as a reason to bring Shearing into town if they needed to question him about the murders.

German called into the Kamloops detachment and told Eastham about the newest details they had on Shearing. Eastham and some other detectives were coming into Dawson Creek the next day and asked them to get Shearing into custody so they could question him.

The next day, when German spotted Shearing's truck, he pulled him over. Driving was Jason Hill, and along with Shearing, there was a girl. He arrested Shearing for the possession of the stolen generator and booked him into jail. Eastham did not want Shearing held for the murders of the Johnson-Bentley families and wanted to have the element of surprise on him when they interviewed Shearing.

Unfortunately, the prosecutor in Dawson Creek didn't go along with Eastham's wishes. After charging Shearing with another charge of possession of stolen property, he released him with a promise to appear.

Knowing that Sergeant Eastham was coming up to question him, the Dawson Creek detachment kept Shearing under surveillance. Just as Eastham was about to arrive, Shearing and Hill jumped on a bus to head back to Tumbler Ridge. Eastham called German and asked him to go to Tumbler Ridge and bring Shearing back to town, but he was not to arrest him or tip him off that he was now a suspect in the Johnson-Bentley murders. But how was German going to talk Shearing into coming with him to Dawson Creek?

After several delays due to bad winter weather, Sergeant Eastham and three other detectives finally arrived in Dawson Creek on November 19th. They checked into a hotel and got some rest. The next morning, they were all set to start their interrogation of Shearing.

Shearing had been bussing himself to Dawson Creek with his friend, Jason Hill, and the two arrived in the afternoon. German was alone in town again, so he called up their volunteer Auxiliary Constable, All Kjemhus. After briefing him on the high-risk arrest, German had him stand behind the passenger door of the squad car with a shotgun in hand but out of sight, ready to either use it or operate the action, as Shearing would know the sound of a shotgun racking a shell. It would deter any violence during the encounter with Shearing or Hill. They were the last two off the bus, unhappily surprised to see the police there.

"How are you guys doing?" German said in a very professional manner. The two men didn't answer but nodded as if to say okay.

"Would you mind stepping over to the police car for a minute?" The two slowly wandered over toward the police car before saying anything.

"You're not going to arrest us, are you?" Hill begrudgingly asked.

German looked at Hill and said, "Actually, I'm going to arrest you! There's an outstanding warrant out for you under the name of Hardwood."

Quickly, Hill blurted out, "That's not my name! It's Hill!"

"No, it isn't." German replied, "You're under arrest."

German then searched Hill before he cuffed him and placed him in the back of the squad car.

During this whole time, German focused on getting Shearing back to the detachment for questioning without letting him know anything about Eastham and his detectives.

"You don't want to talk to me?" Shearing asked German after Hill's arrest was complete.

"Yes, actually." German quickly answered before Shearing could walk away.

"You wouldn't know anything about some road damage that was caused by some idiot who walked a D-8 Cat from the BC Rail Service yard to the foot of the trail that leads to your cabin? The cleats of the Cat had torn up the road, and the Department of Highways was really pissed about it!"

"Nah, I don't know anything about it," Shearing replied.

"All right, but members of the Dawson Creek detachment want to talk with you."

Shearing got annoyed and said, "About what?"

"Other matters," German replied.

Shearing replied, getting even angrier, "You aren't going to arrest me, are you?"

Wanting to calm things down and keep Shearing from knowing what was really going on, he calmly answered, "No, I won't need to arrest you if you come on your own."

"You wouldn't lie to me, would you?"

"No," German said, even though he knew he would arrest him if Shearing resisted.

"You did before!"

"When?" German asked in a confused state.

"Well, it wasn't you."

"Look, I'll drive you down there, and when they're done talking with you, I'll drive you back up here."

That seemed to relax Shearing some, "Well, okay then."

German grabbed his briefcase and his dog,

an Old English Sheepdog named Max. The dog got in the back seat, and Dave got in the car's passenger seat and asked if he had to wear a seatbelt.

"Yes, you have to wear a seat belt." They had some small talk for the first 45 minutes until they came across a dead moose on the side of the road. To keep Shearing thinking things were pretty casual, German stopped to look. The two of them stepped out of the truck and approached the carcass.

"Jason [Hill] said that he saw this on his way in," Shearing said.

The two talked about roadkill for a few minutes, then returned to the truck and continued their trip to Dawson Creek. A little further down the road, they came across a pack of coyotes. German thought it would be a good opportunity to talk rifles.

"I have a .22 Cooey for shooting grouse."

"Single-shot?" Shearing questioned.

"Yeah, I'd really like to have one of those pump-action ones. That way, I could take a couple of shots at once if I had to."

"I've got one," Shearing proudly claimed. "A. 22 Remington. It is pretty accurate and good for hunting deer. It's my dad's rifle and has hardly been used that I know of."

Sounding like he was almost trying to sell the rifle.

When they arrived at the Dawson Creek detachment, they walked in the back door. Standing at the desk was Sergeant Eastham, whom German greeted with a smile as he introduced Shearing. Shearing's eyes went wide with fear, as Eastham's name had been all over the media as the lead detective on the Bentley-Johnson murder case. A different officer escorted Shearing to the interview room while German and Eastham exchanged information about him.

The most crucial thing German could tell Eastham about Shearing was that he always looked down when confronted about a crime he was guilty of. After mentioning the rifle information he had discovered during their drive there, Eastham was ready to start the interview.

SGT. EASTHAM

(BEFORE CONVICTION)

Before entering the interview room, it was vitally important for Sergeant Eastham to know precisely how he would conduct the interrogation and what questions he wanted to ask Shearing. Eastham had seen plenty of cases dismissed or thrown out of court for the smallest of mistakes, and he didn't want Shearing to end up out on the streets to kill again.

Eastham also knew they had been working on this case for about 15 months and only had circumstantial evidence. They would need more, a lot more, and if this interview went how they wanted it to go, they would have it. He had gone over the procedure in his head, trying to prepare for everything that could happen. He had to be relaxed yet professional. He would have to be assertive yet passive. He would have to create the perfect balance with Shearing to intimidate him enough into talking, but not enough to ask for a lawyer.

Today was Saturday, so the courts were closed, and all the legal aid lawyers were off. So if they played their cards right, they would have about 48 hours to complete the job. He was finally primed and ready. It was time to go to work.

Eastham entered the interview room where Shearing had been seated for a while now, across from Detective Ken Leibel. It was essential to start the interview with good things in life, such as God or Shearing's mother. While they talked about these things, avoiding the crimes, the detectives could look for any weaknesses in their suspect.

Shearing was seated in an old, creaky wooden chair, with both of his legs and arms crossed. He was smoking a cigarette, and by the smell of the room, he had already had a few before Eastham walked in. Leibel was sitting with his chair leaning against the wall, saying nothing.

When Eastham opened the door, his eyes caught Leibel's, and they nodded towards each other. While doing this, he saw Shearing moving in his chair to face Eastham. Just then, Eastham turned to look Shearing in the eyes, reached out his hand, and said, "Hi Dave." Shearing stood up, and the two men shook hands firmly. The contest between who would be in charge had now begun.

"You can call me Mike." He continued, "You've met Detective Ken Leibel?" Shearing nodded his head yes as he sat back into his chair. "We're detectives from Kamloops." Eastham then showed Shearing his badge and identification card, and sat in a third chair beside Leibel.

Eastham noticed Shearing's body tightening, and his lips pinched tightly together. He knew he needed to relax Shearing, so he started with some light talk by asking him some basic information.

"Now, Dave, I can really be forgetful sometimes. I am not very bright, and I tend to forget things a lot. So I'm going to write down our conversation, and Kenny here is going to help me. You don't mind, do you?"

Shearing shook his head to say no.

"What is your full name?"

"David William Shearing."

Back in the eighties, detectives usually used a cassette tape recorder to keep a record of everything that went on in the interview room, but in this case, Eastham didn't want to. For one reason, it might scare Shearing, who didn't know the real reason he was there. Secondly, he knew lawyers liked to use the recording to try and find any minor detail they could to get the case dismissed.

"When exactly were you born?"

"Uh, April 10, 1959."

"How long have you been around Tumbler Ridge?"

"Since about the 24th of July."

"Have you got a job in town down there?"

"I did have one there up until about two weeks ago. I was working for Sun Country Construction, putting up forms for basements."

"Alright, Dave, tell me a little more about yourself."

"What do you want to know?"

"Well, tell me about your parents. Where are your parents?"

Finally, with that question, Shearing uncrossed his arms and adjusted his seating to where he appeared more relaxed. "Dad died of cancer last spring." He said with a quiet, soft-spoken tone.

"What about your mother, David. Where is she?"

"My mother still lives in Clearwater. She's

been in an old folks' home for some time, and she's not coming out of there, I don't think."

"Any brothers or sisters?"

"One of each. My sister and I don't get along so good. We haven't talked since I left Clearwater. And my brother Greg, we get along pretty good." *(At the time of the interview, Greg was 37 years old and had recently become unemployed)* Shearing, with some pride in his tone, added, "Greg was a sheriff."

"What about you, what kinds of things have you done?"

Shearing lit another cigarette and began to list his accomplishments. "I completed Grade 12 in high school." And he proudly said, "and finished college for heavy-duty mechanics." *(a 6-month course).* He continued by listing off some of the construction jobs he had also done.

"You've done quite a few things in your time, Dave? You must be a real handyman outside?"

"Yeah, I know a lot of stuff."

"Have you had any problems with the law?"

Shearling lit another cigarette and started to spread his legs apart before answering. "Well, there's been a couple of problems, I don't have much money, so I've got to get by." He then mentioned he had been involved with some theft of construction tools and possession of stolen property, but figured he would get off with a simple slap on the wrist for that. "I was just being stupid. Some of it was just me, but I had some help from the crowd that I was hanging out with. Not a great crowd, I guess for that sort of thing."

"Ever been to jail?"

"A couple of times in Clearwater, just overnight."

"So, Dave, when were you going to head back to Clearwater to see your mum again?"

"Well, I'd like to go back for Christmas, but I couldn't stay. There isn't much work there, and I kind of like it up here in Tumbler Ridge."

"Do you have a car?"

"A couple of different ones. I just put a new cab on this '72 Ford four by four, but I still need a passenger-side door and some fenders."

This statement got Eastham's attention, as the Bentley's truck had its bumper removed from it, and the passenger-side door had a bullet hole through it. Could he have been trying to fix up the Bentley truck before burning it?

Shearing went on talking about his vehicles. "I've got another Ford, a '75 that I drive right now. I've had a couple of other cars, like a 1965 Chevy Bel-Air. That was my first, and it was all right. I also had a '68 Chevy and a GMC pickup truck."

"Who did you hang out with back in Clearwater?"

"Well, I got along with pretty much everybody. My best bud is probably Allan Smith. I've known him my whole life, but I haven't seen him in about two years."

"Anyone else?"

"Well, let's say that if I walked into a bar in Clearwater, I'd know somebody."

"How about close friends? There's your friend Allan, and?"

"All my friends are close."

"So, what do you like to do in your spare time? Got any hobbies?"

"Well, I like to play guitar. Had to learn that on my own, but it was something I wanted to learn for a long time. I work on my trucks all the time, you know. I like fishing and..."

Eastham interrupts, "And hunting?"

"No," Shearing answered quickly.

"Do you have any firearms?"

"No, I don't have any guns." Then there was a long silence before he finished, "I'm not much of a hunter – just fishing. I spent a lot of time down at the Clearwater River. I like it down there. Best damn trout fishing I've ever seen though was in Dreyfells Lake. I was there this spring."

"I've fished a few times, caught a couple of big ones in my days. Takes a lot of patience." Eastham replied, trying to keep the friendly conversation going.

Shearing sat up straight. "Yeah, patience is a lot of the game. That and a good lure, you have to have the right lure for the water conditions."

"Ever married?"

"Nah."

"Any sweethearts? Girlfriends?"

"Well, there was this one girl in Kamloops, Janet Duncan, she's about 20. I'm terrible with numbers and ages."

"How about names?"

"Well, I'm good with faces, not so much with names," Shearing added while starting to laugh.

"Who knows about you, David? Who do you talk with?"

"You know you guys know more about me than anyone. Except maybe my mother or my brother, and maybe Al."

Eastham then started to explain more. "We want to get to know you, Dave. We want to understand you. The more you tell us, the more we'll understand you. We're doing pretty good right now, don't you think?"

Shearing got a weird look on his face before replying, "It's pretty good."

"It looks like you hit the booze pretty good last night. Do you like to drink?"

"Well, lately, yeah, beer mostly."

"Any favorites?"

"Well, probably Budweiser."

"Any liquor?"

"If any, probably rye. Silver Tassel or Canadian Club."

"How about drugs?"

"Haven't done much since high school. I tried acid once and didn't like it. It kind of made me... Well, nothing really. I was just scared to get into stuff like that. Mostly pot back then."

"What about prescription drugs? Have you been taking any medication?"

"No, nothing like that. I don't like taking those kinds of drugs. Don't take them unless I really have to. Like two months ago or so, I was hitting it pretty hard and fell into a fire pit. Stupid really. Burned my back and arm. That was just stupid."

Shearing then continued by telling them about an accident that he had. "This pickup was kind of spinning around and hit my truck.

My legs smashed into the dash, and I fractured my pelvis. I don't drink and drive anymore."

Leibel broke his silence and asked. "Was there anybody else in the truck with you?"

"Robert Cliff was there with me."

"Ever been to a psychiatrist?" Eastham came back at him.

"Well, no!" Shearing responded both with surprise, and he had a look on his face as if to say only 'weirdos' do that.

"There's nothing wrong with seeing a psychiatrist, you know. Policemen do it all the time. We have a lot of problems ourselves. Alcoholism, depression, I've seen both of these in my 22 years of policing." Eastham snapped back.

Shearing relaxed a bit. "I guess I thought of seeing a hypnotherapist once to try and quit smoking, but I never ended up doing that, as you can tell. I'd like to quit by the end of the year, but I have a ways to go before then."

Eastham suddenly turned serious again. "Do you know what we're doing here, Dave? Considering the distance that we came, we must be here for a good reason."

Shearing was surprised by the question and sudden change of tone. He started to look down at his feet. "No, I'm not sure." He answered. "I don't have anything to hide, you know I'm an honest guy."

"We're honest, too, David. We don't tell lies, but then, we won't tell you everything we know either. We have a job to do, we're professionals, and we're good at what we do. We aren't going to threaten you. We aren't going to beat you, but we won't make promises either. We can't do anything for you. We're always fair. We won't bring any heavies down on you. I know you're no dummy. You've got the same education as me."

"Really!" Shearing replied with surprise in his voice.

"It means that you don't have to talk unless you want to. It means nobody can make you talk to us." Eastham let the room go quiet for a moment before he started up again. "You understand that at any time you want a lawyer, you just say so. If you don't want to answer our questions, you don't have to. Do you understand?"

"Yeah."

"If a lawyer was here right now, he'd tell you not to say anything if you are guilty. He'd tell you to just shut your mouth and not talk to the cops. He says that for a reason, you know?"

"Yes," Shearing said while he nodded his head yes.

"All right, I just wanted to warn you and make sure you understand. It's important that you know where you are coming from. I want to be honest with you. We're always honest and straightforward."

Shearing just nodded his head as if to agree with what Eastham had been saying again.

"Any time you want to leave, you can. We are going to be talking to you about a lot of criminal things, and I want you to know that that warning applies to all of it. You know you can call a lawyer at any time, and we can't make you any promises. We aren't going to threaten you in any way. Understand?"

"Yeah."

"Any time we're talking, you can get up and leave, okay?"

"Okay."

"We're detectives, GIS - General Investigation Section. We assist several different detachments of the RCMP in the Southern Interior, such as Kamloops, Williams Lake, Merritt, and Clearwater. We're professionals, and we're very good at what we do."

Shearing then asked a surreal question. "Are you guys investigating the Johnson/Bentley murders?"

Again, Eastham let the room go silent for a

minute before continuing, "Did anyone talk to you about it last year?"

"Yeah, some cop talked to me about it briefly before, sometime last year."

"A uniformed officer? Or plainclothes?"

"Uh-huh. Uniformed."

"Do you know Trophy Mountain?"

Shearing nodded, yes.

"How about Battle Mountain?"

Shearing continued to nod his head.

"You know that's where we found the truck, camper, and car?"

"Yeah."

"You know, we have a lot of members in Clearwater. We know a lot more about you than you think. Everyone wants to help us, even the shit rats. We're getting anonymous calls, a lot of those. Everyone wants to help."

Eastham again let the room go silent for a minute before continuing. "We've been looking under all kinds of rocks. Getting stolen property, drugs, money. Bikers are calling in with all the information they can give us. Bikers!"

This revelation made Shearing look up, finally.

"I want to see if you are an honest guy. I'm going to start back a couple of years ago and see what you will do. Remember, you can leave at any time."

Shearing nodded, yes.

"We discovered that a kid was killed that summer on Wells Gray Road. It was a hit and run, or criminal negligence, or whatever. The guy didn't stop. I know all about it; otherwise, I wouldn't be up here in Dawson Creek on a weekend."

There was noticeable relief in Shearing's body, as he probably thought the hit and run was why they were there, not the Johnson/Bentley murders. "I know."

"What happened, Dave?" Eastham asked as he leaned forward on the desk to get his face closer to Shearing's. "Tell me what happened."

"I was driving," Shearing admitted. "I guess you knew that."

"Which way were you going?"

Shearing took a little while, probably to try to remember what happened that night.

"Well, I was driving home, going up the top of the hill, going about 45 or 50 miles an hour. I took my foot off the gas."

"Then what happened?"

"I was scared shitless. I'd been drinking. I knew he was dead."

"How did you know?"

"The whole car ran over him. My whole car

bounced; I mean really bounced! He had to be dead instantly."

"Who was with you?"

"You know who was with me." Shearing snapped back.

"Hey, you won't be getting any answers from me, David."

"But I don't want to involve the guy."

"Well, that's up to you." Just then, Eastham sat back in his chair.

"All right, well, you already know it was Doug Elliot."

Without addressing the name Shearing just shared, Eastham continued questioning, "Then what did you do?"

"Well, we were scared to go to the police."

"Why?"

"Cause I had a few drinks. I hadn't been drinking that much, I mean, I could still drive, but I thought the cops would think that I didn't see the body and didn't try to stop. I just didn't have time. We drove into a turn-off and up the road a bit. We were confused. I didn't know what to do."

Shearing paused for a moment before he started up again. "We drove around, but there was a piece of chrome under the door, dragging along the road. I stopped to pull that off." Shearing suddenly stopped talking again. "Shit, what did I do then? Well, we talked about it for a bit, then we agreed that we shouldn't tell the police about it. I was really scared and confused. I drove Doug home, and I went home shortly after." Shearing then looked at Eastham, "I would imagine you want to ask me more questions about that?"

"Who was the guy you ran over?"

"Dave Carter."

"Did you know him?"

"Yes."

"How did it make you feel?"

"Really confused. I was sad. Well, not sad, I don't know what. I was upset."

"Has it changed your life?"

"I don't know."

"Have you had a tough time living with that?"

Shearing let out a big sigh, "Yeah. I've thought about it."

"Have you had nightmares?"

"No nightmares, but I think about it."

"How many people know?"

"I don't know. I thought it was just Doug and I."

"Well, I'm going to tell you it's no big secret. A lot of people know, except the cops, of course."

"Golly."

"How do you feel now?"

"The shits."

"Well, you've told me and Ken, does that mean anything to you?"

"Yeah, but I'm not sure what."

"Well, a lot of people feel, well, you told me. Do you think that you might want to write down what happened that night in your own words?"

"I guess so."

Eastham then slid a pad of paper and a pen across the table to Shearing. "Do you want a coffee?"

"Yeah," Shearing mumbled.

Eastham got up from his chair and headed to the door, "Let's get one thing straight," he stopped and turned back to face Shearing, "I'm not giving you anything. I'm getting you a coffee because we were going to have one. What do you want in it?"

"Two sugars."

Eastham left to get the coffees and take a bit of a break. When he came back into the interrogation room with the three coffees in his hand, he was shocked to see that Shearing was crying as he was writing out his statement. He placed the coffees on the table, one in front of Shearing, and didn't mention the crying.

"Having some troubles?" Eastham said as he sat back down in his chair.

"No," Shearing answered slowly, still sniffling away and writing.

Eastham sat and sipped his coffee for a while before leaving the room again. This time for a bathroom break. When he returned to the room, Shearing had his head resting in his left hand, elbow on the table, still writing, sobbing, and taking puffs from his burning cigarette.

Shearing adjusted his chair, sat up, and said, "My stomach is hungry."

"What?"

"My stomach, can't you hear it growling like that?"

Eastham shook his head, "No, sorry."

Shearing continued to write his statement for about 50 minutes before talking again, "Do you have a tissue?"

"Guess what I have in my back pocket?" Eastham replied with a smile as he pulled out a packet of tissues and handed it to Shearing. Shearing blew his nose a few times, threw away the tissue, and lit another cigarette.

"Jesus, kid. Do you ever smoke?"

Shearing finished blowing his nose and wiping his eyes, "Well, half of them are yours."

Both Eastham and Shearing smiled and chuckled lightly.

After another short silence, Eastham asked, "How are you getting along there?"

"Getting there, I guess. I don't know how detailed you want it."

"It's your statement, not mine. You put down what you think you should put down."

Shearing ripped the first two pages off the paper pad, numbered them on the top right of the pages, and handed them to Eastham. "Well, I've described that night anyway, I think."

"Do you want to sign it, or not? It really doesn't matter."

Shearing signed the bottom of the page, along with Eastham and Leiber, and they put the time at 6:39 p.m. "What happens now?" Shearing asked as if he was ready to leave.

"We'll have to discuss this. Okay, David. You understand everything we've done. I told you when we started that we know a lot about you. We wouldn't be here, especially on a weekend, unless there was a good reason. When we started, we gave you a warning: anything you say can be used as evidence on everything. I also told you we were investigating the Johnson and Bentley murders, and this is where it all stems from. The warning we gave you still stands. As long as you realize that?"

Shearing nodded his head in the affirmative again.

"First, I want to go over this statement."

Eastham slowly read over the statement, only stopping when he needed to clarify some of the words that Shearing had written sloppily or misspelled. "So, this is basically it?"

"Yes, as I remember it."

"Bet that feels good to get that off your shoulders? How do you feel?"

"Pretty tired."

"Have you ever written a statement for the police before?"

"No."

"Well, I guess there's a first time for everything, heh?"

They both laughed.

Eastham asked, "Do you have any questions?"

"I'd like to know what happens next."

"At this point, we'd have to take it up with the prosecutor."

"Am I going to jail?"

"I don't know. It could be criminal negligence or hit and run. My job is to collect the evidence and take it to the prosecutor. The judge then decides what will happen. Both charges are very serious. I don't know which you'll be charged with. It's not up to us."

"What's going to happen to Doug?"

"Again, that's up to the prosecutor. The

passenger doesn't have any control over the gas or brake. You know what happened. You did it, you're the one, in your mind. What happens, happens. All things will work out in the end. It's fate. Do you believe in God, David?"

"No," Shearing answered quietly.

"How about your mum?"

"Not really."

"She's an honest person who believes in principles?"

"I believe in principles."

"How do you think this will affect your mother, David?"

"I don't know, she'll worry."

"But she knows you, Dave, a mother knows. She taught you right from wrong. We are taught responsibility. She knows you understand what you did was wrong. She knows you'll take responsibility. That makes you a good person. It's not the people like you we worry about, David. It's the people who don't know they did something wrong, or who don't want to take responsibility for it. I did a profile on you, David. Basically, you were pretty quiet up until 1980."

"Yes," Shearing responded while looking towards the floor.

"Two things changed your life, David. One was the death of your father."

Shearing mumbled another yes.

"You know, cops go to shrinks for a number of different reasons: stress, alcoholism. We're not unlike anyone else. We did a background check on you. We know you have fights. We know someone stabbed you in the chin. We know about the guy you threw out the window, leaving him without the use of his thumb. We know a lot about you, you know that, and you know what we are here for."

"You knew that I had all the details of the hit and run?" Shearing asked with surprise in his voice.

"Yeah."

"Did you talk to Doug?"

"I don't tell lies, David."

"Is that the answer?"

"Ah, but David! Like a lawyer, you should never ask a question you don't know the answer to."

Shearing let out a big sigh and lit another cigarette.

"David, what do you think about the Johnson and Bentley murders? What do you think about them being killed in your front yard, so to speak?"

"Well, it was pretty bad for the community."

"Do you know where the car was found?"

"Yeah."

"You know where the truck was found?"

"Yeah."

"You also know where they were killed?"

"Bear Creek." *(At this particular time, nobody in the RCMP actually knew where the family had been murdered)*

"I think I need to speak to a lawyer now." Shearing blurted out.

"David, I think you need a lawyer," Eastham answered. "But I want you to listen to me for a minute. You don't need to talk; you just need to listen to me. But first, I'm going to get some coffee. You guys want another mug?" Everyone answered yes, so Eastham got up, grabbed the empty mugs, and left the room.

(Technically, Shearing never actually asked for a lawyer. He just suggested that he might need one. Therefore, it allowed the detectives an opportunity to keep him talking. Shearing could have gotten up and left any time unless they arrested him on the hit and run charges.)

By the time Eastham returned to the room with fresh coffee, both Shearing and Leibel had left the room to use the bathroom and stretch their legs. He sat in his chair and started to sip on his coffee, and about 10 minutes later, they walked back into the room. "Just had to check the fluids," Leibel said.

After the two men were seated, Eastham leaned towards Shearing and spoke, "David, stupid things happen sometimes. We all do stupid things. It was stupid, David, but I don't know what triggered you to do it. I know it happened. I just don't know why it happened. You do need a lawyer, David; there's no question about it, you need one. But I know what happened, and so do you. The difference is, you know all the details, and I don't."

Shearing tucked his chin into his chest, crossed his arms, and his lip started to quiver slightly.

"If you want to cry, okay, I want to cry too. It's a delicate subject, David. We have to do it sometimes. We don't like it any better than you do. You know that we know. It's changed you, David. You've been boozing it pretty heavy since then. I know you've been trying to put it in the back of your mind."

Shearing's body began to tremble some now.

"I know you want to tell us about it. I know that you do. You just don't know how to right now, and I understand. You don't understand why you did it, and I know you think about it." Eastham continued. "Don't make me involve your mother. I don't want to go and search her place or your brother's place. I know what happened, and I know it was something that got right out of hand."

Shearing began to cry loud enough that Eastham had to raise his voice.

"I know you're scared, David. There's a lot of pressure on you about this. Most of that pressure is from yourself. You don't have to talk to us, but you want to tell me. You already told me about Doug Carter. You wrote it down, and we discussed it."

Shearing now had his eyes covered with one of his hands, and his mouth with the other hand.

"You knew we'd come for you, didn't you, David?"

"Yeah." Shearing blurted out between sobs.

"Every time you saw a police car, you wondered when we were coming."

Shearing nodded, yes.

"It isn't easy, David; you can't just close your eyes and hope we'll all go away. We won't. We've been going through this for the past 15 months, too." Pushing on, Eastham said, "I know that you aren't that kind of person, David. That's why you'll have to explain it. We've got to do this. I don't like it, but we've got to. When I told you that we were from Kamloops, you knew why we were here, didn't you?"

Shearing nodded again.

"There are two ways to do this, David. You could write it out, or we could tape this. You're shaking, though, David. You're upset. I don't think that you could write it. I might be able to write it, or we could tape it. I know you want to help us, David. I know you want to tell us what happened."

The room went silent for a few minutes. Eastham was waiting for Shearing to say something.

"I know you're scared, David, and I know that you're worried about us. You're scared because of what you've done."

All of a sudden, Shearing blurted out loudly, "I could fucking shoot myself! Just go get me your fucking gun and leave me alone with it for a few minutes. I'll take care of everything."

"We don't want you to do that. Your life is important, regardless of what you did. Look, we all make mistakes, and life is quite indifferent about them. The world isn't going to crash to a halt because David Shearing made a mistake. If I had to start all over again every time I made a mistake, I'm not sure where I'd be. Probably still learning to walk. Mistakes are what make us learn. Do you want to do this question-and-answer style, or would you rather just do this by yourself?"

"I don't know," Shearing answered.

"David, when did you first see the Johnson and Bentley family?

Shearing said nothing.

"Where did you first see them?"

"Shit, what fucking life?" Shearing shouted out.

"You have a life, David."

"Not anymore, I don't." Shearing looked directly into Eastham's eyes for the first time.

"Your life is important, Dave. Important to you and your family. Don't think for one minute it's not. We're going to go through this together, Dave. I told you I was going to be fair, and I don't lie."

Just then, Eastham reached his hand out across the table and offered it to Shearing, who hesitated for a moment before grabbing hold of it.

"All right, will you tell me about it now?"

"I don't know."

"You know it's going to come out. I know it. I can't tell you to do anything. It's your decision, but we both know you have to tell me.

Did you ever think about turning yourself over to the police?"

"No."

"Why not?"

"Don't know."

"What is done is done, David. You can't bring back six lives, no matter what. I know you're an honest person. I know you've been drinking. It's not easy to forget something like that. You won't forget. Sometimes people do things, and they don't know why – crimes of passion, or things that just get out of hand. You can't keep hiding from this, David. It's far too late for that now. Do you think you need help?"

"Yeah." Shearing quickly answered.

"Do you know what made you do it, Dave?"

"No."

"Can you remember it very well?"

"Yeah."

"You poor bugger. Let's do it, Dave. It's tough for you, and it's tough for me. Where did you first see the Johnson and Bentley family?"

"Bear Creek."

"Do you remember what day it was when you first approached them? Daytime? Nighttime?"

"Oh God," Shearing screamed out.

"It's difficult for us, Dave. Will you help us out? You know you're going to tell us, and I know you will too. I know it's hard for you, trying to figure out how you're going to tell us."

"It ain't easy," Shearing said in between his sobs.

"There is no easy way," Leibel added. "You saw them. What time of the day was it, David?"

"I gotta think for a while," Shearing exclaimed. He sat, saying nothing, looking like he was deep in thought. "What happens if I tell you?"

"Well, you will be charged with murder. You'll be in custody, and we will obviously have to have you checked out by a psychiatrist to see why you did it."

Shearing agreed by nodding his head again.

"Where's the gun, David?"

"At the ranch."

"Is it a pump?"

"Yes."

"And the boat and motor?"

"At the ranch."

"Where on the ranch, David?"

"I can draw you a map."

Eastham gave Shearing a piece of paper and

a pen. While Shearing drew the map, he explained all the details to the detectives.

"Is the boat under anything, or concealed?" Leibel asked.

"Yes, it's under some bushes."

"Where's the equipment that came with the boat? The gas tank and life jackets?"

"Underneath it." Shearing finished the drawing and signed at the bottom of the map.

Eastham left the room to get more coffee. This time, he was going for the whole jug, as it would take all night to get through all the details of the murders. When he came back into the room, Leibel had Shearing drawing another map.

"All right," Shearing started talking, "This is where they were."

"Where did you come in? The main gate?"

"No, the fence over here." He pointed at a place on the map.

"I came in the campsite through these bushes over here."

"Who did you shoot first?"

"I don't remember."

"These four over here?" Eastham pointed on the map. Shearing nodded, yes. *(Four circles represented the adults in the camp, sitting around the fire)*

Shearing had approached from behind the

truck and fired from a position between it and the tent. The tent was just slightly to the right of the camper. "Then I shot the two in the tent," Shearing said while pointing at the map.

"What then?"

"I put them in the car. The adults I put in the back seat, the two girls I put in the trunk."

"Then?"

"I drove the car down to the clearing and parked it there. I then went back and got the truck and parked it there too."

"When does the bullet hole in the truck show up?"

"What?" Shearing asked.

"The bullet hole in the passenger side door. It wasn't done with a .22."

"It wasn't?"

"How many guns did you have?"

"Just the one."

"This was at nighttime that you drove the vehicles?"

"Yeah, well, yes."

"You took the truck to the bare clearing there?"

"Yeah, down there." Shearing tried to show where he parked them, but it was outside of the area of the map he had drawn.

"Do you need another map?"

Shearing grabbed another piece of paper and started drawing a continuation of his map.

"Do you feel like having something to eat?"

"I don't know," Shearing answered while still drawing his new map. "I parked the vehicles here." He stopped drawing and pointed out the spot.

"How far was it from there?"

"About three or four hundred feet."

"How long did you leave the vehicles there?"

"I left them there. I think it was the next day I came down and started sorting through the tools and stuff. I wanted to keep the key for the camper. I don't know why. I'm not sure if it was that day or another day I drove the car up to Battle Mountain."

"Okay, what tools did you keep?"

"A plastic sort of tray of wrenches and stuff."

"Like what?"

"Well, wrenches and pliers. A bunch of tools."

"Where are these now?"

"Probably, some might be in the shed by my house."

"What color was the plastic tray?"

"A bright color. Orange, I think."

"What else was there?"

Shearing went quiet and started to think. Then he began to write down some items on his map. It was vital for Eastham to get as much detail of the things Shearing had taken so that he could get a search warrant for Shearing's house and shed.

"What else do you have at your house or ranch?"

"The camera."

"Where is it?"

"The house."

"What about the film?"

"I tossed it away."

"Where did you throw it?"

"In the camper, I think."

"What else is there?"

"I don't remember."

"Fishing equipment?"

"Didn't keep it."

"Spare tire?"

Shearing had to think for a minute. "Now what the hell did I do with that?" he asked out loud. "It still may be down at the boat."

"Anything else that you can think of?"

"Not really."

"Do you want to do us a map of Battle Mountain, then Trophy Mountain, where the vehicles ended up?"

Shearing nodded yes and started to draw the fourth map.

"All right, insofar as the car is concerned, what did you do?"

"I stopped and walked over to the area. I wanted to see if I could get it there. I decided it would make it and went back to drive it in there."

"What else did you do?"

"I had to move some logs and a couple of rocks."

"Did you have anything when you went in there?"

"A flashlight."

"How about an ax?"

"I might have, but I don't think so."

"Did you chop anything? Any trees?"

"I don't remember." *(A tree was cut down to put the car where it was burned)*

"Then what?"

"I drove it in."

"Did you get stuck?"

"Yeah, on some logs."

"Then?"

"I poured some gas inside the car."

"Did it explode when you lit it?"

"You mean, right away? Well, it went 'whomp.'"

"What did you do with the keys?"

"Jesus, I don't know."

"Did you leave any door open?"

"Yeah, I think I left the drivers-side open."

"Okay, so you're there. You get stuck and get out of your car. You open the trunk, and where was the gas?"

"I don't know."

"Where did you put it first?"

"In the front."

"How did you light it up?"

"A piece of paper, or birch bark."

"It would have been pretty dark at the time, heh?"

"Yeah."

"After you lit the car on fire, where did you go?"

Shearing pointed at a spot on the road.

"Then what happened?"

"I watched it burn for a while, then headed back."

"All right, how about Trophy Mountain? Do you want to mark down what happened to the truck and camper?"

Shearing nodded again, then started to draw out a new map, this one of Trophy Mountain. He then explained how he burned the truck with a full jerry can of gas. He watched it burn for a while before he headed back home.

"Were you drinking when you did this?"

"No."

"What about the camper? What do you remember about the camper? Was there anything else that you took from the camper to Tumbler Ridge?"

"There's the tools in my truck."

"No. In Tumbler Ridge."

"That's what I meant. Did you mean my cabin?"

"Yes."

"No."

"Where's the gun?"

"In the rack at my house, in the front room."

"What kind of a gun is it?"

"An old .22 pump action." *(The detectives now had enough to draw up a search warrant for all of Shearing's residences and vehicles)*

"Now, you can either write out a statement, like you did the other one, or you can talk, and I'll write everything down?"

"All right, sure."

Eastham grabbed a pen and paper. "All right, don't go too fast."

Shearing went through the series of events from beginning to end.

Shearing's Story About What Happened That Night

Shearing spotted the truck and camper one night in August, on his way home from work. That same evening, he decided to go for a walk and somehow found himself at the campsite where he'd spotted the campers earlier. He moved around in the bush until he found a spot that looked down over the camper.

Shearing watched the campers briefly until he was spooked when he thought one of them spotted him. He quickly got away, running across a field and hiding in some shrubs. He waited about 15 minutes just in case he had been followed. Once he was sure nobody had followed him, he returned home.

The next night, he went back. This time he had a .22 rifle. He followed the same paths; this time, instead of hiding and watching from the bush, he walked right out into the campsite and started firing his weapon. When the four people by the fire pit were down, he went to the tent, crouched down, and shot the two girls. He loaded the bodies into the car, placing the four adults in the back seat and the girls into the trunk.

Shearing collected all of the family's possessions, which had been lying around the campsite, and threw them into the back of the camper. He moved the car and truck with the camper a couple hundred feet away, into the clearing of the field he had run through the night before.

When he returned the next day, he rummaged through the car and removed everything he wanted to keep. He then drove the car up to Battle Mountain and lit it on fire. Two days later, he got the truck and drove it to Trophy Mountain. But when it got stuck in the mud, he parked it and torched it where it was.

Shearing claimed that he just stalked the family of six for a couple of nights before shooting them, loaded their bodies in the car, stole some property, drove the vehicles into the night, and torched both the vehicles and the bodies.

But there was much more to the story of what he did that night.

The trial was set to start on Monday, April 16, 1984, in the Supreme Court located in Kamloops. Shearing retained lawyer Fred Kaatz from the Mair Jensen Blair law firm, which is considered one of the best in B.C. Fred Kaatz was a very well-respected defense attorney who had spent several years as an investigator for the RCMP.

A few days before the trial started, prosecutor Bob Hunter called all the detectives who had worked the case into his office. Hunter wanted to commend them all for doing such a great job, collecting the evidence so well that there wasn't a possibility Shearing would get off on any of the murder charges. However, that wasn't why Hunter called them into his office. He wanted to tell them that the case was not going to go to trial. The defense team, led by Fred Kaatz, was copping pleas to all six counts of second-degree murder. It would be up to the prosecution to secure a sentence of life without a chance of parole for 25 years. The norm for a case like this was life with possible parole in 15 years, so they still had their work cut out for them.

This left some unfinished business in Sergeant Eastham's mind. Experience told him there was more to this story. He knew Shearing had not been completely honest and forthcoming about everything that happened that night. It was time to visit Shearing and find out if he would tell him everything.

Eastham visited Shearing in jail on April 16, 1984, before his court appearance.

"How ya feeling, Dave?"

"Well, not bad, I guess, considering."

"I'm going to be straight with you, David. You know I've been around for a long time. I've been a cop for 22 years, and you know cops hear a lot of stories. Look, I don't have any reason to think that you lied to me. David, but I got a feeling gnawing in my guts that something else happened that night, and you're not telling me what that is."

Shearing put his head down and pointed his eyes towards his feet. Eastham knew that meant Shearing was hiding something. "You told me once that you might tell me the whole story one day, and I left it at that. Well, David, the day you're sentenced, I'm going to come and collect." Eastham stood and walked to the cell door. "Think about it, David, I'll be back."

Conviction

Detectives Bylo and Dalen drove up to the courthouse. They had Shearing in the back seat of their unmarked police car. The sidewalks and lawns surrounding the courthouse were covered with reporters. The courtroom was already full, including members of the Johnson and Bentley families. Extra security was taken to ensure that nobody would try to shoot or attack Shearing while they were bringing him into the courthouse.

The courtroom went silent as Shearing was brought in. Everyone stood as Justice Harry McKay walked onto the bench. The court clerk stood and read out all of the charges against Shearing. McKay asked how Shearing pleaded. His defense attorney stood and told the court that Shearing would be pleading guilty to all charges. Before McKay could accept the pleas, he would have to ask Shearing himself if he understood the full extent of what he was doing. "You understand that you are admitting fully and unequivocally to having committed the murders charged against you?"

Shearing stood and answered. "Yes."

"And you understand that, as I have already mentioned to counsel, what the possible penalties are?" McKay continued.

"Yes," Shearing replied.

McKay then asked Shearing to be seated before he accepted the pleas of guilty on all six counts. The judge adjourned for the lunch break, and when everyone returned, both the prosecution and defense took turns on presenting their recommendations of what the sentence should be, and their reasons.

The next morning, Tuesday, April 17, 1984, the court proceedings continued. Judge McKay returned and was going to impose his sentence on Shearing.

"Mr. Shearing, would you please stand?" Shearing and his lawyer both stood facing the judge.

> "The prisoner has pleaded guilty to six counts of second-degree murder. The facts as they emerge from his statement show the senseless, ruthless, cold-blooded slaughter of six innocent and defenseless victims, a slaughter that devastated three generations of a single family.
>
> Two of the victims, the grandparents, Mr. and Mrs. Bentley, were enjoying their retirement years. Mr. and Mrs. Johnson were raising a family and in the prime of their life. The other two young girls, one 11 and the other 13, had their whole lives ahead of them. The victims were enjoying a family reunion and a camping trip in one of our wilderness areas when this senseless slaughter occurred. The adults were sitting around a campfire

at the end of a no doubt enjoyable day, and the young girls had retired to their tent for the night.

What a tragedy. What a waste, and for what? As best as I am able to judge, the only motive for this mass killing was that the prisoner coveted their possessions. The sentence for second-degree murder is life imprisonment. The only issue before me is as to the period the prisoner must serve before becoming eligible for parole."

The judge went over all of the points that both the defense and prosecutors brought up in court on the previous afternoon, then continued.

"Dealing with the nature of the offenses and the circumstances surrounding their commission, I must, of course, be careful to ensure that I do not treat these murders as though they were first-degree murders, thus requiring a period of ineligibility of 25 years. The crown elected to charge second-degree murder in each case, and I assume that was because of the perceived frailty in the evidence relating to the planning and deliberation as those words have been defined in the jurisprudence on the subject.

Parliament has decreed that sentencing judges may, on conviction for a second-degree murder, having regard to the criteria set out in section 671, increase the period of ineligibility for parole from 10 years up to a maximum of 25 years. Obviously, an increase to the maximum of 25 years would be a rare event. I am unaware of it being done in any other case to date. In my view, however, this is an appropriate case for such a drastic action. The enormity of the crimes demands the maximum sentence.

Mr. Shearing, with respect to each of the six counts of murder that you have pleaded guilty to, I sentence you to concurrent terms of imprisonment for life without eligibility for parole until you have served 25 years of your sentence."

Shearing was taken to a room at the back of the courthouse, where he and his lawyers met. At this point, it was safe to assume they were planning how to get Shearing into the general population of whichever prison he would be sent to so he could spend his time comfortably and not be caged in solitary confinement.

They also knew Eastham wanted to talk with Shearing about what else happened on the night of the murders. His lawyer knew that Eastham would be writing the parole reports for Shearing and figured it might be better for Shearing to tell him his secrets to get some leniency on those future reports, perhaps.

SGT. EASTHAM

(AFTER CONVICTION)

Shearing's lawyer, Fred Kaatz, told him he was free to tell Eastham anything he wanted. He reassured Shearing that nothing could be done to him legally, as he had already been tried and convicted of the crimes. After Kaatz left, Eastham entered the room to talk with Shearing. As soon as Eastham had a seat, Shearing told him he would tell him everything.

Shearing started, "I guess I was at the Bear Creek site one of those nights on my way home from work."

Eastham asked, "You remember which night?"

"I think it was Thursday or Friday I saw the family there – a couple of older folks with these two young girls. I guess I got it in my mind that

I wanted them. I went back, and I'm not sure if it was that night or the following night. I knew I was going to have to kill those other four to get the girls. I watched them for about 45 minutes, sitting upon this sort of hill, where I'd watched them the nights before. I showed it to you back when we went to the park. When I was there, one of the women saw me."

"Which one?"

"I don't know. It was pretty dark."

"What happened then?"

"Well, she started standing up. And I said, 'Don't move! I got a gun.' Then the younger guy stood up, and I shot him."

"Where did you shoot him, David?"

"I think I hit him in the throat because he was gurgling and making a lot of noise. Then the older guy started running over to the truck, and I shot him next to the passenger-side door. The mother of the girls was running for the tent, and I shot her in the head about halfway between the fire and the tent. Then I headed around to get the older woman, who was trying to get into the camper. I just came up behind her and shot her in the head, too. Once they were all dead, I went over to the tent. The girls were in there, kind of sitting up on their elbows. They asked me what all the noise was, and I said there were some bad people out there, and your parents told me to stay back so that they could go get some help. They asked me if it was motorcycle people, and I said, 'Yeah, don't come out. Whatever you do, don't come out.' Then I went back out and had to shoot the young guy."

"Bob Johnson? He's got a name, David!"

"Yeah, Bob Johnson. I'm not good with names. Anyway, I shot him again because he was making all the noise. Then I had to put the bodies in the car."

"That had to be pretty tough."

"It wasn't easy. I had a little blood on my hands. I covered them up with a blanket when I was done, and then went back and cleaned up some of the other stuff. There wasn't too much sitting around, so it didn't take long. I went over to the tent when I was done, and crawled in."

Shearing then described the sexual assault that he had committed against the girls in more detail.

"After I got dressed, I got them to help me take down the tent. They asked where their parents were a couple of times, and I told them they got away to get help. We cleaned up the rest of the site and put most things inside the camper. I guess they believed me as they did everything I said. They didn't see me shoot the parents, so I guess they didn't have any reason not to believe me."

"We got in the car, and I told them to sit in the front beside me."

(How Shearing thought anybody would believe this story is beyond me. First off, when he started shooting the parents at the campsite, I'm sure there would have been screaming from the mother, for instance, when she first spotted Shearing, or from the three other adults when he shot the first woman. So, for Shearing to say that the girls didn't know what was happening outside their tent is ridiculous. Then, for Shearing to go into the tent after all of that and sexually assault the girls? They were 11 and 13 years old, and they would have known right then that Shearing was a bad man. Add that to the fact that they would have seen the four dead adult bodies piled in the back seat, all bleeding out in the car. And the girls wouldn't realize what was happening? More lies!)

Shearing continued with his story. "We drove back around Wells Gray Road and headed up to the ranch. When I got to where I wanted us to be, I got the girls out of the car and had them set up the tent. I told them that the biker people were still around and looking for them, so they weren't to leave. They were so scared they did everything I told them to."

He then told Eastham that he walked back to the campsite, got the truck and camper, and drove them to where he wanted to hide them on the ranch. When he returned to the ranch, he told the girls that he had saved their parents and helped them escape. "They really thought that I was their hero." He then told the girls they shouldn't leave the tent, as there were bears, wolves, and bikers out there that would get them. If the bears showed up, he told them that they could hide in the camper. "They were scared shitless, and would do anything I wanted them to, and once they were settled in the tent, I went back home. The next morning, Shearing went to work as usual and left the girls alone. "I brought them bread and milk and stuff. When I came home, I think it was Wednesday night, or maybe it was Thursday from work."

"And you murdered the parents on?"

"I'm pretty sure it was Monday."

"All right."

"That next day, Tuesday, I mean, I came back that night. I came back to see them, and I was still their hero. I told them that I had talked to their parents and that they told me it was safest for them to stay there with me. They were pretty happy with that story, and they trusted me. We talked a lot at night before they went to sleep, and I had some beer with me to drink in the camper. Both the girls slept out in the tent as the younger one feared the camper and was kind of claustrophobic."

On Friday night, Shearing returned to tell them that their parents would meet them at a remote fishing cabin. They left the ranch and began working their way through the dense brush in the dark. "It was raining like hell," Shearing exclaimed. "I tried to light a fire for them because they were really cold and wet, but I couldn't." Shearing then explained how they camped out in the woods, where he covered them with a sheet of plastic that he had brought with them. He also claimed that the two girls slept in one sleeping bag, while he slept in the other.

The next day, he said they continued to travel through the woods until they came to the river. At the river, they turned downstream and went for about a mile until they reached his cabin. There, they hung their clothing and sleeping bags out to dry. That night, they stayed inside the cabin. Again, he was in one sleeping bag; the two girls were in the other.

It was now Sunday morning. Shearing said he had spotted some prisoners fishing in the river when they got up. "My dad was a prison guard, so I wasn't too worried about it," Shearing claimed. Later that day, Don Gordon, a prison guard for the Clearwater Corrections Centre, came up to the cabin door and told Shearing some real mild prisoners were fishing in the river, and he didn't need to be worried about them. Shearing also said that the guard didn't see the girls with him.

"Where were the girls?"

"I hid them behind the door and told them to be quiet. They did everything I said."

After Gordon left and returned to his prisoners, Shearing took the girls and left, heading back to the ranch. "The girls were really slow on the way back. I guess they were really tired from all of the walking that we had been doing. When we got back to the ranch, everything was still set up the way we had left it."

Not too long after they returned, Shearing asked Karen to go for a walk with him to talk about a personal matter. Karen followed him, and they stopped once they got out of range of the ranch. "I told her that I had to take a piss, so she turned around. I had the .22 stashed there, so when she wasn't looking, I shot her in the back of the head. When I went back to the camp, I had a beer and sat around. When Janet asked where Karen was, I told her I had tied Karen to a tree. And that night, Janet and I were in the camper. Janet was a virgin and didn't know a lot about sex at all. She didn't know how to do anything, so we just stayed up most of the night and talked about everything. That morning, Tuesday, I think, I asked Janet to come for a walk with me down the trail. She came, and when we got to the spot where I hid the rifle, I asked her to turn around so that I could take a piss. When she did, I shot her in the back of the head and killed her also. I loaded the two bodies in the trunk, then went into the ranch and went to bed."

The next night, Shearing returned to the car and drove it up to Battle Mountain. It had been ten days now that the bodies had lain in the back seat of the car. Shearing wanted to drive the car far into the woods before he burned it, but he got stuck in the mud so badly that he gave up trying and burned it where it sat.

It was now about August 23rd, and the tourist alert had gone out, which might have been the signal for Shearing to take the truck and camper up the mountain and torch it. "I knew the area pretty well," Shearing explained. "There was a big gully there, and I wanted to drive the truck right off the cliff. That way, nobody would ever find it." It had rained hard the night before, and the ground had turned to mud. So, when he drove it up to the spot where he wanted it to be, he got stuck again. After trying hard to get the truck out of the rut in the ground, he gave up and lit it on fire. After watching it until the fire took hold, he headed for home.

Eastham got up and left the meeting with Shearing, knowing that it was all he would get out of it. He needed to take a long break from hearing about such a horror. He needed some solitude.

After this interview, Detective Leibel went out to check Shearing's cabin. He found a spot where Shearing had carved his initials into the cabin's wooden logs. It said DS + JJ.

There is so much to this story that none of us will ever know. When Eastham presented his findings to other law enforcement members, they weren't considered credible and would never be used in any way. I think that what Eastham was doing was right. After all, he was trying to find out what happened that night.

Some say the trial story was good enough, and the family members didn't need to know the details to get closure and move on with their lives. This statement is absolutely untrue. I've met many of these family members, old neighbors, teachers of the girls, and friends.

There is no such thing as closure when tragic events like this happen. It doesn't end with the trial and conviction. It never ends. What does happen is that all of these people's lives change forever. And after a while, the shock, sadness, and anger fade enough so they can get up in the mornings, have coffee, go to work, and continue their lives.

The truth is, we don't know precisely what happened the night that Shearing went into the Johnson and Bentley campsite. But knowing that a killer describes his story in a way that is angled to try to make us think he wasn't so bad tells us enough. Shearing told his story to make the listeners feel sorry for him.

ALAN WARREN

(BEFORE PAROLE HEARING
OCTOBER 2020)

So, what happened with David Shearing? What was it that made him feel okay with the murder of a family for the reason of having sex with two minors? I don't think we will ever know the answer. But I can add some of the newer things Shearing described to me.

In the Summer of 1982, two girls playing in the old, abandoned prison site in Wells Gray Park, where he was living, caught his attention on his way home from work. He was 23 years old then, and the girls were 13 and 11 years old. It wasn't the case that he heard their laughter while playing, didn't pay much attention, and just went home. He stopped, and instead of making himself known to the girls, he hid behind bushes and watched them.

As they frolicked around the old empty

cells, running in and out of each building, trying to catch each other, and playing some game of tag, Shearing began to make his plans. "I don't know what happened to me. It's like everything in my mind was gone, and all I could think about was those girls," Shearing admitted.

If something took control of his mind, almost like it wasn't his own, had this happened to him before? "I've had dreams both in the day and at night, but nothing like what happened that day. As much as I didn't like what I was thinking, I couldn't stop it. So much happens around us and far away in a day, but all that matters is what happened here. There would be changes in many people's lives made that day, and nothing could ever bring the innocence back to us."

How long did Shearing stay and watch the girls? When did he formulate his plan for what was about to happen? "I'm not sure how long it was. It seemed like it was only five minutes, but I know it was longer. Much longer. When I finally got home that night, it was getting dark, and that doesn't happen until about 9:00 p.m. in August." Shearing said he cleaned up and went to bed. He had no memory of anything else that night. He felt exhausted, so he fell asleep as soon as he lay down. He never stirred the whole night, and nothing disturbed his sleep. He said it would be his last night of what he considered peace for the rest of his life.

According to Shearing, the next day was just like every other day. He rose when the sun came up, sometime around 5:00 a.m., and drank his morning coffee to help wake him up. Then he walked to work. The entire workday was as every other day, except for a storm that seemed to be on the horizon. It was still very hot, but clouds had been building throughout the afternoon. The area would have some wicked thunderstorms in summer. Loud and flashy, but never lasting more than an hour or two.

When Shearing headed back to his cabin after work, he walked by the old prison. That was the first time he had thought about the girls since the night before. "I just wondered if they would be there again, but they weren't. Maybe they had gone home or moved to a different area?"

Shearing said he continued back home to his cabin and made some dinner. It wasn't until later on that evening, somewhere around 7:00 or 8:00 p.m., that he thought about the girls again. "I was really curious if they had left for good or not, so I thought I'd go and check things out." He headed out on a search to find the girls and see if they were still camping around the area.

The evening was pretty cloudy, making things darker than usual at 8:00 p.m. It didn't take long for Shearing to see the flames of the Johnson campfire. He headed toward it until he could hear the voices of people talking and laughing. He crouched down behind a set of bushes, listened to them for a while, and watched when he could. "I just wanted to see if I could spot the same two girls that I had seen before and see if they were there," Shearing said.

"So, you just wanted to see if they were there and not gone from the campsite and nothing more?" I asked.

"Yeah, I had no other intentions at all," he replied.

However, in my research, I had seen several other pieces of information asserting that Shearing sat on the hill behind the bushes and fantasized about the girls while masturbating. When I asked about this, Shearing answered, "No, I would not masturbate. I was unable to get myself up, you know. I have always had a problem with that. I can still think about things, but usually don't get them."

Shearing claimed that after seeing the two girls still at the campsite, he returned to his cabin and went to bed. I can't help but wonder what was really running through his mind that night. Did he just go to sleep thinking nothing more of the girls, or did he continue fantasizing about them? After all, the next day was when it all happened. Could he have just woken up and snapped?

The next morning, the third day that Shearing knew about the girl's location, started the same as the previous day had—he made coffee, got ready, and walked to work. But on this day, he claimed that he never returned to the campsite where the family was after work. Instead, he went straight home. Could it be that because he saw the girls were camping with four adults, two of whom were men, it had swayed him from thinking he could somehow get to the girls? After all, there were four of them and only one of him. The men were both hunters, too, so they would likely have firearms with them. That night, something changed everything, not just for the Johnson and Bentley camping families. But for the whole country. Something that would be talked about for years to come.

We know that later that night, Shearing again walked over to the spot where he had watched the family around their campfire a few nights earlier. And like before, he squatted down, hidden behind the shrubs and shadows that ran through the cloudy night. When he first arrived, he spotted the girls right away, as they were laughing and showing off what looked like some fish they must have caught earlier in the day, as if it were a first-time thing. After a little while, Jackie Johnson got the girls settled down and into the tent for the night.

"So, if you never had any thoughts the night before, or all this day, why did you find yourself at the camp again?" I asked. Shearing replied, "I was just fascinated with who they were and how well they were getting along. Being a family."

Probably only an hour or two later, Shearing walked into their campsite with a gun. So what happened from when he was enjoying watching family time with the Johnsons, to when he actually approached them? "I was like in a trance. I was drawn to the glow of the campfire. I just wanted to get closer to the girls, and maybe somehow, I would be able to see them again or get them to come with me."

Shearing approached the camp from behind the campfire, somewhere between the tent and the camper. It was the perfect spot to keep an eye on all four adults and sneak into the tent, if not now, then after they went to bed in the camper. From Shearing's perspective, three stood, and one was seated around the fire. Suddenly, one of the women stood up and appeared to be looking directly at Shearing. "I was scared and jumped forward. I told them not to move as I had a gun. I didn't know what I was going to do next. I really didn't. But she started to scream, and one of the guys started to run for the truck, so I had to shoot."

Shearing shot Bob Johnson in the neck, which made him fall to the ground while clutching his neck in an attempt to stop the bleeding. He then ran towards the camper to stop the grandfather from getting his rifle and shot him in the back of the head. As he walked around the back of the truck, Grandma Bentley was at the camper door, trying to open it. He shot her in the back of the head, and she fell to the ground. Then, as he walked back to the center of the camp, he saw Jackie Johnson opening up the tent zipper door. So he crept up behind her and shot her in the back of the head, too.

Shearing said he pushed his head into the open tent doorway to check on the girls. "Hey, are you guys alright?" He said, "Both of them were lying on their stomachs and looking up toward the open door. And they looked scared, so I decided to get into the tent with them to calm them down."

What he did when he went into the tent is arguable. Shearing just recounted that there was screaming and yelling and four rifle shots just outside of their tent. The girls were 11 and 13, old enough to know that the sound of shots fired and screams meant something terrible was happening. So, when a gruff-looking man, a stranger, carrying a rifle, came into their tent right after their mother, they'd be at least scared and probably crying frantically.

Shearing initially told the detectives that he shot both girls in the head. He then removed each of the children's bodies and placed them into the trunk of their parents' car. After that, he loaded the four adults in the back seat, covered them with a blanket, and drove the car towards a gully where he burned it to hide all the evidence.

But then, later, he added to his story. Shearing did shoot the four adults as he said he did, but not the two girls. In Shearing's second confession, he told Sergeant Eastham that he got into the tent with the girls, told them some bad people were out there, and their parents went to get help. He also said he told the girls their parents wanted them to stay with him until they returned. Given their ages and what they witnessed, it is unimaginable that the girls didn't know what was going on. They might not have understood why it was happening or what would happen to them, but they knew something was wrong.

Shearing now said that he shot Jackie Johnson while she was opening the tent door, and her body fell in the doorway of the tent, right in front of the girls. Jackie's body held the unzipped tent doors open, and both girls locked eyes with Shearing's as he stood behind their mother's body, still holding the rifle he used to kill her. It's impossible to believe that the girls were in any way calm with Shearing. Not after seeing him shoot their mother and hearing all the other screams and shots that night. But I still asked, "And after they had calmed down and begun to trust you?" He replied, "I just wanted them to trust me. I wasn't going to hurt them. I wanted to keep them safe, is all. All we did was talk and tell stories about fishing and the old prison that they liked to play in."

I wasn't buying it. So, I asked Shearing what he really did in that tent. "I got the older one to tie up the younger girl's hands. She wasn't too calm and kept yelling for no reason. I wanted her (Janet) to remove her clothes so I could make her feel good. I wasn't hurting her. Just feeling her. The other didn't understand it and kept crying, so I had to put something in her mouth."

When asked if he raped them, he replied, "I couldn't get up. I hadn't for a while. I thought maybe I could if I had them with me, but no. Back then, my fantasies were about younger women who couldn't laugh at me, and they let me try to get things to work, you know?"

According to him, after he finished his fantasy play in the tent, he told them to get dressed and stay inside the tent until he called them. He wanted to make sure the bad guys were all gone. He was actually placing the four adult bodies into the car's back seat and covering them with a blanket so the girls wouldn't see them. He called the girls out and told them to dismantle the tent and place it in the trunk of the car.

They all got into the front seat of the Plymouth, and he drove back to his cabin. Shearing then found a place on the property for the girls to set up the tent. He told them to stay close because not only were the bad guys out there, but there were wild animals, too. While they put the tent together, he drove the car away and returned with the truck and camper. "They really trusted me. They believed everything that I told them. We had become friends. I made them sleep in the tent the first night, and if they got cold, they could come to sleep in the camper with me."

I then asked if they had become friends and if they not only trusted but liked each other; what happened to make him kill them? "Karen was not going to understand. She didn't work with me. I don't think she could figure out what we needed to do. I tried so many times, but she kept fighting me. The thing is, I gave her a whole day with me, by myself. Nobody to bother us so that I could show her how she needed to be. It was not just for me, but for her too. I wanted her to be happy and like being with me. I don't know why, but she would not listen or keep stopping to cry. It wasn't sad. It was good." In an effort to explain to Shearing, I said, "I don't know David. She just couldn't comprehend what sex was at 11. She didn't have that same upbringing or lack of parenting that you had."

With this latest claim, it's hard to tell how the killings really happened with the two girls. He claimed that he first killed Janet, the 13-year-old, and then, after spending a day with Karen, he killed her.

We discussed being released from prison and living on parole in the outside world, and why that would be okay for him. "I have always been impotent and never really successful in having sex, proper sex. I used to have fantasies where I could use bondage to control anyone that I would want to have sex with. It was always with young girls because it would be easier to control. I wouldn't have to hurt them. Women tend to be stronger and can put up a fight. It wasn't meant to hurt them, the bondage, it was so that I could control them, help them enjoy it. I wasn't going to rape them. I just wanted to touch them, kiss them, smell them. They would like that too. But these fantasies went away. They started when I was 15, and after Janet, they were gone. I don't have them anymore. When I was 15, they started to grow with intensity and brutality over the years. Together with my hatred for the world and how it treated me and my family, I was able to kill the adults. I just wanted to live out my fantasies of bondage and dominance over Janet, the 13-year-old. This also gave me a sense of worth or power over the world that I hated so much. I no longer have desires for young girls, or to do drugs, or have those kinds of fantasies anymore."

Back in Shearing's parole hearing held in 2008, he said that he wanted the Johnsons and Bentleys to know what really happened to the girls, rather than have them believe things that did not happen. Shearing said, "I struck Janet in the stomach and ordered her to remove her clothes. She did, and then she started to cry. I lost the excitement that I had felt. I wasn't able to continue any of the sadistic parts."

Shearing described his feelings about his sexual fantasies. "I was angry at the world because I thought that I didn't fit in and that I was ugly. I became very shy. I think I was angry at the whole world, and it came out against women. I am not a pedophile and have never had fantasies about children." To Shearing, a child was a girl under 15 years old. He thought Janet was older than 13.

As to the shooting of the two girls in the head and why he did that, he responded, "I was thinking about myself. I reasoned that I had already committed the murders. I couldn't let them go because I would be in a lot of trouble. Now, when I think of it, I wish I hadn't."

Shearing admitted that he continued to fantasize about his assaults on Janet and Karen for about the first ten years in prison. Eventually, they started to diminish in intensity and have now disappeared completely. "For a while, I wished I had been able to fulfill the fantasies I had about Janet and Karen so that I would have known what it meant. Or at least I think I would have understood it better." Shearing said that he never learned how to deal with his feelings or emotions properly as a child.

When Shearing was first caught and on trial, he said it made him feel important for the first time, almost like a celebrity. All the other inmates looked up to him and seemed to admire and respect him. Remember, though, that at the time of the arrest and trial, nothing about the children's sexual assault was known. The other prisoners only knew of him as a killer of six, maybe seven people. If the truth were known to the public at that time, the other inmates would have been trying to kill him.

In a famous, but not so different case, on January 15, 1974, four Otero family members were murdered in Wichita, Kansas. The victims were Joseph Otero, age 38; Julie Otero, age 33; Joseph Otero Jr., age 9; and Josephine Otero, age 11. Their bodies were discovered by the family's eldest child, who was in 10th grade. Dennis Rader, depressed after being laid off, was "trolling" one day when he spotted Julie leaving to take her children to school. He liked the dark hair, skin, and eyes of Latinas. Struck by Julie's beauty and taken with young Josie, he followed them to school. The mother and daughter were his perfect victims. Nearly two months later, fueled by thoughts of bondage, Rader lived out his sexual fantasies through the Otero family. He would later tell police that the basement was "symbolic, like a dungeon." Hanging was a central element of his fantasies. "... So my encore was to just take her down there and hang her. If she had been dead, I would have still hung her, just to hang her." In the basement, a rope was already prepared to hang Josie. To watch her struggle for her life, she was hanged so that her toes barely brushed the ground as the noose was suspended from a sewer pipe. For "a sexual release," he pulled down her panties. Police found his semen traces near her body. Rader, aka The BTK Killer (Bind, Torture, Kill), was sentenced to 10 life sentences, or 175 years – one for each life he took. He is in the most restrictive prison possible, allowed out for one hour a day, five days a week, to shower and/or exercise.

Today, Shearing claims that he now sees the damage that he has done. "Just knowing that I am responsible for all of that devastating loss causes me to be sick to my stomach. I actually hate being in my own skin so much that I'll find myself scratching my arms hard, sometimes until I bleed. I have wanted to apologize to the families in person for so long now. I have taken away their most valuable things to them.

For this loss, I am sincerely sorry. I am so sorry for all of the grief and pain that I have caused."

Shearing said that he wished he could be moved from medium to minimum security and be allowed someday to have day passes. "My wish is to put what time I have left to some good use. I would be thankful and proud to be able to help support my wife." He continued, "My crime was caused by a unique sense of circumstances and problems. And those problems have been resolved. My psychologist says I'm ready to begin the process towards release."

BIBLIOGRAPHY

1. https://web.archive.org/web/20130630031741/http://schadenfreudeuk.blogspot.ca/2011/03/lesley-ann-downey-tape-transcript.html
2. Topping, Peter: *Topping – The Autobiography of the Police Chief in the Moors Murder Case*, Angus & Robertson, London, 1989
3. Syme, Anthony: *Murder on the Moors*, Horwitz Publications, Sydney, 1966
4. Potter, John Deane: *The Monsters of the Moors*, Elek, London, 1966
5. Keightley, Alan: *Ian Brady: The Untold Story of the Moors Murders* (Kindle Locations 7512-7513). Pavilion Books. Kindle Edition.
6. Marchbanks, David: *The Moor Murders*, Leslie Frewin, London, 1966
7. Harrison, Fred: *Brady and Hindley – Genesis of the Moors Murders*, Grafton, London, 1987
8. Goodman, Jonathan: *The Moors Murders: The Trial of Myra Hindley and Ian Brady*, David & Charles, London, 1986
9. Brady, Ian: *The Gates of Janus*, Feral House, Los Angeles, 2001
10. Keightley, Dr. Alan: *Ian Brady: The Untold Story of the Moors Murders*, Robson Books, Great Britain 2017.

11. Moors Murders, *The Sun*, June 28, 2018 - https://www.thesun.co.uk/news/2197861/ian-brady-moors-murders-death-myra-hindley/
12. "Moors Murders: A Notorious Couple and Their Young Prey," *NY Times*, May 17, 2017 - https://www.nytimes.com/2017/05/17/world/europe/moors-murders-ian-brady-myra-hindley-victims.html
13. "Moors Murders," *Manchester Evening News*, Jan. 18, 2019 - https://www.manchestereveningnews.co.uk/all-about/moors-murders
14. "Moors Murders: The Victims of Ian Brady and Myra Hindley," *Sky News*, May 16, 2017 - https://news.sky.com/story/the-moors-murders-the-victims-of-ian-brady-and-myra-hindley-10879310
15. https://www.wusa9.com/article/news/local/dc/911-calls-from-metro-smoke-incident/65-286546066
16. https://www.gisborneherald.co.nz/local-news/20151009/judge-goes-hard-on-domestic-violence/
17. https://listverse.com/2017/10/29/10-faked-crime-scenes-with-good-bad-and-bizarre-motivations/
18. https://en.wikipedia.org/wiki/Stephen_Port
19. https://www.bbc.co.uk/news/resources/idt-d32c5bc9-aa42-49b8-b77c-b258ea2a9205

20. https://www.theguardian.com/uk-news/2021/oct/05/stephen-port-murders-inquest-police-competence
21. https://www.pinknews.co.uk/2016/10/07/alleged-gay-hook-up-killer-eluded-police-by-planted-drug-bottles-and-fake-suicide-note-on-victims/
22. https://www.hulldailymail.co.uk/news/hull-east-yorkshire-news/please-careful-dating-apps-murdered-1696933
23. https://www.bbc.com/news/uk-england-london-37573891
24. https://www.huffingtonpost.co.uk/entry/owen-jones-hits-back-at-police-dating-app-warnings-over-serial-killer-stephen-port_uk_5836b205e4b0ddedcf5c1304
25. https://www.hulldailymail.co.uk/news/hull-east-yorkshire-news/please-careful-dating-apps-murdered-1696933
26. https://www.huffingtonpost.co.uk/entry/owen-jones-hits-back-at-police-dating-app-warnings-over-serial-killer-stephen-port_uk_5836b205e4b0ddedcf5c1304
27. http://simonfieldhouse.com/old-bailey-central-criminal-courts-london/
28. https://www.theguardian.com/uk-news/2016/oct/05/alleged-serial-killer-had-appetite-for-sex-with-unconscious-men
29. https://www.telegraph.co.uk/news/2017/12/26/families-men-killed-serial-killer-stephen-port-insulted-distressed/
30. https://www.cosmopolitan.com/uk/entertainment/a26943007/the-barking-

murders-stephen-port-serial-killer-grindr-stephen-merchant/

31. Bastos, Márcio: "Em program de Fábio Porchat, jovem conta Como descobriu que ex era um serial killer" [In Fábio Porchat's show, a young man tells how he found out that his ex was a serial killer] 26 August 26, 2020.
32. Mr. Justice Openshaw: "R v Stephen Port: Sentencing Remarks of Mr. Justice Openshaw" (PDF) November 25, 2016.
33. Kirk, Tristan: "Stephen Port murder trial: Gay chef murdered four men by injecting them with lethal doses of date rape drug." *London Evening Standard*. October 5, 2016. Retrieved November 25, 2016.
34. "Suspected serial killer Stephen Port appeared on Celebrity MasterChef." *The Independent*. October 21, 2015.
35. Khan, Shehab: "Stephen Port: Grindr serial killer appeals against murder convictions of four men." *The Independent.* August 31, 2018.
36. Osborne, Samuel: "Stephen Port: Police investigate 58 date rape deaths after 'Grindr Serial Killer' found guilty of the murder of four men." *The Independent.* November 24, 2016.
37. Osborne, Samuel: "Stephen Port Guilty: Grindr Serial Killer to be Sentenced for murder of four men." *The Independent*. November 23, 2016.
38. Police interviews with GHB serial killer

Stephen Port, London Scotland Yard, June 2014.

39. "A man has been charged with four counts of murder concerning the deaths of four men," Metropolitan Police Service. Oct 15, 2015.
40. Evans, Martin: "Gay serial killer Stephen Port guilty of date rape drug murders of four young men." *telegraph.co.uk*.
41. Kirk, Tristan: "Stephen Port murder trial: Gay chef murdered four men by injecting them with lethal doses of date rape drug." *London Evening Standard*.
42. Gayle, Damien; Davies, Caroline: "Alleged serial killer Stephen Port 'had the appetite for sex with unconscious men." *The Guardian*.
43. "Stephen Port trial: Alleged serial killer tried to frame a victim." *BBC News*. October 6, 2016.
44. "Families of men killed by serial killer Stephen Port 'insulted and distressed' over lack of police answers." *The Telegraph*. December 26, 2017.
45. Gayle, Damien; Davies, Caroline: "Alleged serial killer Stephen Port 'had an appetite for sex with unconscious men'." *The Guardian*. October 6, 2016. Wilford, Greg (13 May 2017).
46. "Stephen Port: Police missed Grindr serial killer because victims were gay, families say in the lawsuit." *The Independent*. BMJ 2015; 351 DOI: https://doi.org/10.1136/bmj.h5790 (Published November 3, 2015)

47. https://www.truemurderpodcast.com/the-moors-murders/

48. https://razs-midnight-macabre.com/2015/07/06/real-life-horror-the-moors-murders-part-2/

49. https://www.crimeandinvestigation.co.uk/crime-files/myra-hindley

50. https://bukisa.com/articles/1137847_the-grindr-serial-killer-what-s-the-truth-behind-stephen-port-s-murders

51. https://murderandmimosas.buzzsprout.com/1982179/episodes/15442927-grindr-s-grim-reaper-the-lethal-online-enticements-of-stephen-port

52. https://www.kentlive.news/news/kent-news/innocent-young-gravesend-man-enjoying-2462565

53. https://gainsboroughlive.co.uk/news/trial-date-set-as-woman-pleads-no-guilty/

54. https://www.huffingtonpost.co.uk/entry/owen-jones-hits-back-at-police-dating-app-warnings-over-serial-killer-stephen-port_uk_5836b205e4b0ddedcf5c1304

55. https://en.wikipedia.org/wiki/Old_Bailey

56. https://www.neellis.com/2020/08/stephen-port-grindr-killer.html

57. https://www.globaldatinginsights.com/news/accused-gay-dating-site-killer-stephen-port-was-obsessed-with-drug-rape-pornography/

58. https://www.bbc.com/news/uk-45407465

59. https://www.fbi.gov/news/stories/-tracking-animal-cruelty

60. https://www.animallaw.info/article/link-cruelty-animals-and-violence-towards-people

61. Dogs, Cats, and Other Animal Companions | Issues | PETA

62. http://www.paws.org/help/report/connection.php

ABOUT THE AUTHOR

Alan R Warren is a Bestselling Author, Producer, and host of the popular NBC Radioshow *House of Mystery* and *Inside Writing*, both heard on the 106.5 F.M. Los Angeles/102.3 F.M. Riverside/ 1050 A.M. Palm Springs/ 540 A.M. KYAH Salt Lake City/ 1150 A.M. KKNW Seattle/Tacoma and Phoenix.

His bestselling true crime books in Canada include *Beyond Suspicion: The True Story of Colonel Russell Williams*, which will be featured on CNN's *Lies, Crimes, & Videos* (Season 4), and *Murder Times Six: The True Story of the Wells Gray Park Murders*. In America, his bestsellers include *The Killing Game: Serial Killer Rodney Alcala*, which was featured on several television shows such as

Very Scary People with Donny Walberg, Oxygen's *Mark of a Killer*, Reelz' *Killer Trophies*, and soon to be included in a four-part Sundance Channel documentary called *Death's Date*. His bestseller, *Doomsday Cults: The Devil's Hostages*, was featured on Vice's *Dark Side of the '90s*.

His latest series, *Killer Queens*, is a six-part book series covering murders that affect the Gay Community. So far, it includes Book 1 - Leopold & Loeb, Book 2 - Butcher of Hanover: Fritz Haarmann, Book 3 - Grindr Serial Killer: Stephen Port, and Book 4 - Bruce McArthur: Toronto Gay Killer.

ALSO BY ALAN R. WARREN

HOUSE OF MYSTERY RADIOSHOW INTERVIEWS SERIES BOX SET (Books 1 - 7)

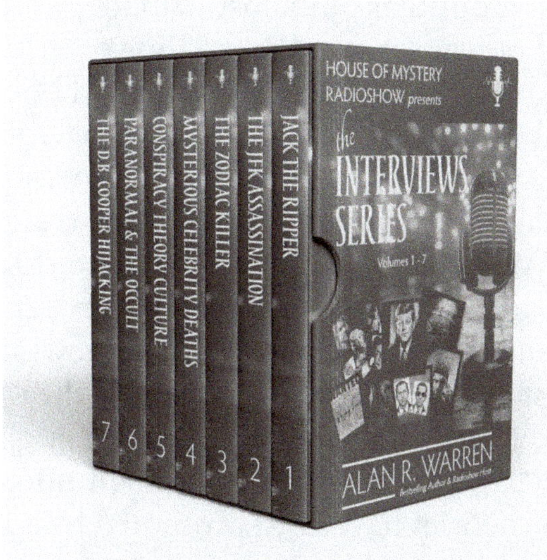

The *House of Mystery Radio Show* has been on the air for ten years, broadcasting in over a dozen cities in the United States, including KKNW 1150 A.M. Seattle/Tacoma, and KCAA 106.5 F.M. Los Angeles 102.3 F.M. Riverside 1050 A.M. Palm Springs. I started the show to find as much information as possible on the world's mysteries in crime, science, religion, history, paranormal, and more. Like most people, the stories and rumors I've heard, books I've read, or documentaries I've watched would seldom provide one direct answer to a question. Throughout my time recording interviews, I would seek out people who had researched a subject enough to have written a book, developed a documentary, or were involved in the event or topic enough to have the knowledge I was seeking.

The strange thing I found was that, in most cases, there was a popular or mainstream idea of what happened or was reported at the time of the event. However, most favorite writers who had books or shows about the event often disagreed with the current theory. They would go as far as to accuse the media of faking the story and hiding the truth from everyone. An example would be the JFK Assassination. There is a common theory reported by different government agencies and news media that most people in America accept as the truth. However, ever since the release of the original Warren Report on the assassination, hundreds of opposing theories have been promoted by authors and researchers.

In this series, each volume focuses on one of the conspiracies discussed on the show. Each book lays out the case details, reviews the official reports, and then follows up with the alternative theories presented during the interviews with the person or people reporting on them. There will be no committed answer at the end of the book. The *House of Mystery Interviews Series* does not attempt to solve the case. Instead, it provides a concise review of the crucial and fascinating points learned during the show's interviews. The book is an excellent reference for other researchers and a good overview for those unfamiliar with the case.

KILLER CRIME SERIES BOX SET (Books 1 - 8)

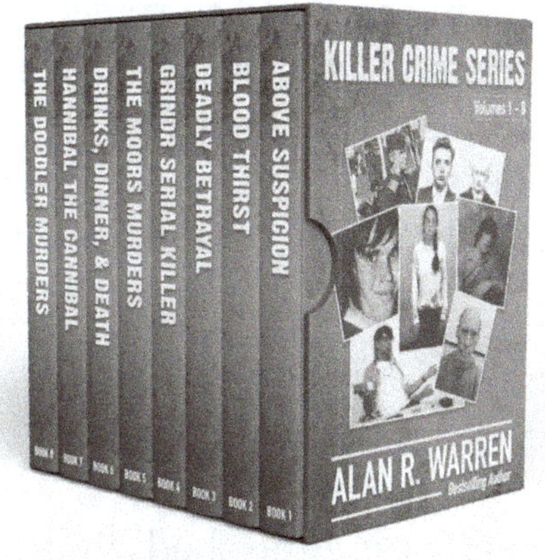

Step into the chilling depths of human depravity with this meticulously crafted box set from bestselling author Alan R. Warren, renowned for his captivating explorations of real-life crimes. This collection of eight unflinching narratives draws readers into the shadowed minds and actions of some of the world's most notorious criminals. From the twisted motivations behind Colonel Russell Williams' crimes in Above Suspicion to the shocking story of Jennifer Pan in Deadly Betrayal, who plotted a tragic betrayal against her own family, Warren delivers each tale with an unmatched intensity that will keep readers riveted.

In Blood Thirst, Warren examines the "Vampire Killer" who terrorized Canada, while Doodler Murders sheds light on the mysterious unsolved murders that haunted 1970s San Francisco. The Grindr Killer follows the grim story of Stephen Port, whose use of dating apps led to tragedy, and in The Moors Murders, Warren revisits the notorious crimes of Ian Brady and Myra Hindley. Rounding out the collection is Hannibal the Cannibal, exploring the dark legacy of one of history's most infamous criminals.

This box set is a journey into the darker side of human psychology, weaving together cases from across different eras and places. Warren's unparalleled storytelling sheds light on these shocking events while honoring the victims and dissecting the minds of those who dared to defy the boundaries of morality and humanity.

KILLER QUEEN SERIES BOX SET (Books 1 - 4)

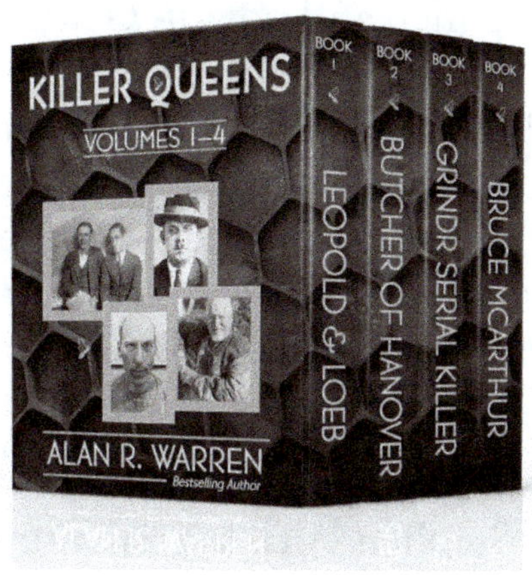

The Killer Queens is a new series of historical fiction books based on true stories. Sources, such as police reports and newspaper articles, are examined to gather as many facts as possible surrounding each case. As with any work of fiction, some creative additions are made when telling these stories, usually within the conversations between the personalities involved. The various sources are the basis of these conversations and, hopefully, make them come alive for the readers to help understand what was meant by those words.

Book 1 of the series focuses on what has been called "The Crime of the Century" in the 1920s United States. At the center of this murder case were Nathan Leopold Jr. and Richard Loeb – two wealthy University of Chicago students who, in May of 1924, kidnapped and murdered 14-year-old Bobby Franks.

Book 2 of the series focuses on the serial killer of at least 27 young men and boys in Germany in the post-World War 1 era. At the center of this murder case were Fritz Haarmann and Hans Grans, who were lovers while committing these murders. It wasn't until the skulls and bones started washing ashore from the Leine River in Hanover that Germany realized they had a cold-blooded serial killer in their country.

Book 3 focuses on more modern times. It is based on the case of Stephen Port, a serial murderer in London, U.K., who was convicted of drugging, raping, and murdering four young men. He was also convicted of drugging and raping several other men. His victims were found through a new type of gay sex parties called 'Party N Play' or 'Chemsex' parties that have become all the rage.

Book 4 This book is based on Toronto's Gay Village and the few times serial killers reigned terror upon it. As much as this series wants to point out the negative aspects of murders in the gay community in countries that don't respect gay people, it's also important to reveal its effects in countries that seemingly support gay people.

MURDER TIMES SIX: The True Story of The Wells Park Murders

"The author even had me (who conducted the interview) on the edge of my seat as I was turning the pages as "the Detective" was trying to unearth the unspeakable truth."

— SGT. MIKE EASTHAM
R.C.M.P.

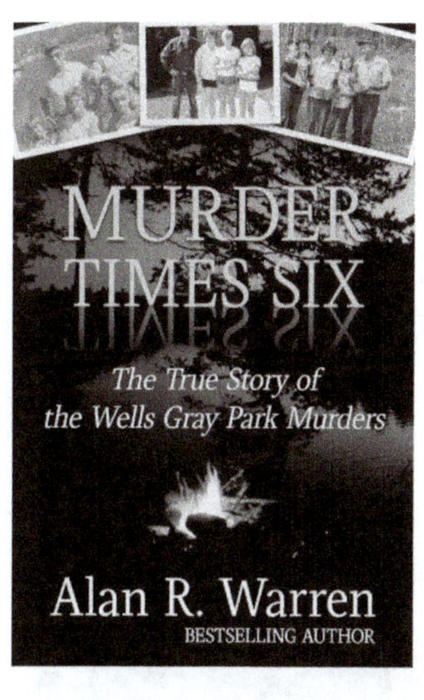

It was a crime unlike anything seen in British Columbia. The horror of the "Wells Gray Murders" almost forty years ago transcends decades.

On August 2, 1982, three generations of a family set out on a camping trip – Bob and Jackie Johnson, their two daughters, Janet, 13, and Karen, 11, and Jackie's parents, George and Edith Bentley. A month later, the Johnson family car was found off a mountainside logging road near Wells Gray Park completely burned out. In the back seat were the incinerated remains of four adults, and in the trunk were the two girls.

But this was not just your average mass murder. It was much worse. Over time, some brutal details were revealed; however, most are still only known to the murderer, David Ennis (formerly Shearing). His crimes had far-reaching impacts on the family, community, and country. It still does today. Every time Shearing attempts freedom from the parole board, the grief is triggered as everyone is forced to relive the horrors once again.

Murder Times Six shines a spotlight on the crime that captured the attention of a nation, recounts the narrative of a complex police investigation, and discusses whether a convicted mass murderer should ever be allowed to leave the confines of an institution. Most importantly, it tells the story of one family forever changed.

THE KILLING GAME: The True Story of Rodney Alcala

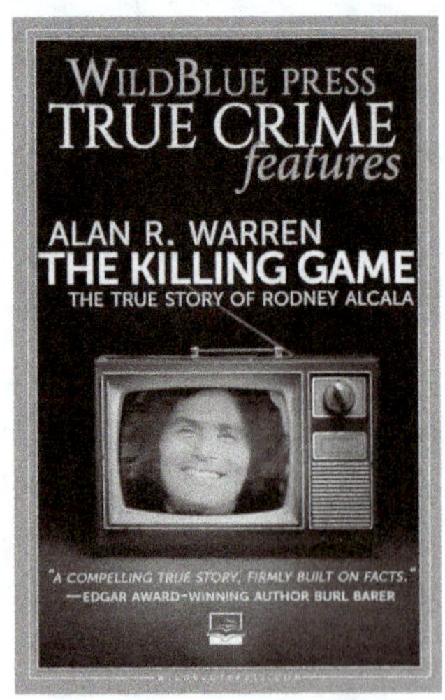

Beginning in 1968 and continuing into the 1970s, a predator stalked California and New York, torturing, raping, and murdering young girls and women. But who was the monster behind these tragedies?

Eventually, a suspect emerged, but he didn't look like a monster. Indeed, Rodney Alcala was a handsome, charming photographer who'd once studied film at New York University under director Roman Polanski. With his wit, easy self-confidence, and humor, he'd even been selected as the "winner" on the popular television show "The Dating Game." But his real game was much more sinister.

In 2010, Alcala was convicted of murdering five women in California during the 1970s; then, in 2013, as he waited on Death Row, he confessed to the murder of two more in New York. Yet, that might not be the end of the nightmare he caused. At his arrest, police found his "portfolio" with thousands of nude and erotic photographs of women and boys, who may also be among his victims.

In *The Killing Game*, bestselling true crime author and radio show host Alan R. Warren reveals the shocking details of Alcala's brutal crimes, as well as the trials and appeals that stretched on for decades and may still not be over.

The "compelling true story" of "The Dating Game Killer" by the radio host and bestselling author of Drinks, Dinner & Death.

— BURL BARER, EDGAR AWARD-WINNING AUTHOR

BEYOND SUSPICION: Russell Williams–A Canadian Serial Killer

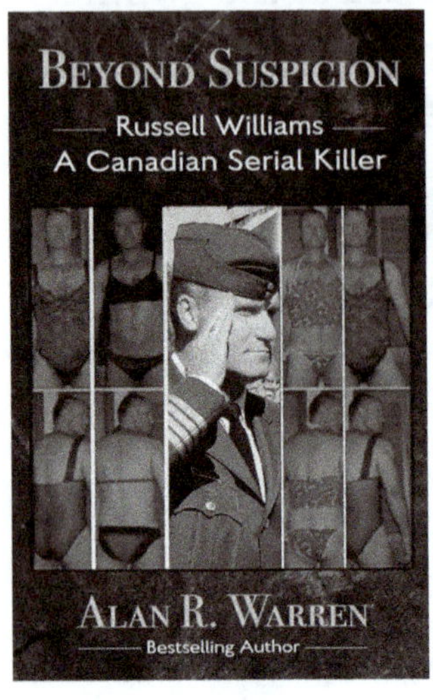

Young girl's panties started to go missing; sexual assaults began to occur, and then female bodies were found! Soon, this quiet town of Tweed, Ontario, panicked. What's even more shocking was when an upstanding resident stood accused of the assaults. This was not just any man but a pillar of the community, a decorated military pilot who had flown Canadian Forces VIP aircraft for dignitaries such as the Queen of England, Prince Philip, the Governor-General, and the Prime Minister of Canada.

This is the story of serial killer Russell Williams, the elite pilot of Canada's Air Force One, and the innocent victims he murdered. Unlike other serial killers, Williams seemed very unaffected by his crimes and leading two different lives.

Alan R. Warren describes the secret life, including the abductions, rape, and murders that were unleashed on an unsuspecting community. Included are letters written to the victims by Williams and descriptions of the assaults and rapes as seen on videos and photos taken by Williams during the attacks.

This updated version also contains the full brilliant police interrogation of Williams and his confession. Also, the twisted way Williams planned to pin his crimes on his unsuspecting neighbor.

MURDEROUS MINDS: Germany

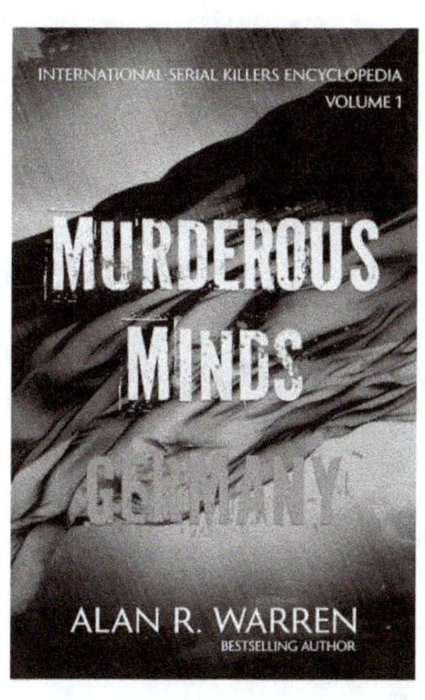

The *International Serial Killers Encyclopedia* series sheds light on the murderous minds of many killers, including their motivations, methods, and madness, through detailed research and explicit retelling of events. Some are notorious names that echo through history books, while others are lesser-known killers whose stories are no less harrowing. Each volume reveals a new layer of darkness.

Volume 1 of the series focuses on the most notorious serial killers from Germany. It contains many cases where the twisted minds and deeds of those who stalked the streets of Germany left a trail of fear and destruction in their wake.

From the infamous Fritz Haarmann, a.k.a. the "Butcher of Hanover," who preyed upon young boys with chilling brutality, to Peter Kürten, a.k.a. the "Vampire of Dusseldorf," whose thirst for blood knew no bounds. Each chapter reveals the brutal tales of individuals consumed by their darkest desires and a compelling blend of true crime and psychological intrigue.

Murderous Minds Germany offers a chilling glimpse into the darkest recesses of the human psyche, reminding us that evil can lurk just beneath the surface, even in the most civilized society.

VOICES OF TRUE CRIME: The O.J. Simpson Murder Case

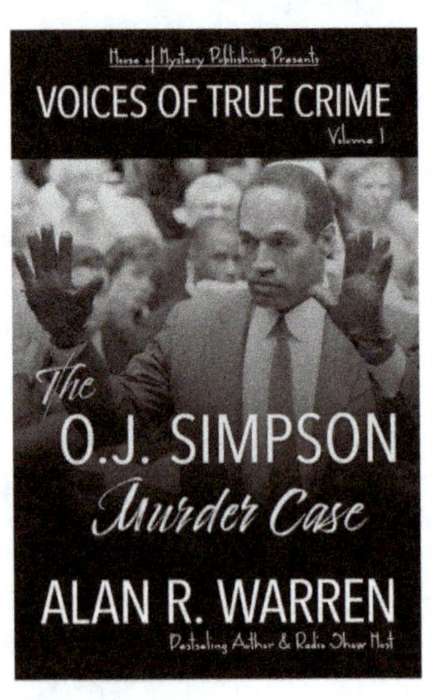

The *House of Mystery Radio Show* has been on the air for ten years, broadcasting in over a dozen cities in the U.S. It started as a way to interview guests knowledgeable in many of the world's mysteries involving crime, science, religion, history, paranormal, conspiracies, etc. *Voices of True Crime* series is a curated collection of interviews from the show. Each volume focuses on an actual criminal case, or several, providing the background and reproducing the main points discussed in the interviews. This series is an excellent reference for researchers and a good overview for those unfamiliar with the case.

Volume 1 covers the O.J. Simpson murder case. Over the last century, there have been plenty of trials called "The Trial of the Century," but of all mentioned, the O.J. Simpson case rose well above the rest. The fact that the accused murderer was a high-profile athlete and celebrity was almost enough to reach that status, but then the brutality of the murders made the world stagger. Throw in the fact that modern technology allowed every aspect of the case to be televised worldwide, including the infamous slow-speed chase and his sensational trial, and it's no wonder this case achieved that title.

House of Mystery interviewed several key players involved in this case: Marcia Clark, the lead prosecutor in the trial; F. Lee Bailey, one of Simpson's "Dream Team" of lawyers; Kim Goldman, sister of victim Ron Goldman; Norman Pardo, Simpson's manager for 15 years who wholeheartedly believes a serial killer murdered Nicole and Ron; and Andy Caldwell, the detective who questioned and arrested Simpson for the robbery in Vegas. Online links to the actual interviews are included.

www.ingramcontent.com/pod-product-compliance
Lightning Source LLC
Chambersburg PA
CBHW070858120626
46546CB00001B/49

* 9 7 8 1 9 9 8 6 8 0 0 3 0 *